TOP 10
OF EVERYTHING
2012

TOP
10
OF EVERYTHING
2012

Caroline Ash and Alexander Ash

hamlyn

Russell Ash (1946–2010), was the originator and author of the *Top 10 of Everything* annual and series. For over 22 years his passion for facts, eye for detail and pursuit of the curious fascinated and entertained millions of readers, and this edition is dedicated to his memory.

Produced for Hamlyn by
Palazzo Editions Ltd
2 Wood Street, Bath, BA1 2JQ

Publishing director: Colin Webb
Art director: Bernard Higton
Managing editor: Sonya Newland
Project editor: Emily Bailey
Picture researcher: Felicity Page

Top 10 of Everything was devised and created by Russell Ash

An Hachette UK Company
www.hachette.co.uk

First published in Great Britain in 2011 by
Hamlyn, a division of
Octopus Publishing Group Ltd
Endeavour House, 189 Shaftesbury Avenue,
London, WC2 8JY

www.octopusbooks.co.uk

Copyright © Octopus Publishing Group Ltd 2011
Text copyright © Russell Ash Ltd 2011

ISBN 978-0-600-62335-9

A CIP catalogue record for this book is available from the British Library.

Printed and bound in China.

10 9 8 7 6 5 4 3 2 1

CONTENTS

INTRODUCTION

23rd EDITION

23 is the smallest prime number with consecutive digits; a human cell has 23 pairs of chromosomes; Julius Caesar was stabbed 23 times when he was assassinated; William Shakespeare was born and died on 23 April; John Forbes Nash, the Nobel Prize-winning mathematician and the subject of the film *A Beautiful Mind*, was obsessed with the number 23; Michael Jordan wore the number 23 throughout his career and David Beckham first started wearing the number 23 when he played for Real Madrid; Psalm 23, the 'Shepherd Psalm' is the best known of all the psalms; there are 23 letters in the Latin alphabet (there is no J, U or W); and this is the 23rd annual edition of *Top 10 of Everything*.

LISTMANIA

We are constantly bombarded with lists. The press and TV programmes present rankings based on market research and polls, lists of the best places to live, the top universities, the greatest films, the bestselling books, the worst crime rates, and so on. Ranked lists have become a way of managing what might otherwise be a daunting mass of facts and figures, putting our world into a perspective that we can readily grasp. *Top 10 of Everything* provides a unique collection of lists in a

diverse array of categories that are – we hope – informative, educational and entertaining.

THIS EVER-CHANGING WORLD

The majority of lists change from year to year – even 'fixed' lists, such as those of the tallest mountains or deepest caves, are revised as more sophisticated measuring techniques are used or as deeper branches are discovered. The minimum entry requirements for Top 10 lists are in a constant state of flux as, for example, rich people get increasingly richer and build ever-bigger yachts, and films with bigger and bigger budgets are released and achieve higher-earning opening weekends.

IT'S A FACT

Top 10 lists provide a shorthand glimpse of what is happing with the world economy, global warming, deforestation, the countries that will have the most people and the densest populations in the future and other issues that concern us all. At the same time, the lists convey a fascinating and entertaining overview of the amazing diversity of our planet and its people, with lists on such subjects as the world's oldest people, the highest waterfalls, the heaviest mammals, the most venomous reptiles, the longest-serving presidents,

the tallest buildings, the longest bridges, the most-visited museums, the highest-grossing films, countries producing the most diamonds, the longest Shakespearean roles, companies with the most employees, the youngest American billionaires, leading chocolate consumers, latest air speed record holders, most widely spoken languages, countries with the most primary schools, bestselling albums and singles of all time, and the fastest men over 100 metres.

MORE THAN JUST THE NO. 1

All these lists follow a rule that has been true since the first edition of *Top 10 of Everything*, which is that every list has to be quantifiable – measurable in some way or other: the biggest, smallest, first, last, tallest, deepest, sunniest, dullest, worst, or chronologically the first or last. All the lists thus offer more than just the No. 1, and provide a perspective in which to compare the subjects of the list. There are no 'bests', other than bestsellers, and 'worsts' are of disasters, military losses and murders, where they are measured by numbers of victims. Unless otherwise stated, film lists are based on cumulative global earnings, irrespective of production or marketing budgets and – as is standard in the movie industry – inflation is not taken into account, which means that recent releases

tend to feature disproportionately prominently. Countries are independent countries, not dependencies or overseas territories. All the lists are all-time and global unless a specific year or territory is noted.

CREDITS AND ACKNOWLEDGEMENTS

Sources encompass international organizations, commercial companies and research bodies, specialized publications and a network of experts around the world who have generously shared their knowledge. As always, their important contribution is acknowledged (see page 256 for a full list of credits), along with that of everyone who has been involved with the book at all stages of its development on this and the previous 22 annual editions.

OVER TO YOU

We hope you enjoy the book. Your comments, corrections and suggestions for new lists are always welcome. Please contact us via the publishers or visit the *Top 10 of Everything* website www.top10ofeverything.com.

The Top 10 Team

1

THE UNIVERSE & THE EARTH

KUAFU SPACE MISSION

Launched by the Chinese in 2012, KuaFu will be the first space mission dedicated to the study of space weather – observing, monitoring and recording activity, particularly solar storms, from their inception at the Sun to their arrival at the Earth's atmosphere. KuaFu comprises three spacecraft, one of which will be permanently situated 1.5 million km (0.9 million miles) away, while the other two will orbit Earth to provide the first continuous imaging of space weather. The erratic behaviour of the Sun leads to solar storms whose effects can wreak havoc on satellites and interfere to a dangerous degree with technology. Being able to accurately predict and monitor these storms will help to reduce their impact.

◄ **Sylvia**
The asteroid Sylvia is about 280 km
(175 miles) in diameter and is orbited
by two small moons.

▼ **Jupiter**
Composed primarily
of hydrogen, Jupiter
is the largest planet.

TOP 10 **LARGEST BODIES IN THE SOLAR SYSTEM**

BODY	MAX. DIAMETER KM	MAX. DIAMETER MILES	SIZE COMPARED WITH EARTH
1 Sun	1,392,140	865,036	109.136
2 Jupiter	142,984	88,846	11.209
3 Saturn	120,536	74,898	9.449
4 Uranus	51,118	31,763	4.007
5 Neptune	49,528	30,775	3.883
6 Earth	12,756	7,926	1.000
7 Venus	12,104	7,521	0.949
8 Mars	6,805	4,228	0.533
9 Ganymede	5,262	3,270	0.413
10 Titan	5,150	3,200	0.404

TOP 10 **LARGEST ASTEROIDS**

NAME	NO.	DISCOVERED	MEAN DIAMETER* KM	MEAN DIAMETER* MILES
1 Ceres	1	1 Jan 1801	952	592
2 Pallas	2	28 Mar 1802	544	338
3 Vesta	4	29 Mar 1807	529	329
4 Hygeia	10	12 Apr 1849	431	268
5 Interamnia	704	2 Oct 1910	326	203
6 Europa	52	4 Feb 1858	301	187
7 Davida	511	30 May 1903	289	180
8 Sylvia	87	16 May 1866	286	178
9 Cybele	65	8 Mar 1861	273	170
10 Eunomia	15	29 Jul 1851	268	167

* Most asteroids are irregular in shape

Asteroids, also known as minor planets, but correctly (along with comets) now called 'small Solar System bodies', are fragments of rock orbiting between Mars and Jupiter. In 2006, Ceres was redesignated as a dwarf planet (bodies over 750 km/466 miles in diameter), along with Pluto and Eris. Up to 6 August 2009, some 217,627 asteroids had been identified, but only 15,361 of them named.

► **Earth**
The third planet from the Sun,
Earth was formed roughly
4.5 billion years ago.

▲ **Mars**
Iron oxide on
its surface
gives Mars
its reddish
appearance.

Asteroid Impact!

Large asteroids with a diameter of 1 km (0.62 mile) are likely to collide with Earth once every 500,000 years, and have the potential to cause extensive damage. Smaller asteroids with a diameter of 5–10 m (16–33 ft) enter the Earth's atmosphere roughly once a year, but frequently explode in the upper atmosphere and so fortunately do not cause much harm.

TOP 10 **BODIES* FURTHEST FROM THE SUN**

BODY	AVERAGE DISTANCE FROM THE SUN KM	MILES
1 Pluto	5,914,000,000	3,675,000,000
2 Neptune	4,497,000,000	2,794,000,000
3 Uranus	2,871,000,000	1,784,000,000
4 Chiron	2,800,000,000	1,740,000,000
5 Saturn	1,427,000,000	887,000,000
6 Jupiter	778,300,000	483,600,000
7 Mars	227,900,000	141,600,000
8 Earth	149,597,870	92,955,793
9 Venus	108,200,000	67,200,000
10 Mercury	57,900,000	36,000,000

* In the Solar System, excluding satellites and asteroids

▲ **Pluto**
Formerly the ninth planet in the Solar System, but now reclassified as a dwarf planet, Pluto is composed of rock and ice.

▲ **Neptune**
Furthest from the Sun, Neptune is the fourth-heaviest planet in the Solar System.

◄ **Saturn**
Saturn is surrounded by nine rings composed primarily of ice particles.

► **Halley's Comet**
Visible from Earth with the naked eye, Halley's Comet can be seen once every 75 years.

THE 10 **BODIES IN THE SOLAR SYSTEM WITH THE GREATEST ESCAPE VELOCITY**

BODY*	ESCAPE VELOCITY (KM/S)
1 Sun	617.50
2 Jupiter	60.22
3 Saturn	32.26
4 Neptune	23.90
5 Uranus	22.50
6 Earth	11.18
7 Venus	10.36
8 Mars	5.03
9 Mercury	4.25
10 Pluto	1.18

* Excluding satellites

Escape velocity is the speed a rocket has to attain upon launching to overcome the gravitational pull of the body it is leaving. The escape velocity of the Moon is 2.38 km/s.

TOP 10 **COMETS COMING CLOSEST TO EARTH**

COMET	DATE*	AU#	DISTANCE KM	MILES
1 Comet of 1491	20 Feb 1491	0.0094	1,406,220	873,784
2 Lexell	1 Jul 1770	0.0151	2,258,928	1,403,633
3 Tempel-Tuttle	26 Oct 1366	0.0229	3,425,791	2,128,688
4 IRAS-Araki-Alcock	11 May 1983	0.0313	4,682,413	2,909,516
5 Halley	10 Apr 837	0.0334	4,996,569	3,104,724
6 Biela	9 Dec 1805	0.0366	5,475,282	3,402,182
7 Grischow	8 Feb 1743	0.0390	5,834,317	3,625,276
8 Pons-Winnecke	26 Jun 1927	0.0394	5,894,156	3,662,458
9 Comet of 1014	24 Feb 1014	0.0407	6,088,633	3,783,301
10 La Hire	20 Apr 1702	0.0437	6,537,427	4,062,168

* Of closest approach to Earth
\# Astronomical Units: 1AU = mean distance from the Earth to the Sun (149,597,870 km/ 92,955,793 miles)

11

STARS & STAR GAZING

▲ *Andromeda galaxy*
The collision of two smaller galaxies formed Andromeda between five and nine billion years ago.

TOP 10 **GALAXIES NEAREST TO EARTH**

	GALAXY	DISCOVERED	APPROX. DIAMETER	DISTANCE FROM EARTH (1,000 LIGHT YEARS)
1	Sagittarius Dwarf	1994	10	82
2	Large Magellanic Cloud	Prehist.	30	160
3	Small Magellanic Cloud	Prehist.	16	190
4 =	Draco Dwarf	1954	3	205
=	Ursa Minor Dwarf	1954	2	205
6	Sculptor Dwarf	1937	3	254
7	Sextans Dwarf	1990	4	258
8	Carina Dwarf	1977	2	330
9	Fornax Dwarf	1938	6	450
10	Leo II	1950	3	660

Source: Peter Bond, Royal Astronomical Society

TOP 10 **BRIGHTEST GALAXIES**

	GALAXY / NO.	DISTANCE FROM EARTH (MILLIONS OF LIGHT YEARS)	APPARENT MAGNITUDE
1	Large Magellanic Cloud	0.17	0.91
2	Small Magellanic Cloud	0.21	2.70
3	Andromeda Galaxy/NGC 224 M31	2.6	4.36
4	Triangulum Galaxy/NGC 598 M33	2.8	6.27
5	Centaurus Galaxy/NGC 5128	12.0	7.84
6	Bode's Galaxy/NGC 3031 M81	12.0	7.89
7	Silver Coin Galaxy/NGC 253	8.5	8.04
8	Southern Pinwheel Galaxy/ NGC 5236 M83	15.0	8.20
9	Pinwheel Galaxy/NGC 5457 M101	24.0	8.31
10	Cigar Galaxy/NGC 55	4.9	8.42

> As the Solar System and Earth are at the outer edge of the Milky Way galaxy, this is excluded.

> Messier (M) numbers are named after French astronomer Charles Messier (1730–1817), who in 1781 compiled the first catalogue of galaxies, nebulae and star clusters. From 1888 onwards, these were replaced by New General Catalogue (NGC) numbers.

TOP 10 **BRIGHTEST STARS***

STAR / CONSTELLATION / DISTANCE[#] / APPARENT MAGNITUDE

1
Sirius
Canis Major
8.61 / -1.44

2
Canopus
Carina
312.73 / -0.62

3
Arcturus
Boötes
36.39 / -0.05[†]

4
Alpha Centauri A
Centaurus
4.40 / -0.01

5
Vega
Lyra
25.31 / +0.03

6
Capella
Auriga
42.21 / +0.08

7
Rigel
Orion
772.91 / +0.18

8
Procyon
Canis Minor
11.42 / +0.40

9
Achernar
Eridanus
143.81 / +0.45

10
Beta Centauri
Centaurus
525.22 / +0.61

* Excluding the Sun
# From Earth in light years
† Variable

> This Top 10 is based on apparent visual magnitude as viewed from Earth – the lower the number, the brighter the star, since by convention 1 was considered a star of first magnitude and 6 the faintest visible to the naked eye. On this scale, the Sun would be -26.73 and the full Moon -12.6.

THE 10 **TYPES OF STAR**

TYPE	SPECTRUM	MAX. SURFACE TEMPERATURE °C	°F
1 **W**	Bright lines	80,000	144,000
2 **O**	Bright and dark lines	40,000	72,000
3 **B**	Bluish-white	25,000	43,000
4 **A**	White	10,000	18,000
5 **F**	White/slightly yellow	7,500	13,500
6 **G**	Yellowish	6,000	11,000
7 **K**	Orange	5,000	9,000
8 **M**	Orange-red	3,400	6,000
9= **C** (formerly R & N)	Reddish	2,600	4,700
= **S**	Red	2,600	4,700

Stars are classified by type according to their spectra – the colours by which they appear when viewed with a spectroscope. These vary according to the star's surface temperature. Within these types there are sub-types, with dwarfs generally hotter than giants.

TOP 10 **STARS NEAREST TO EARTH**

STAR*	LIGHT YEARS	DISTANCE FROM EARTH KM (MILLIONS)	MILES (MILLIONS)
1 Proxima Centauri	4.22	39,923,310	24,792,500
2 Alpha Centauri	4.39	41,531,595	25,791,250
3 Barnard's Star	5.94	56,195,370	34,897,500
4 Wolf 359	7.78	73,602,690	45,707,500
5 Lalande 21185	8.31	78,616,755	48,821,250
6 Sirius	8.60	81,360,300	50,525,000
7 Luyten 726-8	8.72	82,495,560	51,230,000
8 Ross 154	9.69	91,672,245	56,928,750
9 Ross 248	10.32	97,632,360	60,630,000
10 Epsilon Eridani	10.49	99,240,645	61,628,750

* Excluding the Sun

Source: Peter Bond, Royal Astronomical Society

A spaceship travelling at 40,237 km/h (25,000 mph) – faster than any human has yet reached in space – would take more than 113,200 years to reach Earth's closest star, Proxima Centauri.

The World's Largest Telescope

The European Extremely Large Telescope (E-ELT) is currently being designed, and should be operational by 2018. The telescope's 'eye' will be 42 m (138 ft) in diameter, made up of 906 hexagonal segments, and will gather 15 times more light than any of today's largest optical telescopes. It has an innovative design that includes advanced adaptive optics to correct for the Earth's turbulent atmosphere, giving exceptional image quality. It is likely to revolutionize our perception of the Universe.

Space Exploration

THE 10 **FIRST ANIMALS IN SPACE**

	NAME / ANIMAL / STATUS	COUNTRY	DATE
1	**Laika** (female Samoyed husky) Died in space	USSR	3 Nov 1957
2 =	**Laska** and **Benjy** (mice) Re-entered Earth's atmosphere, but not recovered	USA	13 Dec 1958
4 =	**Able** (female rhesus monkey) and **Baker** (female squirrel monkey) Successfully returned to Earth	USA	28 May 1959
6 =	**Otvazhnaya** (female Samoyed husky) and an **unnamed rabbit** Successfully returned to Earth	USSR	2 Jul 1959
8	**Sam** (male rhesus monkey) Successfully returned to Earth	USA	4 Dec 1959
9	**Miss Sam** (female rhesus monkey) Successfully returned to Earth	USA	21 Jan 1960
10 =	**Belka** and **Strelka** (female Samoyed huskies) plus 40 mice and two rats First to orbit and return safely	USSR	19 Aug 1960

The first animal to be sent up in a rocket – but not into space – was Albert 1, a male rhesus monkey, in a US Air Force converted German V2 rocket in 1948. He and his successor, Albert 2, died during the tests, as did a monkey and mice in 1951 tests, but a monkey and 11 mice were recovered after a launch in a US Aerobee rocket on 20 September 1951. The earliest Soviet experiments with launching animals in rockets involved monkeys, dogs, rabbits, cats and mice, most of which died as a result. Laika, the first dog in space, went up in *Sputnik 2*, with no hope of coming down alive. Able and Baker, launched in a *Jupiter* missile, were the first animals to be recovered (although Able died a few days later).

▲ **Space pioneers**
Laika (top) is actually the name of the breed to which the dog named Kudryavka, a female Samoyed husky, belonged. Baker (above) lived until 1984 after her safe return to Earth.

MOONWALKERS

Six of the 11 US *Apollo* manned missions resulted in successful Moon landings (*Apollo 13* was aborted after an oxygen tank exploded). During the last of these (*Apollo 17*, 7–19 December 1972), Eugene A. Cernan (b. 14 March 1934) and Harrison H. Schmitt (b. 3 July 1935) became the final astronauts to date to have walked on the surface of the Moon, both spending a total of 22:04 in EVA.

◄ **Farewell to the Moon**
Eugene Cernan was the last of only 12 men to have left their footprints on the lunar surface.

INTERNATIONAL SPACE STATION

Completion of the International Space Station (ISS) is scheduled for 2012. This low Earth orbit research facility is the result of a collaboration between five space agencies – those of the USA, Russia, Japan and China as well as the European Space Agency. Construction began in 1998, when the first two modules were launched and joined in space. Two years later, the first crews arrived and the ISS has been manned constantly since then, with astronauts and cosmonauts conducting experiments that will help with future space exploration.

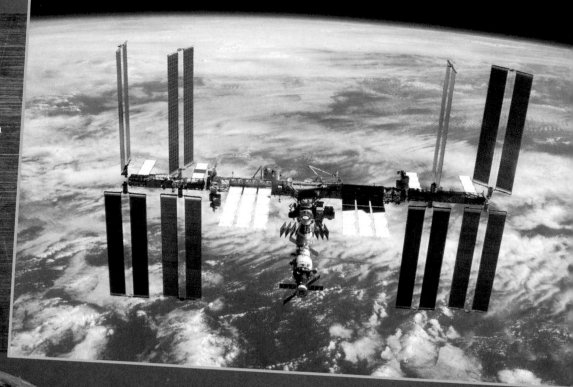

TOP 10 **BODIES MOST VISITED BY SPACECRAFT**

BODY / SPACECRAFT

1	Moon	66
2	Mars	32
3	Venus	26
4	Sun	14
5	Jupiter	7
6	Halley's Comet	5
7	Saturn	4
8	= Mercury	1
	= Neptune	1
	= Uranus	1

Venus
Around 80% of the surface of Venus is made up of volcanic lava plains.

Arguably, Earth is the most visited body in the Solar System, with satellites constantly orbiting. With the exception of some visits to the Moon, all the visiting spacecraft were unmanned space probes known as flybys, landers and orbiters. The US space probe *Voyager 2*, for instance, flew by Jupiter, Saturn, Uranus and Neptune over a period of 12 years.

MISSION TO MARS

The Mars Science Laboratory is expected to arrive on the red planet in autumn 2012. This, the latest of NASA's Mars missions, is intended to build on the success of the Mars rovers *Spirit* and *Opportunity*, which have been sending back information from the surface of the planet since 2004. Equipped with the latest technology, the Science Laboratory will be able to convey information about the Martian atmosphere and its rocks and soil, in more detail than ever before.

ELEMENTARY

THE 10 **MOST COMMON ELEMENTS IN THE UNIVERSE**

ELEMENT (SYMBOL) / PARTS PER MILLION*

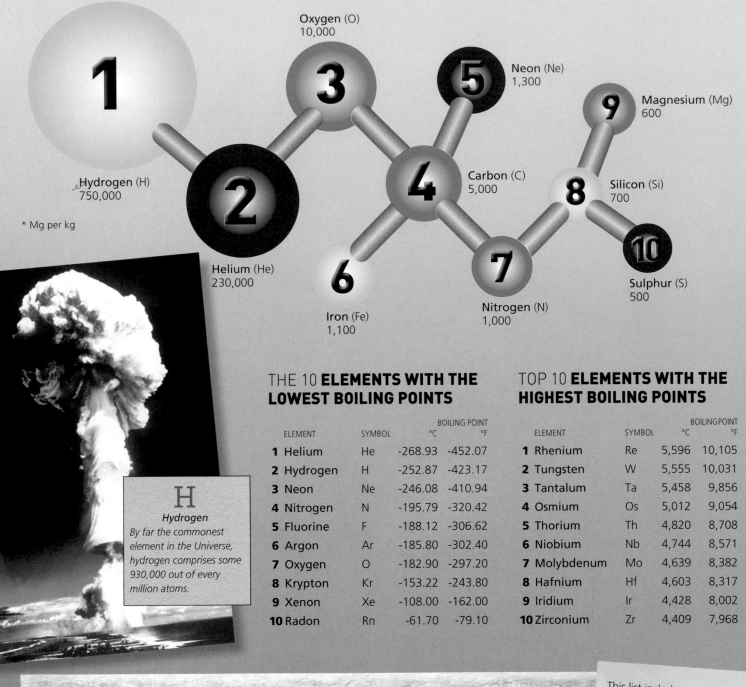

1 Hydrogen (H) 750,000

2 Helium (He) 230,000

3 Oxygen (O) 10,000

4 Carbon (C) 5,000

5 Neon (Ne) 1,300

6 Iron (Fe) 1,100

7 Nitrogen (N) 1,000

8 Silicon (Si) 700

9 Magnesium (Mg) 600

10 Sulphur (S) 500

* Mg per kg

H
Hydrogen
By far the commonest element in the Universe, hydrogen comprises some 930,000 out of every million atoms.

THE 10 **ELEMENTS WITH THE LOWEST BOILING POINTS**

	ELEMENT	SYMBOL	BOILING POINT °C	°F
1	Helium	He	-268.93	-452.07
2	Hydrogen	H	-252.87	-423.17
3	Neon	Ne	-246.08	-410.94
4	Nitrogen	N	-195.79	-320.42
5	Fluorine	F	-188.12	-306.62
6	Argon	Ar	-185.80	-302.40
7	Oxygen	O	-182.90	-297.20
8	Krypton	Kr	-153.22	-243.80
9	Xenon	Xe	-108.00	-162.00
10	Radon	Rn	-61.70	-79.10

TOP 10 **ELEMENTS WITH THE HIGHEST BOILING POINTS**

	ELEMENT	SYMBOL	BOILING POINT °C	°F
1	Rhenium	Re	5,596	10,105
2	Tungsten	W	5,555	10,031
3	Tantalum	Ta	5,458	9,856
4	Osmium	Os	5,012	9,054
5	Thorium	Th	4,820	8,708
6	Niobium	Nb	4,744	8,571
7	Molybdenum	Mo	4,639	8,382
8	Hafnium	Hf	4,603	8,317
9	Iridium	Ir	4,428	8,002
10	Zirconium	Zr	4,409	7,968

TOP 10 **METALLIC ELEMENTS WITH THE GREATEST RESERVES**

	ELEMENT (SYMBOL)	MIN. ESTIMATED GLOBAL RESERVES (TONNES)
1	Iron (Fe)	100,000,000,000
2	Magnesium (Mg)	20,000,000,000
3	Potassium (K)	10,000,000,000
4	Aluminium (Al)	6,000,000,000
5	Manganese (Mn)	3,000,000,000
6	=Chromium (Cr)	1,000,000,000
	=Zirconium (Zr)	1,000,000,000
8	Titanium (Ti)	600,000,000
9	Barium (Ba)	400,000,000
10	Copper (Cu)	300,000,000

This list includes accessible reserves of commercially mined metallic elements (although magnesium is also extracted from seawater, where the reserves are vast), but excludes two, calcium and sodium, that exist in such huge quantities that their reserves are considered 'unlimited' and unquantifiable.

Ne
Neon
Neon is used for signs because it glows red when an electrical discharge is passed through it.

He
Helium
Light, colourless and odourless, helium also has the lowest melting point of any element in the periodic table.

TOP 10 **DEGREES OF HARDNESS**

MOHS SCALE NO. / SUBSTANCE

1	Talc	6	Orthoclase
2	Gypsum	7	Quartz
3	Calcite	8	Topaz
4	Fluorite	9	Corundum
5	Apatite	10	Diamond

The Mohs Scale, named after German mineralogist Friedrich Mohs (1773–1839), is used for comparing the relative hardness of minerals. Each mineral on the scale is softer, and hence capable of being scratched by all those below it.

THE 10 **FIRST ELEMENTS TO BE NAMED AFTER REAL PEOPLE**

	ELEMENT	SYMBOL	NAMED AFTER	YEAR
1	Samarium*	Sm	Vasili Samarsky-Bykhovets (Russia, 1803–70)	1879
2	Gadolinium#	Gd	Johan Gadolin (Finland, 1760–1852)	1880
3	Curium	Cm	Pierre† and Marie Curie† (France 1859–1906; Poland 1867–1934)	1944
4	Einsteinium	Es	Albert Einstein† (Germany, 1879–1955)	1952
5	Fermium	Fm	Enrico Fermi† (Italy, 1901–54)	1953
6	Nobelium	No	Alfred Nobel (Sweden, 1833–96)	1958
7	Lawrencium	Lr	Ernest Lawrence† (USA, 1901–58)	1961
8	Rutherfordium	Rf	Ernest Rutherford† (UK, 1871–1937)	1969
9	Seaborgium	Sg	Glenn T. Seaborg† (USA, 1912–99)	1974
10	Bohrium	Bh	Niels Bohr† (Denmark, 1885–62)	1981

* Named after mineral samarskite, which was named after Samarsky-Bykhovets
\# Named after mineral gadolinite, which was named after Gadolin
† Awarded Nobel Prize

► *Marie Curie*
With her husband, Marie Curie discovered the elements curium, radium and polonium.

OCEANS & SEAS

Persian Gulf
Encompassing the world's largest offshore oilfield, the Persian Gulf adjoins eight countries.

TOP 10 **LARGEST OCEANS AND SEAS**

NAME / APPROX. AREA* (SQ KM / SQ MILES)

1 Pacific Ocean
155,557,000
60,060,900

2 Atlantic Ocean
76,762,000
29,637,977

3 Indian Ocean
68,556,000
26,469,622

4 Southern Ocean#
20,327,000
7,848,299

5 Arctic Ocean
14,056,000
5,427,053

6 Caribbean Sea
2,718,200
1,049,503

7 Mediterranean Sea
2,510,000
969,117

8 South China Sea
2,319,000
895,371

9 Bering Sea
2,291,900
884,908

10 Gulf of Mexico
1,592,800
614,984

* Excluding tributary seas
# As defined by the International Hydrographic Organization

THE 10 **SMALLEST SEAS**

SEA*/OCEAN	APPROX. AREA SQ KM	SQ MILES
1 Gulf of California, Pacific Ocean	153,070	59,100
2 Persian Gulf, Indian Ocean	230,000	88,800
3 Yellow Sea, Pacific Ocean	293,960	113,500
4 Baltic Sea, Atlantic Ocean	382,000	147,500
5 North Sea, Atlantic Ocean	427,090	164,900
6 Red Sea, Indian Ocean	452,990	174,900
7 Black Sea, Atlantic Ocean	507,900	196,100
8 Andaman Sea, Indian Ocean	564,880	218,100
9 East China Sea, Pacific Ocean	664,590	256,600
10 Hudson Bay, Atlantic Ocean	730,120	281,900

* Excludes landlocked seas

TOP 10 **COUNTRIES WITH THE LARGEST AREAS OF CORAL REEF**

COUNTRY / REEF AREA (SQ KM / SQ MILES) / % OF WORLD TOTAL

1 Indonesia
51,020 / 19,700
17.95%

2 Australia
48,960 / 18,900
17.22%

3 The Philippines
25,060 / 9,680
8.8%

World total 284,300 / 109,770 / 100.00%

* Clipperton, French Polynesia, Guadeloupe, Martinique, Mayotte, New Caledonia, Réunion, Wallis and Futuna islands

Source: UNEP World Conservation Monitoring Centre, *World Atlas of Coral Reefs*

THE 10 **DEEPEST DEEP-SEA TRENCHES**

TRENCH*	DEEPEST POINT	
	M	FT
1 Marianas	10,911	35,798
2 Tonga	10,882	35,702
3 Kuril-Kamchatka	10,542	34,587
4 Philippine	10,540	34,580
5 Kermadec	10,047	32,963
6 Bonin	9,994	32,789
7 New Britain	9,940	32,612
8 Izu	9,780	32,087
9 Puerto Rico	8,605	28,232
10 Yap	8,527	27,976

* With the exception of the Puerto Rico Trench (Atlantic), all the trenches are in the Pacific

▲ Canadian coast
More than 50,000 offshore islands lie along Canada's extensive coastline.

TOP 10 **COUNTRIES WITH THE LONGEST COASTLINES**

COUNTRY	COASTLINE LENGTH	
	KM	MILES
1 Canada	202,080	125,567
2 Indonesia	54,716	33,999
3 Greenland	44,087	27,394
4 Russia	37,653	23,396
5 Philippines	36,289	22,549
6 Japan	29,751	18,486
7 Australia	25,760	16,007
8 Norway	25,148	15,626
9 USA	19,924	12,380
10 New Zealand	15,134	9,404
UK	*12,429*	*7,723*
World	*484,058*	*300,780*

Each of the eight deepest ocean trenches would be deep enough to submerge Mount Everest, which is 8,850 m (29,035 ft) above sea level.

▼ Creature of the deep
Fangtooth fish live at depths of up to 5 km (3 miles), where no light penetrates.

5 Papua New Guinea
13,840 / 5,340
4.87%

4 France – overseas territories*
14,280 / 5,510
5.02%

7 Maldives
8,920 / 3,440
3.14%

9 Marshall Islands
6,110 / 2,360
2.15%

6 Fiji
10,020 / 3,870
3.52%

8 Saudi Arabia
6,660 / 2,570
2.34%

10 India
5,790 / 2,240
2.04%

WATER ON THE MOVE

TOP 10 **GREATEST*** RIVER SYSTEMS

RIVER SYSTEM# / CONTINENT	AVERAGE DISCHARGE AT MOUTH (CU M/SEC)	(CU FT/SEC)
1 Amazon South America	219,000	7,733,912
2 Congo (Zaïre) Africa	41,800	1,476,153
3 Orinoco South America	33,000	1,165,384
4 Yangtze (Chang Jiang) Asia	31,900	1,126,538
5 Paraná South America	25,700	907,587
6 Yenisei-Angara Asia	19,600	692,168
7 Brahmaputra (Tsangpo) Asia	19,200	678,042
8 Lena Asia	17,100	603,881
9 Madeira-Mamoré South America	17,000	600,349
10 Mississippi-Missouri North America	16,200	572,098

* Based on rate of discharge at mouth   # Excludes tributaries

Source: University of New Hampshire Global Composite Runoff Data Archive

▲ *Amazing Amazon*
Despite having a drainage area twice the size of India, the Amazon is not crossed by any bridges.

TOP 10 **LONGEST GLACIERS**

GLACIER / LOCATION / LENGTH (KM / MILES)

1 Lambert Antarctica 400 / 249

2 Bering Alaska, USA 190 / 118

3 Beardmore Antarctica 160 / 99

4 Byrd Antarctica 136 / 85

5 Nimrod Antarctica 135 / 84

6 Amundsen Antarctica 128 / 80

7 Hubbard Alaska, USA 122 / 76

8 Slessor Antarctica 120 / 75

9 Denman Antarctica 112 / 70

10 Recovery Antarctica 100 / 62

TOP 10 **LONGEST RIVERS**

RIVER / LOCATION	LENGTH KM	MILES
1 Amazon Bolivia, Brazil, Colombia, Ecuador, Peru, Venezuela	6,992	4,345
2 Nile Burundi, Dem. Rep. of Congo, Egypt, Eritrea, Ethiopia, Kenya, Rwanda, Sudan, Tanzania, Uganda	6,852	4,258
3 Yangtze (Chang Jiang) China	6,300	3,915
4 Mississippi-Missouri USA	6,275	3,899
5 Yenisei-Angara-Selenga Mongolia, Russia	5,539	3,442
6 Huang He (Yellow) China	5,464	3,395
7 Ob-Irtysh China, Kazakhstan, Russia	5,410	3,362
8 Congo-Chambeshi Angola, Burundi, Cameroon, Dem. Rep. of Congo, Rep. of Congo, Central African Republic, Rwanda, Tanzania, Zambia	4,700	2,920
9 Amur-Argun China, Mongolia, Russia	4,444	2,761
10 Lena Russia	4,400	2,734

TOP 10 **HIGHEST WATERFALLS**

WATERFALL* / RIVER / LOCATION / TOTAL DROP (M / FT)

1 Angel
Carrao, Venezuela
979 / 3,212#

2 Tugela
Tugela, South Africa
948 / 3,110

3 Ramnefjellsfossen
Jostedal Glacier, Nesdale, Norway
818 / 2,685

4 Mongefossen
Monge, Mongebekk, Norway
773 / 2,535

5 Gocta Cataracta
Cocahuayco, Peru
771 / 2,531

6 Mutarazi
Mutarazi River, Zimbabwe
762 / 2,499

7 Yosemite
Yosemite Creek,
California, USA
739 / 2,425

8 Østre Mardøla Foss
Mardals, Eikisdal, Norway
657 / 2,154

9 Tyssestrengane
Tysso, Hardanger, Norway
646 / 2,120

10 Cuquenán
Arabopo, Venezuela
610 / 2,000

* Waterfalls with year-round (non-seasonal) flow
and accurately recorded height
Longest single drop 807 m (2,648 ft)

► *Angel Falls*
The Falls are named after American pilot James Angel, who crash-landed his plane there in 1933 and trekked for 11 days back to civilization.

Bobby Leach, a Cornish circus stuntman, became the first man – and second person – ever to go over Niagara Falls in a barrel, on 25 July 1911. He broke both knee-caps and fractured his jaw.

TOP 10 **GREATEST* WATERFALLS**

WATERFALL / COUNTRY	AVERAGE FLOW	
	CU M/SEC	CU FT/SEC
1 Inga Dem. Rep. of Congo	42,476	1,500,000
2 Livingstone Dem. Rep. of Congo	35,113	1,240,000
3 Boyoma (Stanley) Dem. Rep. of Congo	16,990	600,000
4 Khône Laos	10,783	410,000
5 Celilo USA	5,415	191,215
6 Salto Pará Venezuela	3,540	125,000
7 Paulo Afonso Brazil	2,832	100,000
8 Niagara (Horseshoe) Canada/USA	2,407	85,000
9 Iguaçu Argentina/Brazil	1,746	61,660
10 Victoria Zambia/Zimbabwe	1,088	38,430

* Based on volume of water

ISLANDS & LAKES

TOP 10 **HIGHEST ISLANDS**

	ISLAND / LOCATION / HIGHEST POINT	HIGHEST ELEVATION M	FT
1	New Guinea, Indonesia/Papua New Guinea; Puncak Jaya (Mount Carstensz)	4,884	16,024
2	Hawaii, USA; Mauna Kea	4,205	13,796
3	Borneo, Indonesia/Malaysia; Mount Kinabalu	4,101	13,455
4	Taiwan; Jade Mountain (Yu Shan)	3,952	12,966
5	Sumatra, Indonesia; Mount Kerinci	3,805	12,484
6	Ross, Antarctica; Mount Erebus	3,794	12,448
7	Honshu, Japan; Mount Fuji	3,776	12,387
8	South Island, New Zealand; Aorakim (Mount Cook)	3,755	12,320
9	Lombok, Indonesia; Mount Rinjani	3,726	12,224
10	Tenerife, Spain; Pico de Teide	3,718	12,198

▲ High island
Lying between the Himalayas and the Andes, Puncak Jaya embodies one of very few ice-covered areas on the Equator.

THE 10 **SMALLEST ISLAND COUNTRIES**

COUNTRY / LOCATION / AREA (SQ KM / SQ MILES)

1 Nauru
Pacific Ocean 21.0 / 8.1

2 Tuvalu
Pacific Ocean 25.9 / 10.0

3 Marshall Islands
Pacific Ocean 181.0 / 69.9

4 St Kitts and Nevis
Caribbean Sea 261.1 / 100.8

5 Maldives
Indian Ocean 298.1 / 115.1

6 Malta
Mediterranean Sea 316.0 / 122.0

7 Grenada
Caribbean Sea 344.0 / 132.8

8 St Vincent and the Grenadines
Caribbean Sea 389.0 / 150.2

9 Barbados
Caribbean Sea 431.0 / 166.4

10 Antigua and Barbuda
Caribbean Sea 442.6 / 170.9

▼ Island influx
A commuter influx swells Manhattan's population to nearly three million during business hours.

TOP 10 **MOST DENSELY POPULATED ISLANDS***

	ISLAND / LOCATION	AREA SQ KM	SQ MILES	TOTAL	POPULATION# PER SQ KM	PER SQ MILE
1	Salsette, India	435	168	13,180,000	30,291	78,452
2	Manhattan, New York, USA	60	23	1,629,000	27,346	70,826
3	Hong Kong, China	78	30	1,181,000	15,200	39,367
4	Singapore	679	269	4,620,000	6,631	17,175
5	Montreal Island, Canada	500	193	1,800,000	3,601	9,326
6	Long Island, New York, USA	3,629	1,401	7,536,000	2,077	5,379
7	Dakhin Shahbazbur, Bangladesh	1,440	556	1,675,000	1,163	3,013
8	Okinawa, Japan	1,115	446	1,250,000	1,082	2,803
9	Java, Indonesia	138,795	53,589	124,000,000	893	2,314
10	Cebu, Philippines	4,626	1,786	2,5360,000	750	1,942

* Includes only islands with populations of more than 1 million
# Latest available year

TOP 10 **LARGEST LAKES**

LAKE / LOCATION	APPROX. AREA SQ KM	SQ MILES
1 Caspian Sea, Azerbaijan/Iran/Kazakhstan/Russia/Turkmenistan	374,000	144,402
2 Michigan/Huron*, Canada/USA	117,436	45,342
3 Superior, Canada/USA	82,367	31,802
4 Victoria, Kenya/Tanzania/Uganda	69,485	26,828
5 Tanganyika, Burundi/Tanzania/Dem. Rep. of Congo/Zambia	32,893	12,700
6 Baikal, Russia	31,494	12,160
7 Great Bear, Canada	31,153	12,028
8 Malawi (Nyasa), Tanzania/Malawi/Mozambique	30,044	11,600
9 Great Slave, Canada	28,568	11,030
10 Erie, Canada/USA	25,719	9,930

* Now considered two lobes of the same lake

Source: ILEC, World Lake Database

▶ *Exploring Lake Baikal* Scientists use the same submarines that once explored the Titanic.

RUSSIAN ACADEMY OF SCIENCES
P.P. SHIRSHOV INSTITUTE
МЕТРОПОЛЬ
ВЕСТИ

THE 10 **DEEPEST FRESHWATER LAKES**

LAKE / LOCATION	GREATEST DEPTH M	FT
1 Baikal, Russia	1,741	5,712
2 Tanganyika, Burundi/Tanzania/Dem. Rep. of Congo/Zambia	1,471	4,826
3 Vostok, Antarctica	1,000	3,281
4 Malawi (Nyasa) Tanzania/Malawi/Mozambique	706	2,316
5 Great Slave, Canada	614	2,014
6 Crater, Oregon, USA	594	1,949
7 Matana, Celebes, Indonesia	590	1,936
8 Toba, Sumatra, Indonesia	529	1,736
9 Hornindalsvatnet, Norway	514	1,686
10 Sarezskoye (Sarez), Tajikistan	505	1,657

Source: ILEC, World Lake Database

On Location
Containing roughly one-fifth of the world's surface freshwater, Lake Baikal is also the planet's oldest lake – formed more than 25 million years ago.

ON TOP OF THE WORLD

TOP 10 HIGHEST MOUNTAINS

MOUNTAIN / LOCATION	FIRST ASCENT	TEAM NATIONALITY	HEIGHT* M	FT
1 Everest, Nepal/China	29 May 1953	British/New Zealand	8,850	29,035
2 K2 (Chogori), Pakistan/China	31 Jul 1954	Italian	8,611	28,251
3 Kangchenjunga, Nepal/India	25 May 1955	British	8,586	28,169
4 Lhotse, Nepal/China	18 May 1956	Swiss	8,516	27,940
5 Makalu I, Nepal/China	15 May 1955	French	8,485	27,838
6 Cho Oyu, Nepal/China	19 Oct 1954	Austrian	8,188	26,864
7 Dhaulagiri I, Nepal	13 May 1960	Swiss/Austrian	8,167	26,795
8 Manaslu I (Kutang I), Nepal	9 May 1956	Japanese	8,163	26,781
9 Nanga Parbat (Diamir), Pakistan	3 Jul 1953	German/Austrian	8,125	26,657
10 Anapurna I, Nepal	3 Jun 1950	French	8,091	26,545

* Height of principal peak; lower peaks of the same mountain are excluded

In 1852, the Great Trigonometrical Survey of India revealed that Everest was the world's tallest peak at 8,840 m (29,002 ft). Errors in measurement were corrected in 1955 to 8,848 m (29,029 ft) and in 1993 to 8,847.7 m (29,028 ft). In 1999, data beamed from sensors on Everest's summit to GPS satellites established a new height of 8,850 m (29,035 ft), which geographers accept as the current 'official' figure.

TOP 10 LONGEST MOUNTAIN RANGES

RANGE / LOCATION	LENGTH KM	MILES
1 Andes, South America	7,242	4,500
2 Rocky Mountains, North America	6,035	3,750
3 Himalayas/Karakoram/Hindu Kush, Asia	3,862	2,400
4 Great Dividing Range, Australia	3,621	2,250
5 Trans-Antarctic Mountains, Antarctica	3,541	2,200
6 Brazilian East Coast Range, Brazil	3,058	1,900
7 Sumatran/Javan Range, Sumatra, Java	2,897	1,800
8 Tien Shan, China	2,253	1,400
9 Eastern Ghats, India	2,092	1,300
10 = Altai, Asia	2,012	1,250
= Central New Guinean Range, Papua New Guinea	2,012	1,250
= Urals, Russia	2,012	1,250

This Top 10 includes only ranges that are continuous (the Sumatran/Javan Range is divided only by a short interruption between the two islands). The Aleutian Range extends for 2,655 km (1,650 miles), but is fragmented across numerous islands of the north-west Pacific. As well as these ranges that lie above the surface of Earth, there are also several submarine ranges that are even longer.

▶ Machu Picchu
The Andes were originally inhabited by the Incas, and span seven countries and three capitals.

Ojos del Salado
The second highest peak in the
Andes – and in the Southern
Hemisphere – also contains the
world's most elevated lake.

▶ *Piton de la Fournaise*
Meaning 'Peak of the Furnace', this volcano
has erupted 19 times in the last decade.

TOP 10 **HIGHEST VOLCANOES**

VOLCANO	LOCATION	HEIGHT M	HEIGHT FT
1 Ojos del Salado	Chile	6,887	22,595
2 Llullaillaco	Chile	6,739	22,110
3 Tipas	Argentina	6,660	21,850
4 Nevado Incahuasi	Chile	6,621	21,722
5 Cerro el Cóndor	Argentina	6,532	21,430
6 Coropuna	Peru	6,377	20,922
7 Parinacota	Chile	6,348	20,827
8 Chimborazo	Ecuador	6,310	20,702
9 Pular	Chile	6,233	20,449
10 El Solo	Chile	6,190	20,308

Source: Smithsonian Institution

TOP 10 **COUNTRIES WITH THE HIGHEST ELEVATIONS***

COUNTRY	PEAK	HEIGHT M	HEIGHT FT
1 = China	Everest	8,850	29,035
= Nepal	Everest	8,850	29,035
3 Pakistan	K2	8,607	28,238
4 India	Kangchenjunga	8,598	28,208
5 Bhutan	Khula Kangri	7,554	24,784
6 Tajikistan	Garmo (formerly Kommunizma)	7,495	24,590
7 Afghanistan	Noshaq	7,490	24,581
8 Kyrgyzstan	Pik Pobedy	7,439	24,406
9 Kazakhstan	Khan Tengri	6,995	22,949
10 Argentina	Cerro Aconcagua	6,960	22,834

* Based on the tallest peak in each country

TOP 10 **MOST ACTIVE VOLCANOES***

VOLCANO / LOCATION / CONTINUOUSLY ACTIVE SINCE

1 **Mount Etna**
Italy c. 1500 BC

2 **Stromboli**
Italy c. AD 4

3 **Yasur**
Vanuatu c. 1204

4 **Piton de la Fournaise**
Réunion 1920

5 **Santa Maria**
Guatemala 1922

6 **Dukono**
Indonesia 1933

7 **Sangay**
Ecuador 1934

8 **Ambrym**
Vanuatu 1935

9 **Suwanose-jima**
Japan 1949

10 **Tinakula**
Solomon Islands 1951

* Based on years of continuous eruption

Sicily's 3,350-m (10,99-ft)
Mount Etna may have been
erupting for more than
half a million years, with
occasional dormant periods.
Continuous activity has
been recorded for the past
3,500 years, the eruption
of 1843 killing 56, with a
further nine in 1979 and
two in 1987.

LAND FEATURES

TOP 10 **LARGEST DESERTS**

DESERT / LOCATION	APPROX. AREA SQ KM	SQ MILES
1 Sahara, northern Africa	9,100,000	3,513,530
2 Arabian, south-west Asia	2,330,000	899,618
3 Gobi, central Asia	1,295,000	500,002
4 Patagonian, Argentina/Chile	673,000	259,847
5 Great Basin, USA	492,000	189,962
6 Great Victoria, Australia	424,000	163,707
7 Chihuahuan, Mexico/USA	362,600	140,000
8 Great Sandy, Australia	360,000	138,997
9 Karakum, Turkmenistan	350,000	135,136
10 Sonoran, Mexico/USA	311,000	120,078

◀ *Saharan sands*
Covering an area nearly the size of the USA, half of the Sahara receives less than 2 cm (0.8 in) of rain per year.

▼ *Coral collection*
With 1,190 coral islands, the Maldives' average height above sea level is only 1.5 m (4.9 ft).

THE 10 **COUNTRIES WITH THE LOWEST ELEVATIONS**

	COUNTRY*	HIGHEST POINT	ELEVATION M	FT
10	Singapore	Bukit Timah	166.0	544.6
9	Qatar	Qurayn Abu al Bawl	103.0	337.9
8	Kiribati	Unnamed on Banaba	81.0	265.7
7	Vatican City	Unnamed	75.0	246.1
6	Bahamas	Mount Alvernia on Cat Island	63.0	206.7
5	Nauru	Unnamed on plateau rim	61.0	200.1
4	Gambia	Unnamed	53.0	173.9
3	Marshall Islands	Unnamed on Likiep	10.0	32.8
2	Tuvalu	Unnamed	5.0	16.4
1	Maldives	Unnamed on Wilingili island in the Addu Atoll	2.4	7.8

* Excludes overseas possessions, territories and dependencies

Source: CIA, *The World Factbook 2010*

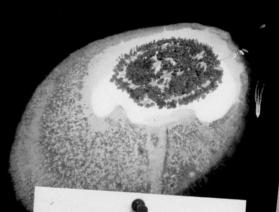

These 10 countries are definitely off the agenda if you are planning a climbing holiday, none of them possessing a single elevation taller than a medium-sized skyscraper.

▼ Great depths
The depth of the Krubera cave is equivalent to seven times the height of the Eiffel Tower

TOP 10 **LARGEST METEORITE CRATERS**

	CRATER / LOCATION	DIAMETER KM	MILES
1	Vredefort, South Africa	300	186
2	Sudbury, Ontario, Canada	250	155
3	Chicxulub, Yucatan, Mexico	170	107
4	= Manicougan, Quebec, Canada	100	62
	= Popigai, Russia	100	62
6	= Acraman, Australia	90	56
	= Chesapeake Bay, Virginia, USA	90	56
8	Puchezh-Katunki, Russia	80	50
9	Morokweng, South Africa	70	43
10	Kara, Russia	65	40

Source: Earth Impact Database, Planetary and Space Science Centre, University of New Brunswick

▼ *Space debris*
Discovered by chance while a farmer was ploughing, Hoba meteorite weighs more than six elephants.

THE 10 **DEEPEST CAVES**

	CAVE SYSTEM / LOCATION	DEPTH M	FT
1	Krubera (Voronja), Georgia	2,191	7,188
2	Illyuzia-Mezhonnogo-Snezhnaya, Georgia	1,753	5,751
3	Lamprechtsofen Vogelschacht Weg Schacht, Austria	1,632	5,354
4	Gouffre Mirolda, France	1,626	5,335
5	Réseau Jean Bernard, France	1,602	5,256
6	Torca del Cerro del Cuevon/ Torca de las Saxifragas, Spain	1,589	5,213
7	Sarma, Georgia	1,543	5,062
8	Shakta Vjacheslav Pantjukhina, Georgia	1,508	4,948
9	Sima de la Conisa/Torca Magali, Spain	1,507	4,944
10	Cehi 2, Slovenia	1,502	4,928

In January 2001, a team of Ukrainian cave explorers in the Arabikskaja system in the western Caucasus mountains of the Georgian Republic found a branch of the Voronja, or 'Crow's Cave', and established that its depth of 1,710 m (5,610 ft) far exceeded anything previously known.

The Largest Meteorites Ever Found

Meteorites have been known since early times: fragments of meteorite have been found mounted in a necklace in an Egyptian pyramid and in ancient Native American burial sites. On 16 November 1492, there was a fall of a 118-kg (260-lb) meteorite, which was later preserved in the museum at Ensisheim in Switzerland. There have been nearly 40,000 documented meteorite finds, with the largest eight weighing over 20 tonnes. Estimates of the size of meteorites creating the largest craters dwarfs those that have actually been discovered. The meteorite producing Vredefort in South Africa is believed to have been between 5–10 km (3–6 miles) wide, weighing trillions of tonnes.

WORLD WEATHER

TOP 10 HOTTEST PLACES – AVERAGE

LOCATION* / AVERAGE TEMPERATURE# (°C / °F)

	LOCATION	°C	°F
1	**Dalol** Ethiopia	34.6	94.3
2	**Assab** Eritrea	30.4	86.8
3	**Néma** Mauritania	30.3	86.5
4	**Berbera** Somalia	30.1	86.2
5	**Hombori** Mali	30.1	86.1
6	**Perm Island,** South Yemen	30.0	86.0
7	**Djibouti** Djibouti	29.9	85.8
8	**Atbara** Sudan	29.8	85.7
9	= **Bender Qaasim** Somalia	29.7	85.5
	= **Kamarãn Island** North Yemen	29.7	85.5

* Maximum of two places per country listed

\# Highest long-term temperature averaged throughout year

Source: Philip Eden

TOP 10 PLACES WITH THE MOST CONTRASTING SEASONS*

	LOCATION#	WINTER °C	WINTER °F	SUMMER °C	SUMMER °F	DIFFERENCE °C	DIFFERENCE °F
1	Verkhoyansk, Russia	-50.3	-58.5	13.6	56.5	63.9	115.0
2	Yakutsk, Russia	-45.0	-49.0	17.5	63.5	62.5	112.5
3	Manzhouli, China	-26.1	-15.0	20.6	69.0	46.7	84.0
4	Fort Yukon, Alaska, USA	-29.0	-20.2	16.3	61.4	45.3	81.6
5	Fort Good Hope, North West Territory, Canada	-29.9	-21.8	15.3	59.5	45.2	81.3
6	Brochet, Manitoba, Canada	-29.2	-20.5	15.4	59.7	44.6	80.2
7	Tunka, Mongolia	-26.7	-16.0	16.1	61.0	42.8	77.0
8	Fairbanks, Alaska, USA	-24.0	-11.2	15.6	60.1	39.6	71.3
9	Semipalatinsk, Kazakhstan	-17.7	0.5	20.6	69.0	38.3	68.5
10	Jorgen Bronlund Fjørd, Greenland	-30.9	-23.6	6.4	43.5	37.3	67.1

* Biggest differences between mean monthly temperatures in summer and winter
\# Maximum of two places per country listed

Source: Philip Eden

TOP 10 DRIEST PLACES – AVERAGE

	LOCATION*	AVERAGE ANNUAL RAINFALL# MM	IN
1	Arica, Chile	0.7	0.03
2	= Al'Kufrah, Peru	0.8	0.03
	= Aswân, Egypt	0.8	0.03
	= Luxor, Egypt	0.8	0.03
5	Ica, Peru	2.3	0.09
6	Wadi Halfa, Sudan	2.6	0.10
7	Iquique, Chile	5.0	0.20
8	Pelican Point, Namibia	8.0	0.32
9	= Aoulef, Algeria	12.0	0.48
	= Callao, Peru	12.0	0.48

* Maximum of two places per country listed
\# Annual total averaged over a long period

Source: Philip Eden

▼ *Iquique*
A commune in northern Chile, Iquique includes a popular port city and the Atacama Desert.

◄ *The Republic of Djibouti*
One of Africa's least populated countries, Djibouti's landscape is mostly semi-desert.

TOP 10 COLDEST PLACES

LOCATION* / LOWEST RECORDED TEMPERATURE (°C / °F)

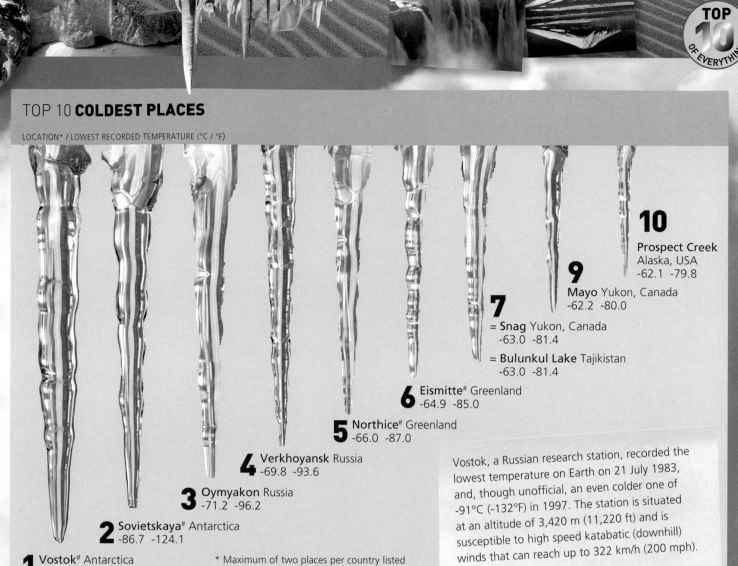

10 Prospect Creek Alaska, USA
-62.1 -79.8

9 Mayo Yukon, Canada
-62.2 -80.0

7 = Snag Yukon, Canada
-63.0 -81.4

= Bulunkul Lake Tajikistan
-63.0 -81.4

6 Eismitte# Greenland
-64.9 -85.0

5 Northice# Greenland
-66.0 -87.0

4 Verkhoyansk Russia
-69.8 -93.6

3 Oymyakon Russia
-71.2 -96.2

2 Sovietskaya# Antarctica
-86.7 -124.1

1 Vostok# Antarctica
-89.2 -128.6

* Maximum of two places per country listed
# Present or former scientific research base

Source: Philip Eden/Roland Bert

Vostok, a Russian research station, recorded the lowest temperature on Earth on 21 July 1983, and, though unofficial, an even colder one of -91°C (-132°F) in 1997. The station is situated at an altitude of 3,420 m (11,220 ft) and is susceptible to high speed katabatic (downhill) winds that can reach up to 322 km/h (200 mph).

▼ **Oymyakon**
Known as the coldest populated place on Earth, Oymyakon has an average winter temperature of -45°C (-49°F).

TOP 10 DULLEST PLACES*

LOCATION#	% OF MAX. POSSIBLE	AVERAGE ANNUAL HOURS SUNSHINE
1 Ben Nevis, Scotland	16	736
2 Hoyvik, Faeroes, Denmark	19	902
3 Maam, Ireland	19	929
4 Prince Rupert, British Columbia, Canada	20	955
5 Riksgransen, Sweden	20	965
6 Akureyri, Iceland	20	973
7 Raufarhöfn, Iceland	21	995
8 Nanortalik, Greenland	22	1,000
9 Dalwhinnie, Scotland	22	1,032
10 Karasjok, Norway	23	1,090

* Lowest yearly sunshine total, averaged over a long period of years
# Maximum of two places per country listed

Source: Philip Eden

THE 10 **DEADLIEST TYPES OF NATURAL DISASTER**

DISASTER /
ESTIMATED DEATHS, 2000–10

Earthquake
680,361

Storm
173,699

Extreme temperature
148,249

Epidemic
66,506

Flood
62,233

Mass movement (wet)
10,856

Drought
1,520

Wildfire
770

Volcanic eruption
560

Mass movement (dry)
126

▶ *Haiti earthquake*
The magnitude 7.0 earthquake caused US$11 billion of damage and left 1.5 million homeless.

There are some discrepancies between the 'official' death tolls in many of the world's worst earthquakes and the estimates of other authorities: a figure of 750,000 is sometimes quoted for the Tangshan earthquake of 1976, for example.

THE 10 **WORST EARTHQUAKES**

	LOCATION	DATE	ESTIMATED NO. KILLED
1	Near East/Mediterranean	20 May 1202	1,100,000
2	Shenshi, China	2 Feb 1556	820,000
3	Calcutta, India	11 Oct 1737	300,000
4	Antioch, Syria	20 May 526	250,000
5	Tangshan, China	28 Jul 1976	242,419
6	Port-au-Prince, Haiti	12 Jan 2010	230,000
7	Nanshan, China	22 May 1927	200,000
8	Yeddo, Japan	30 Dec 1703	190,000
9	Kansu, China	16 Dec 1920	180,000
10	Messina, Italy	28 Dec 1908	160,000

▶ *Indonesian eruption*
Around 50 million cubic metres of volcanic material was released by the 2010 eruption of Mount Merapi.

THE 10 **WORST EPIDEMICS**

	EPIDEMIC	LOCATION	DATE	ESTIMATED NO. KILLED
1	Black Death	Europe/Asia	1347–80s	75,000,000
2	Influenza	Worldwide	1918–20	20–40,000,000
3	AIDS	Worldwide	1981–	>25,000,000
4	Plague of Justinian	Europe/Asia	AD 541–90	<25,000,000
5	Bubonic plague	India	1896–1948	12,000,000
6 =	Antonine Plague (probably smallpox)	Roman Empire	AD 165–180	5,000,000
=	Plague	India	1896–1907	5,000,000
8	Typhus	Eastern Europe	1918–22	3,000,000
9 =	Smallpox	Mexico	1530–45	1,000,000
=	Cholera	Russia	1852–60	1,000,000

THE 10 **COUNTRIES WITH THE HIGHEST FLOOD-DAMAGE COST**

	COUNTRY	ESTIMATED COST (US$) 2000–10
1	China	56,377,821,000
2	India	18,949,347,000
3	USA	15,565,330,000
4	UK	14,949,150,000
5	Germany	11,840,000,000
6	Pakistan	10,206,148,000
7	Italy	9,899,000,000
8	Australia	9,431,500,000
9	Japan	9,397,000,000
10	France	4,322,350,000
	World	212,197,295,000

Source: Emergency Events Database (EM-DAT)

Precise figures for deaths during the disruptions of epidemics are inevitably unreliable, but the Black Death, or bubonic plague, probably transmitted by fleas from infected rats, swept across Asia and Europe in the 14th century, destroying entire populations – including more than half the inhabitants of London, some 25 million in Europe and 50 million in Asia.

THE 10 **COUNTRIES WITH THE MOST DEATHS FROM NATURAL DISASTERS***

COUNTRY / ESTIMATED DEATHS FROM NATURAL DISASTERS / MOST DEADLY TYPE

China 12,710,201
Flood

India 9,114,324
Epidemic

USSR 3,868,439
Epidemic

Bangladesh 2,991,948
Drought

Ethiopia 416,056
Drought

Indonesia 239,462
Earthquake

Japan 221,700
Earthquake

Uganda 203,996
Epidemic

Niger 194,572
Epidemic

Pakistan 170,088
Earthquake

* Includes deaths from drought, earthquake, epidemic, extreme temperature, flood, insect infestation, landslides, storms, volcanoes, wave/surge and wildfires

▲ *Floodwaters in China*
China has suffered over 200 incidents of flooding in the last 100 years – the worst affecting a quarter of a billion people.

2
LIFE ON EARTH

EARTH SUMMIT 2012

The United Nations Conference on Sustainable Development takes place in June 2012 – 20 years after the influential first Earth Summit was held in Rio de Janeiro. The Rio+20 summit will provide a platform for world leaders to come together to address a number of globally important issues, including the financial, food and energy crises, water scarcity, climate change and the loss of biodiversity. The highly ambitious aim of the summit is to seek agreement from heads of state to work towards providing for a future in which each person has a decent standard of living while preserving ecosystems and natural resources.

EXTINCT!

THE FIRST DINOSAUR TO BE NAMED

The first genus of dinosaur to be named was Megalosaurus, which means 'great lizard' in Greek. It was described by William Buckland, a professor at Oxford University, in a paper he wrote in 1824.

TOP 10 **DINOSAUR DISCOVERERS**

	DISCOVERER / COUNTRY	PERIOD	DINOSAURS NAMED*
1	Friedrich von Huene (Germany)	1902–61	46
2	Othniel Charles Marsh (USA)	1870–94	39
3	Dong Zhiming (China)	1973–2003	35
4	= Edward Drinker Cope (USA)	1866–92	30
	= Harry Govier Seeley (UK)	1869–98	30
6	José Fernando Bonaparte (Argentina)	1969–2000	28
7	Richard Owen (UK)	1841–84	23
8	= Barnum Brown (USA)	1873–1963	17
	= Henry Fairfield Osborn (USA)	1902–24	17
	= Yang Zhong-Jian ('C. C. Young') (China)	1937–82	17

* Including joint namings

▲ *Dinosaur discoverer*
Dong Zhiming is the most prolific dinosaur hunter of modern times.

TOP 10 **HEAVIEST DINOSAURS EVER DISCOVERED**

	NAME	ESTIMATED WEIGHT (TONNES)
1	Bruhathkayosaurus	126
2	Amphicoelias	122
3	Puertasaurus	80–100
4	Argentinosaurus	60–88
5	Argyrosaurus	80
6	Antarctosaurus	69
7	Sauroposeidon	50–60
8	Paralititan	59
9	Turiasaurus	40–48
10	Supersaurus	35–40

Fossil remains of Bruhathkayosaurus were found in southern India. Some authorities have estimated it as having weighed as much as 220 tonnes – more than a blue whale – but such claims have been questioned.

▶ *Big bird*
At over 3 m (10 ft) tall, the elephant bird was once the world's largest.

TOP 10 **TIMELINE – LAST SEEN ALIVE**

These are the years when some notable creatures became extinct, especially as a result of human intervention. In the case of those that occurred in captivity, the precise date can be given.

1627
Aurochs
Extensively hunted, the last of these large oxen died in the Jaktorow Forest in Poland.

1649
Aepyornis
Also known as the 'elephant bird', this wingless bird was a native of Madagascar.

1681
Dodo
Perhaps the most famous extinct creature ever, the last of these flightless birds was observed on Mauritius by Benjamin Harry.

1768
Steller's sea cow
This large marine mammal, named after its 1741 discoverer, was hunted to extinction.

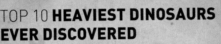

1844
Great auk
The last surviving pair of great auks was killed on Eldey Island for Icelandic collector Carl Siemsen.

TOP 10 **LONGEST DINOSAURS EVER DISCOVERED**

NAME	ESTIMATED LENGTH (M)
1 Puertasaurus	35–40

Provisional estimates by palaeontologist Fernando Novas place this as the longest dinosaur yet discovered.

2 Sauroposeidon	34

It has been estimated that this creature was probably the tallest ever to walk on Earth, able to extend its neck to 18 m (60 ft).

3 Supersaurus	33–34

Claims of a length of up to 40 m (130 ft) have been made by some authorities.

4 Bruhathkayosaurus	28–34

As with claims of its record-breaking weight, those of a length of up to 44 m (145 ft) remain questionable.

5 = Hudiesaurus	30

Although known only from incomplete remains found in China, this may have been one of the longest of all sauropods.

= Turiasaurus	30

This long sauropod was named after Turia, the Latin name of Teruel, Spain, where it was found.

7 Giraffatitan	25–30

This lightly built but long dinosaur was found in Tanzania. A skeleton in the Humboldt Museum, Berlin, is the longest dinosaur on display.

8 Argentinosaurus	22–26

Estimates of the length of Argentinosaurus vary, some early claims putting it at up to 35 m (110 ft).

9 = Argyrosaurus	20–30

This dinosaur from the late Cretaceous period is believed to have stood 8 m (26 ft) tall.

= Diplodocus	20–30

As it was long and thin, Diplodocus was a relative lightweight in the dinosaur world. It was also probably one of the most stupid dinosaurs, having the smallest brain in relation to its body size. Diplodocus was given its name (which means 'double beam') in 1878 by US palaeontologist Othniel C. Marsh.

▼ *Argentinosaurus*
This gigantic plant-eater lived in the forests of South America over 90 million years ago.

► *Back from the dead*
There have been nearly 4,000 unconfirmed sightings of the Tasmanian wolf since 1936.

1875 1883 1914 1932 1936

Tarpan
The last pure-bred tarpan, a European wild horse, died in a Moscow zoo.

Quagga
Found in South Africa, this zebra-like creature became extinct in the wild by 1883.

Passenger pigeon
Once seen in vast flocks, the last specimen died in Cincinnati Zoo on 1 September 1914.

Heath hen
The grouse-like prairie chicken was extensively hunted in New England.

Tasmanian wolf
Also known as the thylacine, the last specimen died in captivity.

Endangered Animals

THE 10 COUNTRIES WITH THE MOST THREATENED ANIMAL SPECIES*

	COUNTRY	MAMMALS	BIRDS	REPTILES	AMPHIBIANS	FISHES	INVERTEBRATES	TOTAL
1	USA	37	74	32	56	177	531	907
2	Australia	55	52	43	47	100	489	786
3	Indonesia	183	119	31	32	138	246	749
4	Mexico	99	55	94	211	150	79	688
5	India	94	78	30	66	122	113	503
6	Malaysia	70	45	24	47	60	242	488
7	Philippines	39	72	38	48	65	213	475
8	Colombia	51	91	19	213	50	30	454
9	Ecuador	43	71	22	171	49	62	418
10	China	74	85	31	87	97	32	406
	UK	5	2	0	0	41	11	59

* Identified by the IUCN as Critically Endangered, Endangered or Vulnerable

Source: IUCN, *2010 Red List of Threatened Species*

▲ **Symbol of hope**
After years of decline, giant panda numbers are thought to be increasing.

▲ **At risk**
The leatherback turtle, ranked as Critically Endangered, is close to extinction in the wild.

THE 10 MOST THREATENED CLASS OF ANIMAL

CLASS / CLASS THREATENED*

1 Amphibians 1,905
2 Fish 1,275
3 Birds 1,222
4 Mammals 1,141
5 Molluscs 978
6 Insects 626
7 Crustaceans 606
8 Reptiles 423
9 Corals 235
10 Arachnids 18

Total (including classes not in Top 10) 8,462

* Identified by the IUCN as Critically Endangered, Endangered or Vulnerable

Source: IUCN, *2010 Red List of Threatened Species*

▶ **Galapagos hawk**
There are less than 150 mating pairs in existence, and these birds are now extinct on several Galapagos islands.

IN THE RED

The IUCN Red List system classifies the degree of threat posed to wildlife on a sliding scale from Vulnerable (at high risk of extinction), through Endangered (at very high risk of extinction), to Critically Endangered (facing an extremely high risk of extinction in the wild). Actual threats to species are many and varied, and include both human activity and natural events, ranging from habitat loss and degradation, invasions by alien species, hunting and accidental destruction due to persecution, pollution and natural disasters.

TOP 10 CHIMPANZEE COUNTRIES

COUNTRY / ESTIMATED CHIMPANZEE POPULATION*

1 **Dem. Rep. of Congo** 80,000–110,000
2 Gabon 27,000–64,000
3 Cameroon 34,000–44,000
4 Guinea 8,100–29,000
5 Côte d'Ivoire 8,000–12,000
6 Uganda 4,000–5,700
7 Mali 1,600–5,200
8 Liberia 1,000–5,000
9 Nigeria 2,000–3,000
10 Sierra Leone 1,500–2,500
   World 172,700–299,700

* Ranked on estimated maximum
Source: IUCN

GLOBAL TIGER INITIATIVE

Faced with threats of poaching, habitat loss and fragmentation, if current trends persist the tiger faces extinction within this decade. The Global Tiger Recovery Programme aims to double the population by 2022, through collaboration of 13 tiger-range countries, charities and institutions. Tigers serve as an umbrella species – setting aside large areas protects many other species. Their habitat overlaps that of many other endangered animals, including Asian elephants, orangutans and greater one-horned rhinoceroses.

▼ *Polar bears at drift*
With its habitat literally melting, global warming is considered the polar bear's most significant threat.

DEATHLY DECLINE

Biodiversity is being lost at 1,000 times the natural rate, with most serious decline in islands, dry forests, polar regions and marine environments. Thirty per cent of species are under threat because of climate change. Of the world's 5,490 mammals, 78 are extinct in the wild, 188 Critically Endangered, 450 Endangered and 492 Vulnerable.

NATURE'S HEAVYWEIGHTS

◄ Land giant
African elephants can be identified by their Africa-shaped ears, which they use to keep cool.

TOP 10 HEAVIEST LAND MAMMALS

MAMMAL* / SCIENTIFIC NAME	LENGTH		WEIGHT	
	M	FT	KG	LB
1 African elephant (*Loxodonta africana*)	7.5	24.6	6,350	14,000
2 Hippopotamus (*Hippopotamus amphibius*)	4.2	14.0	3,629	8,000
3 White rhinoceros (*Ceratotherium simum*)	4.1	13.7	3,592	7,920
4 Giraffe (*Giraffa camelopardalis*)	6.0	19.0	1,270	2,800
5 American buffalo (*Bison bison*)	3.5	11.5	1,000	2,205
6 Moose (*Alces alces*)	3.1	10.1	825	1,820
7 Arabian camel (dromedary) (*Camelus dromedarius*)	3.5	11.5	726	1,600
8 Grizzly bear (*Ursus arctos*)	2.5	8.0	363	800
9 Siberian tiger (*Panthera tigris altaica*)	3.3	10.8	300	660
10 Gorilla (*Gorilla gorilla gorilla*)	2.0	6.5	220	485

* Heaviest species per genus; maximum weight, exclusively terrestrial, excluding seals, etc.

TOP 10 HEAVIEST CARNIVORES

CARNIVORE	LENGTH			WEIGHT	
	M	FT	IN	KG	LB
1 Southern elephant seal	6.0	20	0	4,000	8,800
2 Pacific walrus	3.8	12	6	1,400	3,086
3 Steller sea lion	2.8	9	3	1,100	2,425
4 Polar bear	2.5	8	0	726	1,600
5 Grizzly bear	2.5	8	0	363	800
6 Siberian tiger	3.3	10	7	300	660
7 American black bear	1.8	6	0	270	600
8 Lion	2.0	6	6	191	420
9 Spectacled bear	1.8	6	0	154	340
10 Giant panda	1.5	5	0	136	300

TOP 10 **CARNIVORES WITH THE HEAVIEST NEWBORN**

CARNIVORE / SCIENTIFIC NAME	BIRTH WEIGHT		
	G	LB	OZ
1 Lion (*Panthera leo*)	2,100	4	6
2 Spotted hyena (*Crocuta crocuta*)	1,500	3	5
3 Tiger (*Panthera tigris*)	1,255	2	11
4 Jaguar (*Panthera onca*)	816	1	13
5 Brown (grizzly) bear (*Ursus arctos*)	700	1	9
6 Polar bear (*Ursus maritimus*)	641	1	7
7 Leopard (*Panthera pardus*)	549	1	3
8 Snow leopard (*Panthera uncia*)	442	1	0
9 Grey wolf (*Canis lupus*)	425	0	15
10 Mountain lion (*Puma concolor*)	400	0	14

► **Queen of the jungle**
The gestation period for African lions is around 110 days, with lionesses giving birth to an average litter of two to three cubs.

TOP 10 **HEAVIEST BIRDS**

BIRD* / SCIENTIFIC NAME	HEIGHT		WEIGHT		
	CM	IN	KG	LB	OZ
1 Ostrich (*Struthio camelus*)	255	100.4	156.0	343	9
2 Northern cassowary (*Casuarius unappendiculatus*)	150	59.1	58.0	127	9
3 Emu (*Dromaius novaehollandiae*)	155	61.0	55.0	121	6
4 Emperor penguin (*Aptenodytes forsteri*)	115	45.3	46.0	101	4
5 Greater rhea (*Rhea americana*)	140	55.1	25.0	55	2
6 Mute swan# (*Cygnus olor*)	238	93.7	22.5	49	6
7 Kori bustard# (*Ardeotis kori*)	270	106.3	19.0	41	8
8 = Andean condor# (*Vultur gryphus*)	320	126.0	15.0	33	1
= Great white pelican# (*Pelecanus onocrotalus*)	360	141.7	15.0	33	1
10 European black vulture# (Old World) (*Aegypius monachus*)	295	116.1	12.5	27	5

* By species
\# Flighted – all others are flightless

Source: Chris Mead

◄ *Southern elephant seal*
Adult male members of the southern elephant seal population are typically five to six times larger than the females.

▲ *Biggest bird*
The largest living species of bird, the ostrich also lays the biggest egg and has the top land speed of any living bird.

LONGEST & LARGEST

TOP 10 MAMMALS WITH THE LONGEST TAILS

MAMMAL / MAX. TAIL LENGTH (CM / IN)

1 Asian elephant 150 / 60

2 Leopard 140 / 55

3 African elephant 130 / 51

4= African buffalo 110 / 43
Giraffe 110 / 43
Red kangaroo 110 / 43

7= Langur 100 / 39
Lion 100 / 39
Snub-nosed monkey 100 / 39
Water buffalo 100 / 39
White-cheeked mangabey 100 / 39

► *Deadly grip*
The four largest snakes are all constrictors.

◄ *On the wing*
Weighing as much as 11 kg (25 lb), adult Andean condors can have a 3-m (10-ft) wingspan.

TOP 10 LARGEST BIRDS OF PREY*

	BIRD / SCIENTIFIC NAME	MAX. LENGTH CM	IN
1	Himalayan Griffon vulture (*Gyps himalayensis*)	150	59
2	Californian condor (*Gymnogyps californianus*)	134	53
3	Andean condor (*Vultur gryphus*)	130	51
4 =	Lammergeier (*Gypaetus barbatus*)	115	45
=	Lappet-faced vulture (*Torgos tracheliotus*)	115	45
6	Eurasian Griffon vulture (*Gyps fulvus*)	110	43
7	European black vulture (*Aegypus monachus*)	107	42
8	Harpy eagle (*Harpia harpyja*)	105	41
9	Wedge-tailed eagle (*Aquila audax*)	104	41
10	Ruppell's griffon (*Gyps rueppellii*)	101	40

* By length, diurnal only – hence excluding owls

TOP 10 BIGGEST BIG CATS

	SPECIES / SCIENTIFIC NAME	MAX. LENGTH M	FT
1	Tiger (*Panthera tigris*)	3.70	12.0
2	Lion (*Panthera leo*)	3.30	10.8
3	Leopard (*Panthera pardus*)	2.90	9.6
4	Clouded leopard (*Neofelis nebulosa*)	2.00	6.6
5	Jaguar (*Panthera onca*)	1.90	6.2
6	Snow leopard (*Uncia uncia*)	1.80	5.9
7	Cougar (*Puma concolor*)	1.50	4.9
8	Cheetah (*Acinonyx jubatus*)	1.50	4.9
9	Lynx (*Lynx lynx*, etc.)	1.30	4.2
10 =	Asian golden cat (*Pardofelis temminckii*)	1.00	3.2
=	Bobcat (*Lynx rufus*)	1.00	3.2
=	Ocelot (*Leopardus pardalis*)	1.00	3.2
=	Serval (*Leptailurus serval*)	1.00	3.2

TOP 10 LARGEST WHALES

SPECIES / SCIENTIFIC NAME	ESTIMATED LENGTH M	FT
1 Blue whale (*Balaenoptera musculus*)	32.0	105.0
2 Fin whale (*Balaenoptera physalus*)	26.0	83.3
3 Humpback whale (*Megaptera novaeangliae*)	19.0	62.5
4 Sei whale (*Balaenoptera borealis*)	18.5	60.0
5 = Sperm whale (*Physeter macrocephalus*)	18.0	59.0
= Bowhead whale (*Balaena mysticetus*)	18.0	59.0
7 Northern right whale (*Eubalaena glacialis/Eubalaena australis*)	17.0	55.0
8 Grey whale (*Eschrichtius robustus*)	15.3	50.0
9 Bryde's whale (*Balaenoptera brydei*)	14.5	47.5
10 Baird's whale (*Berardius bairdii*)	12.8	42.0

TOP 10 LONGEST SNAKES

SNAKE / SCIENTIFIC NAME	MAX. LENGTH M	FT
1 Reticulated (royal) python (*Python reticulatus*)	10.0	32.8
2 Indian python (*Python molurus molurus*)	9.0	29.5
3 Anaconda (*Eunectes murinus*)	8.5	27.9
4 Diamond python (*Morelia spilota spilota*)	6.4	21.0
5 King cobra (*Opiophagus hannah*)	5.8	19.0
6 Boa constrictor (*Boa constrictor*)	5.5	18.0
7 Bushmaster (*Lachesis muta*)	3.7	12.1
8 Giant brown snake (*Oxyuranus scutellatus*)	3.4	11.2
9 Diamondback rattlesnake (*Crotalus atrox*)	2.7	8.9
10 Indigo or gopher snake (*Drymarchon corais*)	2.4	7.9

▼ **Spotted climber**
Skilled climbers, leopards can drag whole carcasses into trees.

▲ **Underwater acrobat**
Known for their singing and acrobatics, humpback whales weigh about 3 tonnes per metre.

TOP 10 LONGEST FOUR-LEGGED ANIMALS

ANIMAL* / SCIENTIFIC NAME	MAX. LENGTH M	FT
1 African elephant (*Loxodonta africana*)	7.3	24.0
2 Southern elephant seal (*Mirounga leonina*)	6.0	22.5
3 Estuarine crocodile (*Crocodylus porosus*)	6.3	20.6
4 Giraffe (*Giraffa camelopardalis*)	5.8	19.0
5 White rhinoceros (*Ceratotherium simum*)	4.2	13.8
6 West Indian manatee (*Trichechus manatus*)	4.1	13.5
7 Hippopotamus (*Hippopotamus amphibius*)	4.0	13.1
8 American bison (*Bison bison*)	3.9	12.8
9 Arabian camel (*Camelus dromedarius*)	3.5	11.5
10 Siberian tiger (*Panthera tigris altaica*)	3.3	10.8

* Longest representative of each species

FASTEST & SLOWEST

TOP 10 **FASTEST BIRDS**

BIRD / SCIENTIFIC NAME / MAX. RECORDED SPEED (KM/H / MPH)

1

Grey-headed albatross
(*Thalassarche chrysostama*)
127 / 80

2
Common eider
(*Somateria mollissima*)
76 / 47

3
Bewick's swan
(*Cygnus columbianus*)
72 / 45

4
= Barnacle goose
(*Branta leucopsis*)
68 / 42

= Common crane
(*Grus grus*)
68 / 42

6
Mallard
(*Anas platyrhynchos*)
65 / 40

7

= Red-throated diver
(*Gavia stellata*)
61 / 38

= Wood pigeon
(*Columba palumbus*)
61 / 38

9

Oystercatcher
(*Haematopus ostralegus*)
58 / 36

10
= Ring-necked pheasant
(*Phasianus colchichus*)
54 / 33

= White-fronted goose
(*Anser albifrons*)
54 / 33

▶ *Quick off the mark*
Cheetahs can run at top speed only in very short bursts, but can accelerate from 0 to 100 km/h (62 mph) in about three seconds.

TOP 10 **FASTEST FISH**

FISH / SCIENTIFIC NAME /
MAX. RECORDED SPEED (KM/H / MPH)

1 Sailfish (*Istiophorus platypterus*)
110 / 68*

2 Striped marlin (*Tetrapturus audax*)
81 / 50

3 Wahoo (peto, jack mackerel)
(*Acanthocybium solandri*)
80 / 49

4 Southern bluefin tuna
(*Thunnus maccoyii*)
76 / 47

5 = Bonefish (*Albula vulpes*)
64 / 40

= Swordfish (*Xiphias gladius*)
64 / 40

7 Atlantic needlefish
(*Strongylura marina*)
61 / 38*

8 Four-winged flying fish
(*Hirundichthys affinis*)
60 / 37*

9 Tarpon (ox-eye herring)
(*Megalops cyprinoides*)
56 / 35*

10 Blue shark (*Prionace glauca*)
39 / 25

* 'Flying' or leaping through air

▲ *Fast fish*
Sailfish have the ability to alter their body colour, and turn light blue when excited.

TOP 10 **FASTEST MAMMALS**

MAMMAL / SCIENTIFIC NAME /
MAX. RECORDED SPEED* (KM/H / MPH)

1 Cheetah (*Acinonyx jubatus*)
110 / 62

2 Pronghorn antelope
(*Antilocapra americana*)
86 / 53

3 Grant's gazelle (*Gazella granti*)
82 / 51

4 = Blue wildebeest (brindled gnu)
(*Connochaetes taurinus*)
80 / 50

= Lion (*Panthera leo*)
80 / 50

= Springbok (*Antidorcas marsupialis*)
80 / 50

7 Red fox (*Vulpes vulpes*)
77 / 48

8 Thomson's gazelle
(*Gazella thomsonii*)
76 / 47

9 = Brown hare (*Lepus capensis*)
72 / 45

= Horse (*Equus caballus*)
72 / 45

* Of those species for which data available

TOP 10 **MAMMALS WITH THE LONGEST GESTATION PERIODS***

	MAMMAL / SCIENTIFIC NAME	AVERAGE GESTATION (DAYS)
1	African elephant (*Loxodonta africana*)	660
2	Asian elephant (*Elephas maximus*)	645
3	= White rhinoceros (*Ceratotherium simum*)	480
	= Walrus (*Odobenus rosmarus*)	480
5	= Black rhinoceros (*Diceros bicornis*)	450
	= Arabian camel (dromedary) (*Camelus dromedarius*)	450
7	Giraffe (*Giraffa camelopardalis*)	435
8	Bactrian camel (*Camelus bactrianus*)	410
9	Tapir (*Tapirus*)	400
10	= Ass (*Equus africanus asinus*)	365
	= Grant's zebra (*Equus quagga*)	365

* Excluding whales

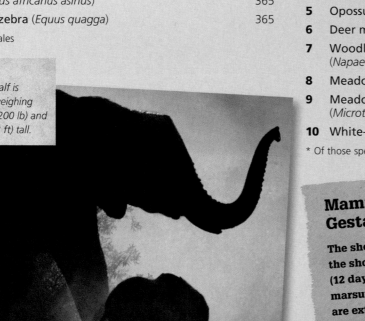

▼ **Big baby**
An elephant calf is enormous – weighing about 91 kg (200 lb) and abount 1 m (3 ft) tall.

▲ **Slow mover**
Three-toed sloths are extremely sedentary, and sleep for 15 to 20 hours a day.

THE 10 **SLOWEST MAMMALS**

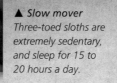

	MAMMAL / SCIENTIFIC NAME	AVERAGE SPEED* KM/H	MPH
1	Three-toed sloth (*Bradypus variegatus*)	0.1–0.3	0.06–0.19
2	Short-tailed (giant mole) shrew (*Blarina brevicauda*)	2.2	1.4
3	= Pine vole (*Microtus pinetorum*)	4.2	2.6
	= Red-backed vole (*Clethrionomys gapperi*)	4.2	2.6
5	Opossum (order *Didelphimorphia*)	4.4	2.7
6	Deer mouse (order *Peromyscus*)	4.5	2.8
7	Woodland jumping mouse (*Napaeozapus insignis*)	5.3	3.3
8	Meadow jumping mouse (*Zapus hudsonius*)	5.5	3.4
9	Meadow mouse or meadow vole (*Microtus pennsylvanicus*)	6.6	4.1
10	White-footed mouse (*Peromyscus leucopus*)	6.8	4.2

* Of those species for which data available

Mammals with the Shortest Gestation Periods

The short-nosed bandicoot and the opossum have the shortest gestation period of any mammal (12 days and 12–14 days respectively). Both are marsupial mammals, whose newborn offspring are extremely small, and transfer to a pouch to complete their development. A baby opossum is no bigger than a bee.

NATURE BY NUMBERS

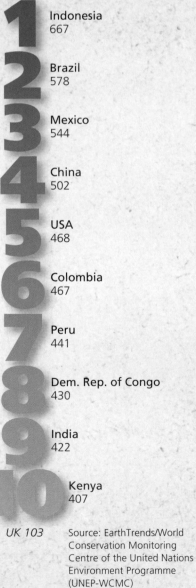

▼ **Old man of the forest** Indonesia's orang-utans are threatened by logging, poaching and forest fires.

TOP 10 **COUNTRIES WITH THE MOST MAMMAL SPECIES**

COUNTRY / MAMMAL SPECIES

1 Indonesia
667

2 Brazil
578

3 Mexico
544

4 China
502

5 USA
468

6 Colombia
467

7 Peru
441

8 Dem. Rep. of Congo
430

9 India
422

10 Kenya
407

UK 103   Source: EarthTrends/World Conservation Monitoring Centre of the United Nations Environment Programme (UNEP-WCMC)

TOP 10 **COUNTRIES WITH THE MOST ELEPHANTS**

COUNTRY / ELEPHANTS

1 Botswana
133,829

2 Tanzania
108,816

3 Zimbabwe
84,461

4 India
28,250

5 Kenya
23,353

6 South Africa
17,847

7 Zambia
16,562

8 Mozambique
14,079

9 Namibia
12,531

10 Uganda
2,337

TOP 10 **LONGEST-LIVED MARINE ANIMALS***

ANIMAL / SCIENTIFIC NAME / LIFESPAN (YEARS)

1 Quahog (marine clam)
(*Arctica islandica*)
221

2 Bowhead whale
(*Balaena mysticetus*)
211

3 Alligator snapping turtle
(*Macrochelys temminckii*)
150

4 Whale shark
(*Rhincodon typus*)
80

5 Sea anemone (*Actinia mesembryanthemum*, etc.)
70

6 European eel
(*Anguilla anguilla*)
85

7 Lake sturgeon
(*Acipenser fulvescens*)
82

8 Freshwater mussel
(*Palaeoheterodonta* – various)
80

9 Dugong
(*Dugong dugon*)
73

10 Spiny dogfish
(*Squalus acanthias*)
70

* Longest-lived of each genus listed

▼ **Old man of the sea** Snapping turtles are among the largest freshwater turtles in the world.

TOP 10 **LONGEST BIRD MIGRATIONS**

SPECIES / SCIENTIFIC NAME / APPROX. DISTANCE (KM / MILES)

1 Pectoral sandpiper
(*Calidris melanotos*)
19,000* / 11,806

2 Wheatear
(*Oenanthe oenanthe*)
18,000 / 11,184

3 Slender-billed shearwater
(*Puffinus tenuirostris*)
17,500* / 10,874

4 Ruff
(*Philomachus pugnax*)
16,600 / 10,314

5 Willow warbler
(*Phylloscopus trochilus*)
16,300 / 10,128

6 Arctic tern
(*Sterna paradisaea*)
16,200 / 10,066

7 Arctic skua
(*Stercorarius parasiticus*)
15,600 / 9,693

8 Swainson's hawk
(*Buteo swainsoni*)
15,200 / 9,445

9 Knot
(*Calidris canutus*)
15,000 / 9,320

10 Swallow
(*Hirundo rustica*)
14,900 / 9,258

* Thought to be only half of the path taken during a whole year

Source: Chris Mead

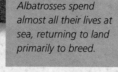

▲ *Royal albatross*
Albatrosses spend almost all their lives at sea, returning to land primarily to breed.

TOP 10 **LONGEST-LIVED RINGED WILD BIRDS**

BIRD / SCIENTIFIC NAME / AGE* (YRS / MTHS)

1 Northern royal albatross
(*Diomedea sanfordi*)
51 / 10

2 Fulmar
(*Fulmarus glacialis*)
40 / 11

3 Manx shearwater
(*Puffinus puffinus*)
37 / 0

4 Gannet
(*Morus bassanus*)
36 / 4

5 Oystercatcher
(*Haematopus ostralegus*)
36 / 0

6 White (fairy) tern
(*Gygis alba*)
35 / 11

7 Common eider
(*Somateria mollissima*)
35 / 0

8 Lesser Black-backed gull
(*Larus fuscus*)
34 / 10

9 Pink-footed goose
(*Anser brachyrhynchus*)
34 / 2

10 Great frigate bird
(*Fregata minor*)
33 / 9

* Elapsed time between marking and report

Source: RSPB

Wild Mammals with the Largest Litters

With up to 32 young per litter, the common tenrec takes the top prize, and females possess up to 29 teats – more than any other mammal. The southern opossum has an average litter size of 10, and can have up to three litters in a single year. The meadow vole probably holds the world record for most offspring produced in a season, as it can have up to 17 litters in rapid succession, bringing up to 150 young into the world.

DEADLIEST ANIMALS

THE 10 TYPES OF SHARK THAT HAVE ATTACKED AND KILLED THE MOST HUMANS

SHARK / SCIENTIFIC NAME	UNPROVOKED ATTACKS* TOTAL	FATALITIES#
1 Great white (Carcharodon carcharias)	244	65
2 Tiger (Galeocerdo cuvier)	88	27
3 Bull (Carcharhinus leucas)	82	25
4 Requiem (Carcharhinus sp.)	39	7
5 Blue (Prionace glauca)	13	4
6 Sand tiger (Carcharias taurus)	32	3
7 =Blacktip (Carcharhinus limbatus)	28	1
=Shortfin mako (Isurus oxyrinchus)	8	1
=Oceanic whitetip (Carcharhinus longimanus)	5	1
=Dusky (Carcharhinus obscurus)	3	1
=Galapagos (Carcharhinus galapagensis)	1	1

* 1580–2009
\# Where fatalities are equal, entries are ranked by total attacks

Source: *International Shark Attack File*, Florida Museum of Natural History

Requiem is actually a family of sharks. However, many Requiem sharks are difficult to identify so the International Shark Attack File groups together attacks by unidentified Requiems, hence its inclusion at No. 4.

▲ **Great white**
These enormous fish are frequently up to 6 m (20 ft) long.

THE 10 BODY PARTS MOST OFTEN INJURED IN SHARK ATTACKS ON DIVERS

BODY PART INJURED / % OF ATTACKS*

1. Calf/knee 35.2
2. Arm 30.2
3. Thigh 23.9
4. Foot 22.0
5. Hand 13.2
6. =Abdomen/stomach 8.8
   =Buttocks 8.8
   =Chest 8.8
9. =Back 6.9
   =Shoulder 6.9

* As of July 2009

Source: *International Shark Attack File*, Florida Museum of Natural History

THE 10 PLACES WHERE MOST PEOPLE ARE ATTACKED BY SHARKS

LOCATION / FATAL ATTACKS / LAST FATAL ATTACK / TOTAL ATTACKS

1	USA (excluding Hawaii) 33 / 2008	**885**
2	Australia 117 / 2008	**330**
3	South Africa 44 / 2009	**212**
4	Hawaii 8 / 2004	**96**
5	Brazil 21 / 2006	**87**
6	Papua New Guinea 24 / 2000	**47**
7	New Zealand 8 / 1968	**44**
8	Mexico 19 / 2008	**35**
9	The Bahamas 1 / 1968	**26**
10	Iran 8 / 1985	**23**

* Confirmed unprovoked attacks, including non-fatal, 1580–2009

Source: *International Shark Attack File*, Florida Museum of Natural History

TOP 10 **MOST VENOMOUS SPIDERS**

SPIDER / SCIENTIFIC NAME / RANGE

1 Banana spider
(*Phoneutria nigriventer*)
Central and South America

2 Sydney funnel web
(*Atrax robustus*)
Australia

3 Wolf spider
(*Lycosa raptoria/erythrognatha*)
Central and South America

4 Black widow
(*Latrodectus* sp.)
Widespread

5 Violin spider/Recluse spider
(*Loxosceles reclusa*)
Widespread

6 Sac spider
(*Cheiracanthium punctorium*)
Central Europe

7 Tarantula
(*Eurypelma rubropilosum*)
Neotropics

8 Tarantula
(*Acanthoscurria atrox*)
Neotropics

9 Tarantula
(*Lasiodora klugi*)
Neotropics

10 Tarantula
(*Pamphobeteus* sp.)
Neotropics

► **Lethal hunter**
Wolf spiders are hunters, chasing their prey, which includes crickets and lizards.

◄ **Killer cobra**
The bite of the Indian cobra is the most venomous of all reptiles.

THE 10 **MOST VENOMOUS REPTILES AND AMPHIBIANS**

	CREATURE*	TOXIN	FATAL AMOUNT (MG)#
1	Indian cobra	Peak V	0.009
2	Mamba	Toxin 1	0.02
3	Brown snake	Texilotoxin	0.05
4 =	Inland taipan	Paradotoxin	0.10
=	Mamba	Dendrotoxin	0.10
6	Taipan	Taipoxin	0.11
7 =	Indian cobra	Peak X	0.12
=	Poison arrow frog	Batrachotoxin	0.12
9	Indian cobra	Peak 1X	0.17
10	Krait	Bungarotoxin	0.50

* Excluding bacteria
\# Quantity required to kill an average-sized human adult

This list ranks spiders according to their 'lethal potential' – their venom yield divided by their venom potency. The banana spider, for example, yields 6 mg of venom, with 1 mg the estimated lethal dose in humans. However, few spiders are capable of killing people – there were just 14 recorded deaths caused by black widows in the USA in the whole of the 19th century – since their venom yield is relatively low compared with that of the most dangerous snakes.

The venom of these creatures is almost unbelievably powerful: 1 mg (the approximate weight of a banknote) of Mamba Toxin 1 would be sufficient to kill 50 people. Other than reptiles, such creatures as scorpions (0.5 mg) and black widow spiders (1.0 mg) fall just outside the Top 10. Were bacteria included, 12 kg of the deadly Botulinus Toxin A (fatal dose just 0.000002 mg) would easily kill the entire population of the world.

CATS & DOGS

TOP 10 PEDIGREE CAT BREEDS IN THE UK

BREED	NO. REGISTERED BY CAT FANCY (2009)
1 British shorthair	5,415
2 Siamese	2,696
3 Ragdoll	2,665
4 Maine coon	2,076
5 Bengal	1,996
6 Persian	1,755
7 Burmese	1,702
8 Birman	1,384
9 Oriental short hair	988
10 Exotic short hair	674

Source: The Governing Council of the Cat Fancy

◀ *Clever Collie*
In 2011 a border collie was reported to have learned the names of 1,022 objects.

▶ *Popular pedigree*
Siamese cats are among the best-loved pedigrees.

THE 10 MOST INTELLIGENT DOG BREEDS

BREED

1 Border collie
2 Poodle
3 German shepherd (Alsatian)
4 Golden retriever
5 Doberman pinscher
6 Shetland sheepdog
7 Labrador retriever
8 Papillon
9 Rottweiler
10 Australian cattle dog

Source: Stanley Coren, *The Intelligence of Dogs* (Scribner, 1994)

▶ *Bottom of the class*
Seemingly based on physical rather than intellectual strength, 39 US universities use a bulldog as their mascot.

THE 10 LEAST INTELLIGENT DOG BREEDS

BREED

1 Afghan hound
2 Basenji
3 Bulldog
4 Chow Chow
5 Borzoi
6 Bloodhound
7 Pekinese
8 = Beagle
 = Mastiff
10 Bassett Hound

Dog owners who have criticized the results of American psychology professor Stanley Coren's intelligence tests (mostly those whose own pets scored badly) maintain that dogs are bred for specialized abilities, such as speed or ferocity, and obedience to their human masters is only one feature of their 'intelligence'.

TOP 10 PET NAMES IN THE UK

1 Charlie
2 Poppy
3 Molly
4 Alfie
5 Max
6 Jack
7 Daisy
8 Ruby
9 Oscar
10 Rosie

Source: Petplan, 2009

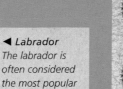

◄ *Labrador*
The labrador is often considered the most popular breed in the world.

TOP 10 **PEDIGREE DOG BREEDS IN THE UK**

BREED / NO. REGISTERED BY THE KENNEL CLUB (2009)

1 Labrador retriever
40,943

2 Cocker spaniel
22,211

3 English springer spaniel
12,700

4 German shepherd dog (Alsatian)
10,338

5 Cavalier King Charles spaniel
8,884

6 Staffordshire bull terrier
8,746

7 Border terrier
8,214

8 Golden retriever
7,804

9 Boxer
5,947

10 West Highland white terrier
5,890

Source: The Kennel Club

THE 10 **LATEST WINNERS OF 'BEST IN SHOW' AT CRUFTS**

YEAR / BREED / NAME

2010 Hungarian vizsla
Hungargunn Bear it'n mind

2009 Sealyham terrier
Efbe's Hidalgo at Goodspice

2008 Giant schnauzer
Jafrak Philippe Olivier

2007 Tibetan terrier
Araki Fabulous Willy

2006 Aust shepherd
Caitland Isle Take a Chance

2005 Norfolk terrier
Cracknor Cause Celebre

2004 Whippet
Cobyco Call the Tune

2003 Pekingese
Yakee a Dangerous Liaison

2002 Standard poodle
Nordic Champion Topscore Contradiction

2001 Basenji hound
Jethard Cidevant

TOP 10 **DOG FILMS**

	FILM	YEAR
1	Scooby-Doo	2004
2	One Hundred and One Dalmatians*	1961
3	Marley & Me	2008
4	101 Dalmatians	1996
5	Bolt	2008
6	Beverly Hills Chihuahua	2008
7	Lady and the Tramp	1955
8	Cats & Dogs	2001
9	Scooby-Doo 2: Monsters Unleashed	2004
10	Eight Below	2006

* Animated version

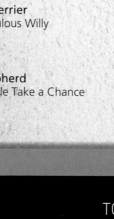

▲ *Pampered pooch*
Drew Barrymore provided the voice for Chloe the Chihuahua in the 2008 film.

LIVESTOCK & AGRICULTURE

TOP 10 TEA-PRODUCING COUNTRIES

COUNTRY / TEA HARVEST (TONNES)*

1 China 1,275,384

2 India 805,180

3 Kenya 345,800

4 Sri Lanka 318,700

5 Turkey 198,046

6 Vietnam 174,900

7 Indonesia 150,851

8 Japan 96,500

9 Argentina# 76,000

10 Thailand 61,557

Source (all lists): Food and Agriculture Organization of the United Nations

* Latest year and countries for which data available
# Estimate

TOP 10 COFFEE-PRODUCING COUNTRIES

COUNTRY / COFFEE PRODUCED*: BEANS (TONNES) / CUPS# (1000)

1 Brazil 2,796,927 / 391,569,780
2 Vietnam 1,067,400 / 149,436,000
3 Colombia 688,680 / 96,415,200
4 Indonesia 682,938 / 95,611,320
5 Peru 273,780 / 38,329,200
6 Ethiopia 273,400 / 38,276,000
7 Mexico 265,817 / 37,214,380
8 India 262,000 / 36,680,000
9 Guatemala 248,614 / 34,805,960
10 Uganda 173,098 / 24,233,720

* Latest year and countries for which data available
# Based on 7g of coffee per cup

TOP 10 STRAWBERRY-PRODUCING COUNTRIES

COUNTRY / PRODUCTION (TONNES)*

1 USA 1,270,694

2 Turkey 291,996

3 Spain 263,700

4 Egypt 200,000

5 Poland 198,907

6 Japan 185,000

7 Russia 158,000

8 Germany 150,100

9 Morocco 130,000

10 Ukraine 57,900

* Latest year and countries for which data available

TOP 10 PIG COUNTRIES

	COUNTRY	PIGS*
1	China	451,177,581
2	USA	67,148,000
3	Brazil	37,000,000
4	Vietnam	27,627,700
5	Germany	26,886,500
6	Spain	26,289,600
7	Russia	16,161,860
8	Mexico	16,100,000
9	France	14,810,000
10	Poland	14,278,647
	UK	4,601,000
	World total	941,212,507

* Latest year and countries for which data available

▲ China pigs
Pigs were domesticated around 10,000 years ago, and provide over a billion Chinese people with their main source of meat.

▶ Ruler of the roost
The world chicken population produces one trillion eggs a year, over 150 per person.

TOP 10 CROPS

	COMMODITY	PRODUCTION (TONNES)*
1	Sugar cane	1,682,577,768
2	Maize	817,110,509
3	Wheat	681,915,838
4	Rice	678,688,289
5	Potatoes	329,556,911
6	Cassava	240,989,481
7	Sugar beet	229,490,296
8	Soybeans	222,268,904
9	Oil palm fruit	207,327,608
10	Barley	150,271,573

* Latest year and countries for which data available; includes semi-official and estimated data

TOP 10 TYPES OF LIVESTOCK

	ANIMAL	WORLD STOCKS*
1	Chickens	18,457,445,000
2	Cattle	1,382,241,378
3	Ducks	1,173,438,000
4	Sheep	1,071,274,348
5	Pigs	941,212,507
6	Goats	867,968,573
7	Turkeys	548,880,000
8	Geese and guinea fowl	357,438,000
9	Buffaloes	188,306,103
10	Horses	59,019,729

* Latest year and countries for which data available; includes semi-official and estimated data

TREES & FORESTS

TOP 10 COUNTRIES WITH THE LARGEST AREAS OF FOREST

COUNTRY	SQ KM	% OF TOTAL	SQ MILES
1 Russia	8,090,900	49	3,123,910
2 Brazil	5,195,220	62	2,005,890
3 Canada	3,101,340	34	1,197,430
4 USA	3,040,220	33	1,173,840
5 China	2,068,610	22	798,690
6 Dem. Rep. of Congo	1,541,350	68	595,120
7 Australia	1,493,000	19	576,450
8 Indonesia	944,320	52	364,600
9 Sudan	699,490	29	270,070
10 India	684,340	23	264,423
_UK_	_28,810_	_12_	_11,120_
World total	_40,330,600_	_31_	_15,571,73_

Source: Food and Agriculture Organization of the United Nations

▲ Brazilian rainforest
The Amazon rainforest covers over a billion acres, with the largest area contained in Brazil.

TOP 10 COUNTRIES WITH THE LARGEST AREAS OF BAMBOO FOREST

COUNTRY / AREA (SQ KM / SQ MILES)

World total / 367,770 / 141,997

Source: Food and Agriculture Organization of the United Nations

1
India
113,610
43,865

2
Brazil
93,000
35,908

3
China
54,440
21,019

4
Indonesia
20,810
8,035

5
Lao People's Dem. Rep.
16,120
6,224

6
Nigeria
15,900
6,139

TOP 10 MOST COMMON TREES IN THE UK

TREE	% OF TOTAL FOREST AREA
1 Sitka spruce (*Picea sitchensis*)	29.1
2 Scots pine (*Pinus sylvestris*)	9.5
3 Oak (*Quercus robur*)	9.4
4 Birch (*Betula pubescens*)	6.7
5 Lodgepole pine (*Pinus contorta latifolia*)	5.7
6 Ash (*Fraxinus excelsior*)	5.4
7 Japanese/hybrid larch (*Larix kempferi/Larix eurolepis*)	4.7
8 Beech (*Fagus sylvatica*)	3.5
9 Norway spruce (*Picea abies*)	3.3
10 Sycamore (*Acer pseudoplatanus*)	2.8

Source: Forestry Commission

TOP 10 TALLEST TREES IN THE UK*

	TREE	LOCATION	HEIGHT M	FT	IN
1	Grand fir (*Abies grandis*)	Ardkingglas Woodland Garden, Inveraray, Argyll and Bute, Scotland	64.3	210	1
2	Douglas fir (*Pseudotsuga menziesii*)	Dunans Estate, Argyll and Bute, Scotland	63.8	209	4
3	Sitka spruce (*Picea sitchensis*)	Doune of Rothiemurchus, Aviemore, Highland, Scotland	59.0	193	7
4	European silver fir (*Abies alba*)	Inveraray Castle estate, Inveraray, Argyll and Bute, Scotland	55.0	180	5
5	Giant sequoia (*Sequoiadendron giganteum*)	Blair Castle, Blair Atholl Pitlochry, Perth and Kinross, Scotland	54.5	178	10
6	Norway spruce (*Picea abies*)	Reelig Glen Wood, Moniack, Inverness, Highland, Scotland	52.0	170	7
7 =	Noble fir (*Abies procera*)	Benmore Estate, Dunoon, Argyll and Bute, Scotland	51.0	167	4
=	Western hemlock (*Tsuga heterophylla*)	Murthly Castle, Perth, Perth and Kinross, Scotland	51.0	167	4
9	Low's white fir (*Abies concolor var. Iowiana*)	Faskally, Pitlochry, Perth and Kinross, Scotland	50.0	164	0
10	Nordmann fir (*Abies nordmanniana*)	Cragside, Rothbury, Morpeth, Northumberland, England	48.0	157	6

* Tallest known example of each of the 10 tallest species

Source: The Tree Register of the British Isles

▼ **Asian devastation**
In the past 20 years, Indonesia has lost 20% of its forest cover.

TOP 10 DEFORESTING COUNTRIES*

COUNTRY	ANNUAL FOREST LOSS 2005–10 SQ KM	SQ MILES
1 Brazil	30,900	11,931
2 Nigeria	4,100	1,583
3 Tanzania	4,030	1,556
4 Zimbabwe	3,270	1,263
5 Dem. Rep. of Congo	3,110	1,201
6 Indonesia	3,100	1,197
7 Myanmar	3,090	1,193
8 Venezuela	2,880	1,112
9 Bolivia	2,710	1,046
10 Argentina	2,520	973
World total	48,410	18,691

* Countries for which data available

Source: Food and Agriculture Organization of the United Nations, *Global Forest Resources Assessment 2010*

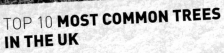

7 Chile	8 Myanmar	9 Ethiopia	10 Vietnam
9,000	8,590	8,490	8,130
3,475	3,317	3,278	3,139

3

THE HUMAN WORLD

DISCOVERING THE DOUBLE HELIX

Fifty years ago – in 1962 – James Watson and Francis Crick were awarded the Nobel Prize for Medicine for their discovery of the molecular structure of DNA (deoxyribonucleic acid). This is the complex molecule that carries genetic information in the body, and is formed of strands of the bases A (adenine), T (thymine), C (cytosine) and G (guanine). Each molecule comprises two twisted strands, which form a spiral configuration (like a spiral staircase or a spring) and run in opposite directions to form a double helix. Watson and Crick's work was a huge scientific breakthrough, and enhanced understanding of how DNA is replicated from cell to cell, and how it passes from generation to generation.

THE HUMAN BODY

◀ **Facing the facts**
Face/neck lift procedures increased by 11.4% in 2010, moving from fourth to third place.

TOP 10 **MOST COMMON ELEMENTS IN THE HUMAN BODY**

ELEMENT / SYMBOL / AVERAGE ADULT* TOTAL (G / OZ)

1 Oxygen#
O
48,800 / 1,721

2 Carbon
C
18,400 / 649

3 Hydrogen#
H
8,000 / 282

4 Nitrogen
N
2,080 / 73

5 Calcium
Ca
1,120 / 39.5

6 Phosphorus
P
880 / 31.0

7 = Potassium
K
160 / 5.6

8 = Sulphur
S
160 / 5.6

9 Sodium
Na
112 / 4.0

10 Chlorine
Cl
96 / 3.4

* 80 kg male
\# Mostly combined as water

TOP 10 **COSMETIC SURGERY PROCEDURES IN THE UK, 2010**

PROCEDURE / NO.

1. Breast augmentation (women) 9,418
2. Blepharoplasty (women) 5,127
3. Face/neck lift (women) 4,493
4. Breast reduction (women) 4,218
5. Rhinoplasty (women) 3,214
6. Abdominoplasty (women) 3,039
7. Liposuction (women) 2,896
8. Brow lifts (women) 1,390
9. Rhinoplasty (men) 993
10. Breast reduction (men) 741

Source: British Association of Aesthetic Plastic Surgeons

The number of surgical procedures in 2010 exceeded 38,200 in the UK – a slow but steady rise of 5% from 2009, when 36,482 procedures were performed. In particular, the demand for certain male surgeries has been growing in recent years.

THE 10 **LATEST PEOPLE TO HOLD THE RECORD AS 'WORLD'S OLDEST'**

	NAME / COUNTRY	YRS	DAYS	BORN	DIED
1	Besse Cooper, USA	114	218	26 Aug 1896	*
2	Eunice Sanborn, USA	115	195	20 Jul 1896	31 Jan 2011
2	Anna Eugénie Blanchard, France	114	261	16 Feb 1896	4 Nov 2010
3	Kama Chinen, Japan	114	357	10 May 1895	2 May 2010
4	Gertrude Baines, USA	115	158	6 Apr 1894	11 Sep 2009
5	Maria (de Jesus) dos Santos, Portugal	115	114	10 Sep 1893	2 Jan 2009
6	Edna Ruth (Scott) Parker, USA	115	220	20 Apr 1893	26 Nov 2008
7	Yone Minagawa, Japan	114	221	4 Jan 1893	13 Aug 2007
8	Emma Fanchon (Faust) Tillman, USA	114	67	22 Nov 1892	28 Jan 2007
9	Emiliano Mercano Del Toro, Puerto Rico	115	156	21 Aug 1891	24 Jan 2007

* Alive as of 1 April 2011

This list is based on the longevity of the successive holders of the record as 'world's oldest' among people for whom there is undisputed evidence of their birth date. None of those in the past 10 years has come within five years of the 122-year 5-month 15-day lifespan of Jeanne Calment (France), who lived from 21 February 1875 to 4 August 1997.

TOP 10 **TALLEST PEOPLE**

	NAME / DATES	COUNTRY	CM	FT	IN
				HEIGHT	
1	Robert Pershing Wadlow (1918–40)	USA	272	8	11.1
2	John William Rogan (1868–1905)	USA	268	8	9.8
3	John Aasen (1887–1938)	USA	267	8	9.7
4	John F. Carroll (1932–69)	USA	264	8	7.6
5	Al Tomaini (1918–62)	USA	255	8	4.4
6	Trijntje Keever* (1616–33)	Netherlands	254	8	3.3
7	Edouard Beaupré (1881–1904)	Canada	250	8	2.5
8	=Bernard Coyne (1897–1921)	USA	249	8	1.2
	=Don Koehler (1925–81)	USA	249	8	1.2
10	=Jeng Jinlian* (1964–82)	China	248	8	1.1
	=Väinö Myllyrinne (1909–63)	Finland	248	8	1.1

* Female; all others male

TOP 10 **HEAVIEST PEOPLE**

	NAME / DATES*	KG	LB
		MAX. WEIGHT	
1	Carol Yager (1960–94)	726	1,600
2	Jon Brower Minnoch (1941–83)	635	1,400
3	Manuel Uribe Garza (b. 1965), Mexico	560	1,234
4	Rosalie Bradford (1943–2006)	544	1,200
5	Walter Hudson (1944–91)	543	1,197
6	Francis John Lang aka Michael Walker (b. 1934)	538	1,187
7	Johnny Alee (1853–87)	513	1,132
8	Michael Hebranko (b. 1953)	499	1,100
9	Patrick Deuel (b. 1962)	486	1,072
10	Robert Earl Hughes (1926–58)	485	1,069

* All USA unless otherwise stated

◄ *Robert Wadlow*
At the time of his death at age 22, Robert Wadlow was still growing.

What weighs 726 kg?

Carol Yager, the world's heaviest person, weighed 726 kg (1,600 lb) at her peak weight. This is roughly the same as:

▪ An adult domestic water buffalo – sometimes referred to as 'living tractors of the East'.

▪ A Smart Fortwo (730 kg/1,609 lb), one of the lightest cars on the European market.

▪ The Rosetta Stone. Though only part of its original size, the stone weighs approximately 760 kg (1,700 lb).

TOP 10 **COUNTRIES SPENDING THE MOST ON HEALTH CARE**

	COUNTRY	HEALTH SPENDING PER CAPITA (US$)
1	Luxembourg	6,763
2	Norway	6,184
3	Monaco	5,492
4	Iceland	4,927
5	Denmark	4,690
6	Ireland	3,676
7	Sweden	3,673
8	France	3,655
9	Switzerland	3,620
10	Netherlands	3,481
	UK	*3,161*

Source: World Health Organization, *World Health Statistics 2010*

◀ *Swiss surgery*
Healthcare in Switzerland is universal, and all Swiss residents are required to purchase basic health insurance.

TOP 10 **DISEASE BURDENS**

	DISEASE	% OF DALYS*
1	Lower respiratory infections	6.2
2	Diarrhoeal diseases	4.8
3	Depression	4.3
4	Coronary heart disease	4.1
5	HIV/AIDS	3.8
6	Cerebrovsacular disease	3.1
7	Premature and low weight birth	2.9
8	=Birth asphyxia and trauma	2.7
	=Road traffic injuries	2.7
	=Neonatal infections	2.7

* All ages; latest available year

Source: World Health Organization

▶ *Medical ratio*
With one doctor for every 170 residents, Cuba has the highest doctor-to-patient ratio in the world.

TOP 10 **COUNTRIES WITH THE MOST DOCTORS** *

	COUNTRY	DOCTORS PER 1,000
1	Cuba	6.4
2	Greece	5.4
3	Belarus	4.9
4	Russia	4.3
5	Belgium	4.2
6	=Lithuania	4.0
	=Switzerland	4.0
8	=Kazakhstan	3.9
	=Netherlands	3.9
	=Norway	3.9

* Where known

Source: World Health Organization, *The World Health Report*

DALYs – Disability-adjusted Life Years – are potential healthy years of life that are lost as a result of contracting diseases or as a result of an injury or other disability. This is used as a measure of the 'burden of disease' that affects not only the individual sufferer, but also has an effect on the cost of the provision of health services and consequent loss to a country's economy. These are world averages, but there are variations from country to country.

THE 10 LEAST HEALTHY COUNTRIES

	COUNTRY	HEALTHY LIFE EXPECTANCY AT BIRTH*
1	Sierra Leone	35
2	Afghanistan	36
3	Zimbabwe	39
4	= Chad	40
	= Lesotho	40
	= Zambia	40
7	= Guinea-Bissau	42
	= Mozambique	42
	= Central African Republic	42
	= Swaziland	42
	= Uganda	42

* Average number of years expected to be spent in good health

Source: World Health Organization, *World Health Statistics 2010*

HALE (Health Adjusted Life Expectancy) is a method used by the WHO to compare the state of health of nations, and illustrates the contrast between developed and developing countries.

◄ Sierra Leone
Almost one out of three children born in Sierra Leone dies before reaching the age of five.

TOP 10 HEALTHIEST COUNTRIES

	COUNTRY	HEALTHY LIFE EXPECTANCY AT BIRTH*
1	Japan	76
2	San Marino	75
3	= Spain	74
	= Sweden	74
	= Australia	74
	= Iceland	74
	= Italy	74
8	= Canada	73
	= France	73
	= Germany	73
	= Ireland	73
	= Israel	73
	= Luxembourg	73
	= Monaco	73
	= Netherlands	73
	= Norway	73
	UK	*70*

* Average number of years expected to be spent in good health

Source: World Health Organization, *World Health Statistics 2010*

▼ Japan
Japan has one of the lowest infant mortality rates in the world.

THE 10 COUNTRIES SPENDING THE LEAST ON HEALTH CARE

	COUNTRY	HEALTH SPENDING PER CAPITA (US$)
1	Myanmar >$1	
2	Dem. Rep. of Congo $2	
3	Guinea $3	
4	= Guinea Bissau $4	
	= Eritrea $4	
	= Sierra Leone $4	
7	= Bangladesh $5	
	= Ethiopia $5	
9	= Central African Republic $6	
	= Liberia $6	
	= Tajikistan $6	

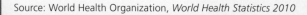

Source: World Health Organization, *World Health Statistics 2010*

BIRTH & DEATH

THE 10 MOST COMMON CAUSES OF DEATH IN ENGLAND AND WALES

DISEASE	NO. OF DEATHS (MALE), 2009
1 Diseases of the circulatory system	41,455
2 Cancers of the upper respiratory system	17,053
3 Cerebrovascular diseases (e.g. stroke)	16,888
4 Chronic lower respiratory diseases	13,165
5 Influenza and pneumonia	11,108
6 Prostate cancer	9,402
7 Diseases of the digestive system	7,559
8 Dementia and Alzheimer's disease	6,709
9 Cancers of the lymphatic and blood systems	5,922
10 Liver disease	4,604
Total (all causes)	248,062

DISEASE	NO OF DEATHS (FEMALE), 2009
1 Diseases of the circulatory system	30,725
2 Cerebrovascular diseases (e.g. stroke)	26,707
3 Dementia and Alzheimer's disease	15,909
4 Influenza and pneumonia	15,711
5 Cancers of the upper respiratory system	12,965
6 Chronic lower respiratory diseases	12,254
7 Breast cancer	10,374
8 Diseases of the urinary system	6,987
9 Heart failure and heart disease	6,536
10 Diseases of the digestive system	6,375
Total (all causes)	253,286

Source: Office for National Statistics, 2010

TOP 10 COUNTRIES WITH THE HIGHEST BIRTH RATE

COUNTRY	ESTIMATED BIRTH RATE (LIVE BIRTHS PER 1,000), 2012
1 Niger	50.1
2 Uganda	47.4
3 Mali	45.2
4 Zambia	43.5
5 Burkina Faso	43.2
6 Ethiopia	42.6
7 Angola	42.5
8 Somalia	42.3
9 Burundi	40.6
10 Dem. Rep. of Congo	40.1
UK	12.3
World average	19.0

Source: US Census Bureau, *International Data Base*

THE 10 COUNTRIES WITH THE MOST DEATHS

COUNTRY	ESTIMATED DEATHS, 2012
1 China	9,631,030
2 India	8,953,697
3 USA	2,650,305
4 Nigeria	2,503,085
5 Russia	2,213,457
6 Indonesia	1,558,798
7 Brazil	1,312,474
8 Japan	1,305,160
9 Pakistan	1,293,980
10 Ethiopia	1,012,275
UK	588,230
World	57,081,617

Source: US Census Bureau, *International Data Base*

The countries with the highest birth rates are amongst the poorest in the world. In these countries, people often deliberately have large families so that the children can help with earning income for the family when they are older. The list of the 10 countries with the highest birth rate therefore corresponds very closely with that of countries with the highest fertility rate – the average number of children born to each woman in the country.

▲ **Happy families**
The total fertility rate (TFR) per woman in Uganda is estimated at 6.69 children in 2011. This represents a slight drop from recent years, but remains one of the highest in the world.

► **Asian baby boom**
China's total fertility rate (TFR) is 1.54 children born for every woman.

THE 10 **COUNTRIES WITH THE MOST BIRTHS**

	COUNTRY	ESTIMATED BIRTHS, 2012
1	India	24,824,516
2	China	16,535,283
3	Nigeria	5,529,888
4	Pakistan	4,624,074
5	Indonesia	4,408,320
6	USA	4,370,790
7	Ethiopia	3,995,623
8	Bangladesh	3,629,218
9	Brazil	3,595,931
10	Dem. Rep. of Congo	3,300,799
	UK	*773,589*
	World	*133,145,854*

Source: US Census Bureau, *International Data Base*

As India's birth rate is maintained and China's subject to curbs, the population of India is set to overtake that of China by 2025.

THE 10 **COUNTRIES WITH THE HIGHEST INFANT MORTALITY**

	COUNTRY	ESTIMATED DEATH RATE (LIVE BIRTHS PER 1,000), 2012
1	Angola	173.7
2	Afghanistan	146.9
3	Niger	110.0
4	Mali	109.1
5	Somalia	103.7
6	Mozambique	99.9
7	Central African Republic	97.2
8	Guinea-Bissau	94.4
9	Chad	93.6
10	Nigeria	90.1
	World average	*40.9*

Source: US Census Bureau, *International Data Base*

Deaths as a ratio of live births is a commonly employed measure of a country's medical and social conditions. In sharp contrast to many western countries, these figures represent the most disadvantaged.

THE 10 **COUNTRIES WITH THE LOWEST INFANT MORTALITY**

COUNTRY / ESTIMATED DEATH RATE (PER 1,000 LIVE BIRTHS), 2012

1 Monaco 1.8   **2** Singapore 2.3   **3** Sweden 2.7   **4** Japan 2.8   **5** Iceland 3.2   **6** France 3.3

7 Spain 3.4   **8** Norway 3.6   **9** Malta 3.7   **10** = Czech Republic = Andorra 3.8

UK 4.7

Source: US Census Bureau, *International Data Base*

MARRIAGE & DIVORCE

TOP 10 TYPES OF MARRIAGE CEREMONY IN ENGLAND AND WALES

CEREMONY	NO. OF MARRIAGES
1 Approved premises	101,158
2 Register office	55,040
3 Church of England	53,591
4 Roman Catholic	8,904
5 Methodist	3,730
6 Church in Wales	3,510
7 Other Christian*	2,692
8 Baptist	1,483
9 Sikh	1,276
10 United Reformed	1,227
Jewish	710
Muslim	197

* Includes Presbyterian, Calvinist, Quakers, Mormons, Congregationalists and others

In 2007 – the latest year for which data are available – a total of 235,367 marriages were solemnized in England and Wales, of which 156,198 were conducted in civil ceremonies and 79,169 in religious ceremonies.

TOP 10 COUNTRIES WITH THE HIGHEST PROPORTION OF TEEN BRIDES

COUNTRY	% OF 15–19-YEAR-OLD GIRLS WHO HAVE EVER BEEN MARRIED*
1 Dem. Rep. of Congo	74.2
2 Niger	61.9
3 Congo	55.5
4 Afghanistan	53.7
5 Bangladesh	51.3
6 Uganda	49.8
7 Mali	49.7
8 Guinea	49.0
9 Chad	48.6
10 Mozambique	47.1
UK	1.7

* In those countries/latest year for which data available

Source: United Nations

▼ *Afghan brides*
According to the UN, between 60% and 80% of marriages in Afghanistan are forced.

TOP 10 COUNTRIES WITH THE MOST MARRIAGES

COUNTRY	MARRIAGES PER ANNUM*
1 China	9,914,000
2 USA	2,205,000
3 Russia	1,262,500
4 Brazil	916,006
5 Iran	841,107
6 Japan	719,822
7 Turkey	638,311
8 Egypt	614,848
9 Mexico	595,209
10 Italy	250,041
UK	235,370

* In those countries/latest year for which data available

Source: United Nations

▲ Hearts and flowers
The average age of first marriage in China is 33.8 for men and 29.1 for women.

THE 10 COUNTRIES WITH THE LOWEST MARRIAGE RATES

COUNTRY	MARRIAGES PER 1,000 PER ANNUM*
1 Qatar	2.6
2 Andorra	3.1
3 Slovenia	3.2
4 = Panama	3.4
= Venezuela	3.4
6 = Argentina	3.5
= Bolivia	3.5
= Ireland	3.5
9 = China	3.9
= Bulgaria	3.9

* In those countries/latest year for which data available

Source: United Nations

THE 10 COUNTRIES WITH THE HIGHEST DIVORCE RATES

COUNTRY	DIVORCE RATE PER 1,000*
1 Russia	4.5
2 Ukraine	3.8
3 Moldova	3.5
4 = Belarus	3.3
= Lithuania	3.3
6 = Cuba	3.2
= Latvia	3.2
8 Czech Republic	3.1
9 = Belgium	2.8
= Estonia	2.8
UK	3.1

* In those countries/latest year for which data available

Source: United Nations

THE 10 COUNTRIES WITH THE LOWEST DIVORCE RATES

COUNTRY	DIVORCE RATE PER 1,000*
1 Guatemala	0.1
2 Chile	0.2
3 = Tajikistan	0.4
= Bosnia and Herzegovina	0.4
5 Georgia	0.5
6 Mongolia	0.6
7 = Jamaica	0.7
= Mexico	0.7
= Macedonia	0.7
10 Ireland	0.8

* In those countries/latest year for which data available

Source: United Nations

The countries that figure among those with the lowest divorce rates represent a range of cultures and religions, which either condone or condemn divorce to varying extents, thus affecting its prevalence or otherwise. In some countries, legal and other obstacles make divorce difficult or costly.

NAME GAME

TOP 10 FIRST NAMES IN ENGLAND AND WALES, 2009

BOYS		BIRTHS
1	Oliver	7,364
2	Jack	7,090
3	Harry	6,143
4	Alfie	5,536
5	Joshua	5,526
6	Thomas	5,520
7	Charlie	5,409
8	William	5,247
9	James	4,544
10	Daniel	4,444
	Top 10 total	56,823

Source: Office for National Statistics, 2010

GIRLS		BIRTHS
1	Olivia	5,201
2	Ruby	4,555
3	Chloe	4,479
4	Emily	4,462
5	Sophie	4,452
6	Jessica	4,291
7	Grace	4,208
8	Lily	3,967
9	Amelia	3,625
10	Evie	3,389
	Top 10 total	42,629

Since 2008, Jack has been replaced by Oliver as the most popular boys' name, after 14 years in the top position. However, regionally, Jack remains in top place in Wales and the north-east and north-west of England. Olivia is the top girls' name for the second year running. Regionally, Isabella appears at No. 6 in London, while Ava and Lucy are popular in the north-east of England, listed at Nos. 8 and 10 respectively.

TOP 10 FIRST NAMES IN THE USA

	BOYS / BIRTHS		GIRLS / BIRTHS
1	Jacob 20,858	1	Isabella 22,067
2	Ethan 19,664	2	Emma 17,716
3	Michael 18,677	3	Olivia 17,246
4	Alexander 18,025	4	Sophia 16,743
5	William 17,696	5	Ava 15,730
6	Joshua 17,418	6	Emily 15,204
7	Daniel 17,336	7	Madison 15,097
8	Jayden 17,082	8	Abigail 14,232
9	Noah 17,061	9	Chloe 11,785
10	Anthony 16,139	10	Mia 11,319
	Top 10 total 179,902		Top 10 total 157,139

TOP 10 **FIRST NAMES IN ENGLAND AND WALES 100 YEARS AGO**

	GIRLS	BOYS
1	Mary	John
2	Margaret	William
3	Doris	George
4	Dorothy	Thomas
5	Kathleen	James
6	Florence	Arthur
7	Elsie	Frederick
8	Edith	Albert
9	Elizabeth	Charles
10	Winifred	Robert

TOP 10 **FIRST NAMES IN AUSTRALIA**

GIRLS		BOYS
Isabella	1	William
Ruby	2	Jack
Chloe	3	Oliver
Olivia	4	Joshua
Charlotte	5	Thomas
Mia	6	Lachlan
Lily	7	Cooper
Emily	8	Noah
Ella	9	Ethan
Sienna	10	Lucas

* Based on registrations in New South Wales, 2010

TOP 10 **FIRST NAMES IN CANADA** *

GIRLS		BOYS
Olivia	1	Ethan
Ava	2	Liam
Isabella	3	Jacob
Emily	4	Logan
Sophia	5	Noah
Alexis	6	Alexander
Ella	7	Benjamin
Sarah	8	Owen
Chloe	9	William
Hailey	10	Lucas

* Based on registrations in Alberta, 2009

TOP 10 **LONGEST-REIGNING LIVING MONARCHS**

MONARCH / COUNTRY*	ACCESSION	YRS	REIGN# MTHS	DAYS	MONARCH / COUNTRY*	ACCESSION	YRS	REIGN# MTHS	DAYS
1 Bhumibol Adulyadej Thailand	9 Jun 1946	64	6	21	**6** Carl XVI Gustaf Sweden	15 Sep 1973	37	3	16
2 Elizabeth II UK	6 Feb 1952	58	10	25	**7** Juan Carlos Spain	22 Nov 1975	35	1	9
3 Haji Hassanal Bolkiah Brunei	5 Oct 1967	43	2	26	**8** Beatrix Netherlands	30 Apr 1980	30	8	1
4 Sayyid Qaboos ibn Said al-Said Oman	23 Jul 1970	40	5	7	**9** Mswati Swaziland	25 Mar 1986	24	9	6
5 Margrethe II Denmark	14 Jan 1972	38	11	17	**10** Emperor Akihito Japan	7 Jan 1989	21	11	2

* Sovereign states only
\# As of 31 March 2011

THE 10 **LATEST COUNTRIES TO ABOLISH MONARCHIES**

	COUNTRY	LAST MONARCH	MONARCHY ABOLISHED
1	Nepal	Gyanendra I	2008
2	Samoa	Malietoa Tanumafili II	2007
3	Central Africa	Bokassa I	1979
4	Iran	Mohammad Reza Pahlavi	1979
5	Laos	Savang Vatthana	1975
6	Ethiopia*	Haile Selassie I	1974
7	Afghanistan	Mohammed Zahir Shah	1973
8	Greece#	Konstantinos II	1973
9	Cambodia†	Norodom Sihanouk	1970
10	Libya	Idris I	1969

* Emperor deposed 1974
\# King exiled 1967
† Restored 1993

This list excludes countries that detached from British rule and became republics or no longer exist as a state.

◀ *Bokassa I*
A dictator who ruled with an iron fist, Bokassa I was overthrown in 1979.

▶ *Ruler of Brunei*
One of the richest men in the world, the sultan has an estimated fortune of US$20 billion.

▶ *Heads of state*
The portrait used for the Queen's Head stamp is the most reproduced work of art in the world.

TOP 10 LONGEST-REIGNING QUEENS

	QUEEN*	COUNTRY	REIGN	REIGN YEARS
1	Victoria	UK	1837–1901	63
2	Elizabeth II	UK	1952–	59#
3	Wilhelmina	Netherlands	1890–1948	58
4	Wu Chao	China	AD 655–705	50
5	Salote Tubou	Tonga	1918–65	47
6	Elizabeth I	England	1558–1603	44
7	Maria Theresa	Hungary	1740–80	40
8	Maria I	Portugal	1777–1816	39
9	Joanna I	Italy	1343–81	38
10	Suiko Tenno	Japan	AD 592–628	36

* Queens and empresses who ruled in their own right, not as consorts of kings or emperors
# As of 31 March 2011

TOP 10 LONGEST-SERVING BRITISH ROYAL CONSORTS

	CONSORT / MONARCH	BECAME CONSORT	CEASED TO BE CONSORT	YRS	MTHS	DAYS
1	Duke of Edinburgh / Queen Elizabeth II	6 Feb 1952	–	59	1	24*
2	Charlotte of Mecklenburg-Strelitz / George III	8 Sep 1761	17 Nov 1818	57	2	9
3	Philippa of Hainault / Edward III	24 Jan 1328	15 Aug 1369	41	6	22
4	Eleanor of Provence / Henry III	14 Jan 1236	16 Nov 1272	36	10	2
5	Eleanor of Aquitaine / Henry II	25 Oct 1154	6 Jul 1189	34	8	11
6	Anne of Denmark / James I	23 Nov 1589	4 Mar 1619	29	3	9
7	Margaret of Anjou / Henry VI	23 Apr 1445	21 May 1471	26	0	28
8	Mary of Teck / George V	6 May 1910	20 Jan 1936	25	8	14
9	Catherine of Aragon / Henry VIII	11 Jun 1509	23 May 1533	23	11	12
10	Henrietta Maria of France / Charles I	13 Jun 1625	30 Jan 1649	23	7	17

* As of 31 March 2011

▲ *Queen and consort*
The royal couple celebrate their 64th wedding anniversary on 20 November 2011.

PRESIDENTS & POLITICIANS

▲ **Kennedy's last moments**
Kennedy's assassination spawned a wealth of conspiracy theories that continue to this day.

THE 10 LAST US PRESIDENTS AND VICE-PRESIDENTS TO DIE IN OFFICE

	NAME / PRESIDENT/ VICE-PRESIDENT	DEATH DATE
1	John F. Kennedy* (P)	22 Nov 1963
2	Franklin D. Roosevelt (P)	12 Apr 1945
3	Warren G. Harding (P)	2 Aug 1923
4	James S. Sherman (V-P)	30 Oct 1912
5	William McKinley* (P)	14 Sep 1901
6	Garret A. Hobart (V-P)	21 Nov 1899
7	Thomas A. Hendricks (V-P)	25 Nov 1885
8	James A. Garfield* (P)	19 Sep 1881
9	Henry Wilson (V-P)	10 Nov 1875
10	Abraham Lincoln* (P)	15 Apr 1865

* Assassinated

John F. Kennedy was the 15th and last US president or vice-president to die in office, and the fourth to die by an assassin's bullet. Prior to Lincoln, two presidents (Zachary Taylor and William Harrison) and three vice-presidents (William Rufus de Vane King, Elbridge Gerry and George Clinton) had all died in office.

TOP 10 LONGEST-SERVING PRESIDENTS TODAY*

	PRESIDENT / COUNTRY	TOOK OFFICE
1	Colonel Mu'ammar Gaddafi# Libya	1 Sep 1969
2	Ali Abdullah Saleh Yemen	18 Jul 1978†
3	Teodoro Obiang Nguema Mbasogo Equatorial Guinea	3 Aug 1979
4	José Eduardo dos Santos Angola	21 Sep 1979
5	Paul Biya Cameroon	7 Nov 1982
6	Yoweri Museveni Uganda	29 Jan 1986
7	Blaise Compaoré Burkina Faso	15 Oct 1987
8	Robert Mugabe Zimbabwe	1 Dec 1987
9	Omar al-Bashir Sudan	30 Jun 1989
10	Idriss Déby Chad	2 Dec 1990

* As of 31 March 2011
# Since a reorganization in 1979, Colonel Gaddafi has held no formal position, but continues to rule under the ceremonial title of 'Leader and Guide of the Revolution'
† Became president of North Yemen; of combined country since 22 May 1990

Youngest US Presidents

When Barack Obama assumed the office of president on 20 January 2009, he was 47 years old. He became the fifth youngest US president, and was almost exactly a year older than Bill Clinton, who was 46 when he took office. John F. Kennedy holds the title of the youngest president – he was 43 years old when he was elected. The US Constitution requires that a president must be at least 35 years old on taking office.

► **Young couple**
The Obamas' daughter Sasha (b. 2001), is the youngest child to live in the White House since John F. Kennedy, Jr.

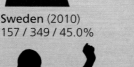

This list is based on the most recent general election results for 145 democratic countries, based on the lower chamber where the parliament or equivalent body comprises two chambers.

TOP 10 **PARLIAMENTS WITH THE HIGHEST PERCENTAGE OF WOMEN MEMBERS***

PARLIAMENT / LATEST ELECTION / WOMEN MEMBERS / TOTAL MEMBERS / % WOMEN

1 Rwanda (2008)
45 / 80 / 56.3%

2 Sweden (2010)
157 / 349 / 45.0%

3 South Africa (2009)
178 / 400 / 44.5%

4 Cuba (2008)
265 / 614 / 43.2%

5 Iceland (2009)
27 / 63 / 42.9%

6 Netherlands (2010)
61 / 150 / 40.7%

7 Norway (2009)
67 / 169 / 39.6%

8 Belgium (2010)
59 / 150 / 39.3%

9 Mozambique (2009)
98 / 250 / 39.2%

10 Angola (2008)
85 / 220 / 38.6%

UK (2010) 143 / 650 / 22.0%

* As of 30 September 2010   Source: Inter-Parliamentary Union

THE 10 **YOUNGEST BRITISH PRIME MINISTERS**

PRIME MINISTER / DATES	TOOK OFFICE	AGE* YRS	AGE* DAYS
1 William Pitt (1759–1806)	1783	24	205
2 Duke of Grafton (1735–1811)	1768	33	16
3 Marquess of Rockingham (1730–82)	1765	35	61
4 Duke of Devonshire (1720–64)	1756	c. 36	–
5 Lord North (1732–92)	1770	37	290
6 Earl of Liverpool (1770–1828)	1812	42	1
7 Henry Addington (1757–1844)	1801	43	291
8 David Cameron (b. 9 Oct 1966)	2010	43	214
9 Tony Blair (b. 6 May 1953)	1997	43	360
10 Sir Robert Walpole (1676–1745)	1721	44	107

* Where a prime minister served in more than one ministry, only the first is listed

► **Young blood**
On 11 May 2010, David Cameron became the youngest prime minister for nearly 200 years.

To the Ends of the Earth

THE 10 FIRST PEOPLE TO REACH THE SOUTH POLE

NAME / AGE / NATIONALITY / DATE

1 Roald Amundsen 47	Norwegian	14 Dec 1911	6 Robert Falcon Scott 43	English	17 Jan 1912
2 Olav Bjaaland 50	Norwegian	14 Dec 1911	7 Henry Bowers 29	Scottish	17 Jan 1912
3 Helmer Hanssen 41	Norwegian	14 Dec 1911	8 Edgar Evans 36	Welsh	17 Jan 1912
4 Sverre Hassel 35	Norwegian	14 Dec 1911	9 Lawrence Oates 31	English	17 Jan 1912
5 Oscar Wisting 40	Norwegian	14 Dec 1911	10 Edward Wilson 39	English	17 Jan 1912

In 1910, Robert Falcon Scott set out to reach the South Pole, and 'secure for the British Empire the honour of this achievement'. After hauling a sledge for more than 1,290 km (800 miles), on 17 January 1912 he was greeted by the Norwegian flag. He had been beaten by Roald Amundsen.

▶ **Pole position**
Making use of sled dogs and skis, Amundsen's 99-day journey was relatively uneventful.

▶ **Scott's team**
8,000 people applied to be part of Scott's Terra Nova expedition, many volunteering to help and contributing to its funds.

THE FIRST EXPEDITIONS TO REACH THE NORTH POLE OVERLAND

American Robert Peary claimed to have reached the pole on 7 April 1909. However, due to the speeds and route claimed, this is widely disputed, and later studies suggest he was several dozen kilometres short. The first undisputed surface conquest, verified by the United States Air Force, was made by Ralph Plaisted, Walt Pederson, Gerry Pitzl and Jean Luc Bombardier, on 19 April 1968. Travelling by snowmobile, the expedition lasted 43 days and covered 1,328 km (825 miles).

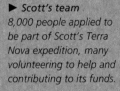

ski-doo
OLYMPIQUE

SCOTT'S LAST JOURNEY

Upon reaching the pole, Scott proclaimed 'Great God! This is an awful place'. After planting the flag, they returned homeward the next day. Faced with abnormally cold weather, all five members perished, succumbing to frostbite, gangrene and starvation. Scott's last diary entry reads:

Since the 21st we have had a continuous gale from W.S.W. and S.W. We had fuel to make two cups of tea apiece and bare food for two days on the 20th. Every day we have been ready to start for our depot 11 miles away, but outside the door of the tent it remains a scene of whirling drift. I do not think we can hope for any better things now. We shall stick it out to the end, but we are getting weaker, of course, and the end cannot be far. It seems a pity, but I do not think I can write more.
R. Scott

▲ *Captain Scott's depot*
Scott's hut at Cape Evans, which survives to this day, is insulated by quilted seaweed.

THE HEROIC AGE OF ANTARCTIC EXPLORATION

In 1895, the Sixth International Geographic Congress meeting in London proclaimed that 'This congress record its opinion that the exploration of the Antarctic Regions is the greatest piece of geographical exploration still to be undertaken.'

SHACKLETON AND THE ENDURANCE

'Men wanted for hazardous journey. Low wages, bitter cold, long hours of complete darkness. Safe return doubtful. Honour and recognition in event of success.'
Advertisement for Shackleton's expedition

Two years after Scott's expedition, Ernest Shackleton attempted to cross the Antarctic continent via the pole. However, his ship got trapped and crushed in the ice, leaving the crew of 28 marooned, far from land and with only three lifeboats for survival. After months in makeshift camps on the ice, the party reached the uninhabited Elephant Island. From there, Shackleton and five others sailed to reach help at a whaling station on South Georgia, some 1,300 km (800 miles) away. They returned four months later with a borrowed Chilean boat to pick up the remaining crew.

▲ Endurance
Hailed as the strongest wooden ship ever built, Endurance lasted eight months trapped in ice.

MURDER!

THE 10 MOST PROLIFIC POISONERS

POISONER* / CIRCUMSTANCES / VICTIMS

1 Harold Shipman
In January 2000, Manchester doctor Shipman was found guilty of the murder of 15 women patients; the official enquiry into his crimes put the figure at 215, with 45 possible further cases, but some authorities believe that the total could be as high as 400.

215

2 Susannah Olah
Hungarian nurse Susi Olah 'predicted' the demise of up to 100 people, who subsequently met their deaths as a result of arsenic poisoning. When the law finally caught up with her in 1929, she committed suicide.

100

3 Gesina Margaretha Gottfried
Having poisoned her first husband and two children with arsenic in 1815, German murderess Gesina Mittenberg then killed her next husband, Michael Gottfried. After a trial, at which she admitted to more than 30 murders, she was executed.

>30

4 Nora Kelley (aka Jane Toppan)
Boston-born Nora Kelley trained as a nurse. After numerous patients in her care had died bodies were exhumed, revealing traces of morphine and atropine poisoning. She may have claimed as many as 30 victims.

30

5 Hélène Jegado
Jegado was a French housemaid who was believed to have committed some 23 murders by arsenic. She was tried at Rennes in 1851, found guilty and guillotined in 1852.

23

▲ **Harold Shipman**
Shipman is the only British doctor to be found guilty of murdering his patients.

6 Mary Ann Cotton
Over a 20-year period, it seems probable that former nurse Cotton (b. 1832) disposed of 14–20 victims, including her husband, children and stepchildren by arsenic poisoning.

20

7 =Dr William Palmer
Dubbed the 'Rugeley Poisoner', Palmer (b.1824) may have killed at least 13, including his wife, brother and children, in order to claim insurance. He was hanged at Stafford on 14 June 1856.

14

=Sadamichi Hirasawa
On 26 January 1948, Hirasawa entered the Shiinamachi branch of the Imperial Bank of Tokyo. Posing as a doctor, he administered what he claimed was a medicine but was in fact cyanide to 16 members of staff, 14 of whom died.

14

9 Johann Otto Hoch
German-born Hoch (1862–1906) preyed on widows, many of whom he married before murdering them, usually with poison. He certainly killed 12 and, according to some authorities, as many as 50 before being hanged in 1906.

>12

10 Marie Becker
In the autumn of 1932 Becker poisoned her husband Charles with digitalis, followed by her lover Lambert Bayer. In order to finance her own extravagant lifestyle, she then embarked on a series of murders of elderly women whom she nursed, using the same drug.

12

* Excluding poisoners where evidence is so confused with legend (such as that surrounding the Borgia family) as to be unreliable

◀ **Arsenic**
The fact that it is odourless and flavourless has made arsenic a favourite method for poisoners.

▲ **Seung-Hui Cho**
Cho's killing spree was America's worst school shooting.

◄ *El Salvador*
More than 60% of homicides in El Salvador are gang-related.

THE 10 **WORST GUN MASSACRES***

PERPETRATOR / LOCATION / DATE / CIRCUMSTANCES / NO. KILLED

1 **Woo Bum Kong**, SangNamdo, South Korea, 28 Apr 1982
Off-duty policeman Woo Bum Kong (or Wou BomKon), 27, went on a drunken rampage with rifles and hand grenades, killing 57 and injuring 38 before blowing himself up with a grenade. **57**

2 **Martin Bryant**, Port Arthur, Tasmania, Australia, 28 Apr 1996
Bryant, a 28-year-old Hobart resident, used a rifle in a horrific spree that began in a restaurant and ended with a siege in a guesthouse. He held hostages and set the guesthouse on fire before being captured by police. **35**

3 **Seung-Hui Cho**, Virginia Tech, Blacksburg, Virginia, USA, 16 Apr 2007
South Korean-born Cho used handguns to kill 27 fellow students and five faculty members of Virginia Tech before turning a gun on himself. **32**

4 = **Baruch Kappel Goldstein**, Hebron, occupied West Bank, Israel, 25 February 1994
Goldstein, a 42-year-old US immigrant doctor, carried out a gun massacre of Palestinians at prayer at the Tomb of the Patriarchs before being beaten to death by the crowd. **29**

= **Matsuo Toi**, Tsuyama, Japan, 21 May 1938
21-year-old Toi used a rifle and swords to kill 29 of his neighbours before committing suicide.

6 **Campo Elias Delgado**, Bogota, Colombia, 4 Dec 1986
Delgado, a Vietnamese war veteran and electronics engineer, stabbed two and shot a further 26 people before being killed by police. **28**

7 = **George Jo Hennard**, Killeen, Texas, USA, 16 Oct 1991
Hennard drove his pickup truck through the window of Luby's Cafeteria and, in 11 minutes, killed 22 with semi-automatic pistols before shooting himself.

= **James Oliver Huberty**, San Ysidro, California, USA, 18 Jul 1984
Huberty, aged 41, opened fire in a McDonald's restaurant, killing 21 before being shot dead by a SWAT marksman. A further 19 were wounded, including a victim who died the following day. **22**

9 = **Thomas Hamilton**, Dunblane, Stirling, UK, 13 Mar 1996
Hamilton, 43, shot 16 children and a teacher in Dunblane Primary School before killing himself in the UK's worst ever shooting incident. **17**

= **Robert Steinhäuser**, Erfurt, Germany, 26 Apr 2002
Former student Steinhäuser returned to Johann Gutenberg Secondary School and killed 14 teachers, two students and a police officer before shooting himself.

* By individuals, excluding terrorist and military actions; totals exclude perpetrator

THE 10 **COUNTRIES WITH THE HIGHEST MURDER RATES**

COUNTRY / MURDERS PER 100,000 POPULATION*

1 Honduras 60.87
2 Jamaica 59.50
3 El Salvador 51.83
4 Venezuela 47.21
5 Guatemala 45.17
6 Trinidad and Tobago 39.67
7 Colombia 38.77
8 Lesotho 36.69
9 South Africa 36.54
10 St Kitts and Nevis 35.25

* In latest year for which data available

Source: United Nations

THE 10 COUNTRIES REPORTING THE MOST BURGLARIES

COUNTRY / BURGLARIES REPORTED

1. USA
2,222,200

2. UK
581,546

3. Germany
380,684

4. France
298,173

5. Australia
241,690

6. Canada
209,755

7. Spain
174,761

8. Japan
162,111

9. Poland
124,066

10. Turkey
114,234

Source: United Nations Office on Drugs and Crime

▲ American prisoners
With numbers increasing four-fold over the last 20 years, the USA houses a quarter of the world's prison population.

THE 10 COUNTRIES WITH THE MOST KIDNAPPINGS

COUNTRY* / KIDNAPPINGS

1. India
23,911

2. Turkey
10,509

3. Canada
4,671

4. France
2,074

5. UK
2,034

6. Belgium
1,165

7. United Arab Emirates
971

8. Australia
782

9. Mexico
713

10. Russia
698

* For which data is available

Source: United Nations Office on Drugs and Crime

THE 10 **COUNTRIES WITH THE HIGHEST PRISON POPULATIONS**

COUNTRY	PRISONERS PER 100,000 OF POPULATION	TOTAL PRISONERS*
1 USA	748	2,297,400
2 China	120	1,620,000
3 Russia	585	829,300
4 Brazil	253	494,237
5 India	32	384,753
6 Mexico	202	222,550
7 Thailand	313	212,058
8 Iran	223	166,979
9 South Africa	319	160,026
10 Ukraine	334	152,169
England and Wales	*155*	*85,454*

* As at date of most recent data

Source: International Centre for Prison Studies

▲ **Crowded conditions**
Despite an official capacity of 438, the national penitentiary in Port-au-Prince, Haiti, actually houses 3,100 inmates.

THE 10 **COUNTRIES WITH THE MOST OVERCROWDED PRISONS**

COUNTRY / PRISON OCCUPANCY RATE (%)*

Haiti
335.7

Benin
307.1

Bangladesh
275.0

Burundi
268.1

Sudan
255.3

El Salvador
253.5

Pakistan
232.7

Kenya
223.3

Mali
223.0

Uganda
218.0

* Occupancy level based on official capacity

Source: International Centre for Prison Studies

THE 10 **LARGEST POLICE FORCES IN ENGLAND AND WALES**

POLICE FORCE	OFFICERS
1 Metropolitan Police	33,367
2 West Midlands	8,626
3 Greater Manchester	8,148
4 West Yorkshire	5,758
5 Merseyside	4,516
6 Thames Valley	4,434
7 Northumbria	4,187
8 Kent	3,787
9 Hampshire	3,748
10 Lancashire	3,649
Total	*143,734*

THE 10 **COUNTRIES WITH THE HIGHEST PROPORTION OF FOREIGN PRISONERS**

COUNTRY / % FOREIGN PRISONERS

1 United Arab Emirates 92.2
2 Monaco 91.2
3 Andorra 81.7
4 Saudi Arabia 72.0
5 Switzerland 70.2
6 Luxembourg 69.5
7 Gambia 66.7
8 Qatar 59.7
9 Cyprus 59.6
10 Austria 45.8

Source: International Centre for Prison Studies

WORLD WAR I

▲ **Facing the enemy**
An estimated 2,000,000
German soldiers lost their
lives in the war.

THE 10 COUNTRIES WITH THE GREATEST MERCHANT SHIPPING LOSSES IN WORLD WAR I

	COUNTRY	VESSELS SUNK NO.	TONNAGE
1	UK	2,038	6,797,802
2	Italy	228	720,064
3	France	213	651,583
4	USA	93	372,892
5	Germany	188	319,552
6	Greece	115	304,992
7	Denmark	126	205,002
8	Netherlands	74	194,483
9	Sweden	124	192,807
10	Spain	70	160,383

THE 10 LARGEST ARMED FORCES OF WORLD WAR I

	COUNTRY	PERSONNEL*
1	Russia	12,000,000
2	Germany	11,000,000
3	British Empire	8,904,467
4	France	8,410,000
5	Austria-Hungary	7,800,000
6	Italy	5,615,000
7	USA	4,355,000
8	Turkey	2,850,000
9	Bulgaria	1,200,000
10	Japan	800,000

* Total at peak strength

THE 10 SMALLEST ARMED FORCES OF WORLD WAR I

	COUNTRY	PERSONNEL*
1	Montenegro	50,000
2	Portugal	100,000
3	Greece	230,000
4	Belgium	267,000
5	Serbia	707,343
6	Romania	750,000
7	Japan	800,000
8	Bulgaria	1,200,000
9	Turkey	2,850,000
10	USA	4,355,000

* Total at peak strength

THE 10 COUNTRIES SUFFERING THE GREATEST MILITARY LOSSES IN WORLD WAR I

	COUNTRY	KILLED
1	Germany	1,773,700
2	Russia	1,700,000
3	France	1,357,800
4	Austria-Hungary	1,200,000
5	British Empire*	908,371
6	Italy	650,000
7	Romania	335,706
8	Turkey	325,000
9	USA	116,516
10	Bulgaria	87,500

* Including Australia, Canada, India, New Zealand, South Africa, etc.

THE 10 COUNTRIES WITH THE MOST PRISONERS OF WAR, 1914–18

COUNTRY	POWS
Russia	2,500,000
Austria-Hungary	2,200,000
Germany	1,152,800
Italy	600,000
France	537,000
Turkey	250,000
British Empire	191,652
Serbia	152,958
Romania	80,000
Belgium	34,659

TOP 10 GERMAN AIR ACES OF WORLD WAR I

PILOT / KILLS CLAIMED

1	Rittmeister Manfred von Richthofen	**80**
2	Oberleutnant Ernst Udet	**62**
3	Oberleutnant Erich Loewenhardt	**53**
4	Leutenant Werner Voss	**48**
5	= Hauptmann Bruno Loerzer / = Leutnant Fritz Rumey	**45**

7	Hauptmann Rudolph Berthold	**44**
8	Leutnant Paul Bäumer	**43**
9	Leutnant Josef Jacobs	**41**
10	= Hauptmann Oswald Boelcke / = Leutnant Franz Büchner / = Oberleutnant Lothar Freiherr von Richthofen	**40**

The claims of top World War I ace Rittmeister Manfred, Baron von Richthofen, (right) – whose brother also merits a place in this list – of 80 kills has been disputed, since only 60 of them have been completely confirmed. Richthofen, known as the 'Red Baron' and leader of the so-called 'Flying Circus' (because the aircraft of his squadron were painted in distinctive bright colours), shot down 21 allied fighters in the single month of April 1917. His own end a year later, on 21 April 1918, has been the subject of controversy, and it remains uncertain whether he was shot down in aerial combat with British pilot Captain A. Roy Brown (who was credited with the kill), or by shots from Australian machine gunners on the ground.

WORLD WAR II

TOP 10 BRITISH AND COMMONWEALTH AIR ACES OF WORLD WAR II

KILLS CLAIMED

PILOT / NATIONALITY

1 Sqd Ldr Marmaduke Thomas St John Pattle
South African — **>40**

2 Gp Capt James Edgar 'Johnny' Johnson
British — **33.91**

3 Wng Cdr Brendan 'Paddy' Finucane
Irish — **32**

4 Flt Lt George Frederick Beurling
Canadian — **31.93**

5 Wng Cdr John Randall Daniel Braham
British — **29**

6 Gp Capt Adolf Gysbert 'Sailor' Malan
South African — **28.66**

7 Wng Cdr Clive Robert Caldwell
Australian — **28.5**

8 Sqd Ldr James Harry 'Ginger' Lacey
British — **28**

9 Sqd Ldr Neville Frederick Duke
British — **27.83**

10 Wng Cdr Colin F. Gray
New Zealander — **27.7**

▶ *Success in the skies*
The Battle of Britain was a turning point for Britain, as the RAF defeated the Luftwaffe.

Kills expressed as fractions refer to those that were shared with others, the number of fighters involved and the extent of each pilot's participation determining the proportion allocated to him. Thus, while some overall totals may be approximations, as a result of this precise reckoning of the shared kills, British pilot James Harry 'Ginger' Lacey, with 28, misses sharing 10th place with Gray by one-third of a kill.

TOP 10 TANKS OF WORLD WAR II

	TANK / INTRODUCED	COUNTRY	WEIGHT (TONNES)	NO. PRODUCED
1	M4A3 Sherman (1942)	USA	34.7	41,530
2	T34 Model 42 (1940)	USSR	31.9	35,120
3	T34/85 (1944)	USSR	35.8	29,430
4	M3 General Stuart (1941)	USA	13.7	14,000
5	Valentine II (1941)	UK	19.6	8,280
6	M3A1 Lee/Grant (1941)	USA	30.0	7,400
7	Churchill VII (1942)	UK	44.8	5,640
8	= Panzer IVD (pre-war)	Germany	22.4	5,500
	= Panzer VG (1943)	Germany	50.2	5,500
10	Crusader I (1941)	UK	21.3	4,750

The Sherman's weaponry comprised two machine guns and, originally, a 75-mm cannon, but after 1944 about half the Shermans in operation had their cannons replaced by one capable of firing a powerful 7.7 kg shell or a 5.5-kg armour-piercing shell.

TOP 10 LARGEST ARMED FORCES OF WORLD WAR II

	COUNTRY	PERSONNEL*
1	USSR	12,500,000
2	USA	12,364,000
3	Germany	10,000,000
4	Japan	6,095,000
5	France	5,700,000
6	UK	4,683,000
7	Italy	4,500,000
8	China	3,800,000
9	India	2,150,000
10	Poland	1,000,000

* Total at peak strength

Allowing for deaths and casualties, the total forces mobilized during the course of the war is, of course, greater than the peak strength figures: that of the USSR, for example, has been put as high as 20 million, the USA 16,354,000, Germany 17.9 million, Japan 9.1 million and the UK 5,896,000.

◄ *Ground control*
Swiftly designed and mass produced by the USA, the iconic Sherman tank was technically uncomplicated but extremely reliable.

TOP 10 US NAVY SUBMARINE COMMANDERS OF WORLD WAR II

COMMANDER / SUBMARINES COMMANDED / SHIPS SUNK

1 Richard H. O'Kane — Tang — 31
2 Eugene B. Fluckley — Barb — 25
3 Slade D. Cutter — Seahorse — 21
4 Samuel D. Dealey — Harder — 20.5
5 William S. Post Jr — Gudgeon and Spot — 19
6 Reuben T. Whitaker — S-44 and Flasher — 18.5
7 Walter T. Griffith — Bowfin and Bullhead — 17*
8 Dudley W. Morton — R-5 and Wahoo — 17*
9 John E. Lee — S-12, Grayling and Croaker — 16
10 William B. Sieglaff — Tautog and Tench — 15

* Gross tonnage used to determine ranking order

THE 10 COUNTRIES SUFFERING THE GREATEST MILITARY LOSSES IN WORLD WAR II

COUNTRY / LOSSES

10 Italy 279,800
9 USA 292,131
8 Yugoslavia 305,000
7 Poland 320,000
6 Romania 350,000
5 British Empire# (UK 264,000) 357,116
4 Japan 1,140,429
3 China 1,324,516
1 USSR 13,600,000*
2 Germany 3,300,000

Total 21,268,992

* Total, of which 7.8 million battlefield deaths
# Including Australia, Canada, India, New Zealand, etc.

MODERN MILITARY

TOP 10 **COUNTRIES WITH THE MOST ATTACK HELICOPTERS**

	COUNTRY	HELICOPTERS
1	USA	1,273
2	Spain	665
3	Russia	646
4	France	228
5	Germany	192
6	Ukraine	139
7	Egypt	120
8	Israel	103
9	Taiwan	101
10	Japan	80
	UK	*79*
	World	*5,015*

Source: CIA, *The World Factbook 2010*

◄ Air combat
America's Boeing Apache fleet has clocked over two million flight hours in numerous global peacekeeping operations.

TOP 10 **COUNTRIES WITH THE LARGEST ARMIES**

	COUNTRY	PERSONNEL
1	China	1,400,000
2	India	1,100,000
3	North Korea	1,002,000
4	South Korea	560,000
5	Pakistan	520,000
6	USA	512,000
7	Vietnam	412,000
8	Turkey	402,000
9	Iran	350,000
10	Myanmar	325,000
	UK	*112,000*

▼ People's Army
In addition to its million-plus active members, North Korea's People's Army has over eight million reserve personnel.

TOP 10 RANKS OF THE ROYAL NAVY, ARMY AND ROYAL AIR FORCE

ROYAL NAVY	ARMY	ROYAL AIR FORCE
1 Admiral	General	Air Chief Marshal
2 Vice-Admiral	Lieutenant-General	Air Marshal
3 Rear-Admiral	Major-General	Air Vice-Marshal
4 Commodore	Brigadier	Air Commodore
5 Captain	Colonel	Group Captain
6 Commander	Lieutenant-Colonel	Wing Commander
7 Lieutenant-Commander	Major	Squadron Leader
8 Lieutenant	Captain	Flight Lieutenant
9 Sub-Lieutenant	Lieutenant	Flying Officer
10 Acting Sub-Lieutenant	Second Lieutenant	Pilot Officer

TOP 10 CONTRIBUTORS TO UN PEACEKEEPING OPERATIONS

COUNTRY	PERSONNEL
1 Bangladesh	10,862
2 Pakistan	10,733
3 India	8,783
4 Nigeria	5,837
5 Egypt	5,258
6 Nepal	5,186
7 Ghana	3,911
8 Jordan	3,769
9 Rwanda	3,663
10 Uruguay	2,516

Source: United Nations

Some of these titles have parallels in the US military, but with certain differences: in the Royal Navy, for example, the rank of Commodore, first recorded in 1695, is a temporary one applied to senior officers in command of detached squadrons, and is divided into two classes, the upper of which receives pay equivalent to that of a Rear-Admiral and has a Captain under him, while the second class does not. Since 1862, in the US Navy, a commodore may command a naval division or station, or a first-class warship.

▼ **American arms**
The USA's four largest arms companies – Lockheed Martin, Boeing, Northrop Grumman and General Dynamics – employ over half a million people.

TOP 10 ARMS-EXPORTING COUNTRIES

COUNTRY	EXPORTS VALUE (US$)	MAIN TRADE PARTNER
1 USA	6,090,000,000	Singapore
2 Russia	4,469,000,000	India
3 Germany	2,473,000,000	South Korea
4 France	1,851,000,000	Singapore
5 UK	1,024,000,000	Saudi Arabia
6 Spain	925,000,000	Norway
7 China	870,000,000	Pakistan
8 Israel	760,000,000	Turkey
9 Netherlands	608,000,000	Portugal
10 Italy	588,000,000	Malaysia
World	*22,640,000,000*	

Source: Stockholm International Peace Research Institute

TOP 10 ARMS-IMPORTING COUNTRIES

COUNTY	IMPORTS VALUE (US$)
1 India	2,116,000,000
2 Singapore	1,729,000,000
3 Malaysia	1,494,000,000
4 Greece	1,269,000,000
5 South Korea	1,172,000,000
6 Pakistan	1,146,000,000
7 Algeria	942,000,000
8 USA	831,000,000
9 Australia	757,000,000
10 Turkey	675,000,000
UK	*288,000,000*
World	*22,640,000,000*

Source: Stockholm International Peace Research Institute

RELIGIONS OF THE WORLD

TOP 10 **LARGEST JEWISH POPULATIONS**

COUNTRY	JEWS
1 Israel	5,282,757
2 USA	5,241,553
3 France	626,370
4 Argentina	504,271
5 Canada	478,038
6 UK	290,057
7 Germany	223,343
8 Russia	183,235
9 Ukraine	176,653
10 Brazil	147,406
Top 10 total	*13,674,871*
World total	*14,822,687*

Source: World Christian Database

▲ *Jewish state*
Israel was formed in 1948 following the Arab-Israeli War.

If considered an independent country, the territory of Palestine (the West Bank and Gaza Strip) would come in at No. 4, with 521,188 Jews. The Diaspora, or scattering of Jewish people, has established Jewish communities in almost every country in the world. In 1939, the estimated total Jewish population was 17 million. Some 6 million fell victim to Nazi persecution, reducing the figure to about 11 million, since when it has grown to more than 14 million.

▶ *Christian symbol*
About one-third of the world's population is Christian.

TOP 10 **BELIEFS IN THE UK**

RELIGION	FOLLOWERS
1 Christians	49,530,864
2 Agnostics	8,021,337
3 Muslims	1,640,725
4 Atheists	891,525
5 Hindus	635,888
6 Sikhs	410,949
7 Jews	290,057
8 Buddhists	196,647
9 Spiritists	75,362
10 Chinese folk-religionists	61,404

Source: World Christian Database

TOP 10 **LARGEST HINDU POPULATIONS**

COUNTRY / HINDUS

UK / 635,888
Top 10 total / 936,719,230
World total / 942,871,282

Source: World Christian Database

1 India 887,059,081

2 Nepal 20,249,772

3 Bangladesh 15,587,198

4 Indonesia 3,429,712

5 Sri Lanka 2,662,954

6 Pakistan 2,436,797

7 Malaysia 1,749,669

8 USA 1,478,555

9 South Africa 1,204,106

10 Myanmar 861,386

▼ *Brazilian worship*
Nearly 75% of the Brazilian population claims to be Roman Catholic.

TOP 10 **LARGEST CHRISTIAN POPULATIONS**

	COUNTRY	CHRISTIANS
1	USA	257,935,642
2	Brazil	177,737,086
3	China	114,364,041
4	Russia	114,041,632
5	Mexico	106,058,166
6	Philippines	83,077,538
7	Nigeria	72,023,815
8	Dem. Rep. of Congo	64,685,125
9	Germany	58,016,298
10	India	57,550,490
	UK	*49,530,864*
	Top 10 total	*1,105,489,833*
	World total	*2,159,141,594*

Source: World Christian Database

TOP 10 **COUNTRIES WITH MOST ATHEISTS AND AGNOSTICS**

	COUNTRY	ATHEISTS	AGNOSTICS	TOTAL
1	China	96,860,601	428,644,836	525,505,437
2	USA	1,328,803	38,695,319	40,024,122
3	Germany	2,056,011	17,773,652	17,793,663
4	Vietnam	5,888,435	11,258,775	17,147,210
5	North Korea	3,737,875	13,360,858	17,098,733
6	Japan	3,643,341	12,919,880	16,563,221
7	India	1,937,586	14,076,698	16,014,284
8	France	2,589,310	10,281,764	12,871,074
9	Russia	1,484,731	8,495,922	9,980,653
10	Italy	2,162,156	7,749,533	9,911,689
	UK	*891,525*	*8,021,337*	*8,912,862*
	Top 10 total	*121,688,849*	*563,257,237*	*682,910,086*
	World total	*137,845,884*	*659,922,513*	*797,768,397*

Source: World Christian Database

TOP 10 **LARGEST MUSLIM POPULATIONS**

	COUNTRY	MUSLIMS
1	Indonesia	183,700,584
2	Pakistan	177,658,575
3	India	166,097,980
4	Bangladesh	146,090,117
5	Iran	74,021,861
6	Turkey	73,745,237
7	Egypt	73,609,345
8	Nigeria	71,845,953
9	Algeria	34,685,807
10	Morocco	32,012,962
	UK	*1,640,725*

Source: World Christian Database

▼ *Islamic domes*
The domes on the mosques of Islam symbolize the vaults of heaven and the sky.

4

TOWN & COUNTRY

POPULATION EXPLOSION

On 1 September 1962, the UN announced that the world population totalled more than 3 billion people. By the end of the 20th century this figure had reached 6 billion, meaning that the number of people in the world had doubled in a little under 40 years. If this astronomical population growth continued it would be unsustainable for our planet, but fortunately the growth rate has slowed substantially, although the actual population will continue to rise. There will be an estimated population of just over 7 billion people by June 2012, rising to 9.3 billion by 2050.

COUNTRIES OF THE WORLD

TOP 10 LARGEST COUNTRIES

	COUNTRY	SQ KM	% OF AREA SQ MILES	WORLD TOTAL (%)
1	Russia	17,098,242	6,601,669	11.5
2	Canada	9,984,670	3,855,103	6.7
3	USA	9,629,091	3,717,813	6.5
4	China	9,596,961	3,704,408	6.4
5	Brazil	8,514,877	3,287,613	5.7
6	Australia	7,692,024	2,969,907	5.2
7	India	3,287,263	1,269,219	2.3
8	Argentina	2,780,400	1,073,519	2.0
9	Kazakhstan	2,724,900	1,052,090	1.8
10	Sudan	2,505,813	967,500	1.7
	UK	*242,900*	*93,784*	*0.16*

Source: United Nations Statistics Division

THE 10 MOST RECENT INDEPENDENT COUNTRIES

	COUNTRY	INDEPENDENCE
1	Kosovo	17 Feb 2008
2	Montenegro	3 Jun 2006
3	Serbia	5 Jun 2006
4	Timor-Leste	20 May 2002
5	Palau	1 Oct 1994
6	Eritrea	24 May 1993
7	= Czech Republic	1 Jan 1993
	= Slovakia	1 Jan 1993
9	Bosnia and Herzegovina	1 Mar 1992
10	Kazakhstan	16 Dec 1991

Kazungula, on the Zambezi River, is a point at which the borders of Botswana, Namibia, Zambia and Zimbabwe all meet, each thus theoretically having a border length of zero. There are also many island countries that have no borders with any other countries.

TOP 10 SHORTEST BORDERS

	COUNTRIES	LAND BORDERS KM	MILES
1	Vatican City/Italy	3.2	2.0
2	Monaco/France	4.4	2.7
3	Azerbaijan/Turkey	9.0	5.6
4	North Korea/Russia	19.0	11.8
5	Cuba/USA (Guantanamo Bay)	29.0	18.0
6	Liechtenstein/Austria	34.9	21.7
7	Armenia/Iran	35.0	21.7
8	San Marino/Italy	39.0	24.2
9	Liechtenstein/Switzerland	41.1	25.5
10	Andorra/France	56.6	35.2

Source: CIA, *The World Factbook 2010*

▶ *Small state*
Monaco is the second smallest country in the world (after Vatican City), covering an area of only 2 sq km (0.78 sq miles).

▲ Brazil
The entire Brazilian coastline – stretching nearly 7,500 km (4,660 miles) lies on the Atlantic Ocean.

THE 10 COUNTRIES WITH THE LOWEST COASTLINE/AREA RATIO

	COUNTRY	AREA (SQ KM)	COASTLINE (KM)	RATIO (M/SQ KM)
1	Dem. Rep. of Congo	2,267,600	37	0.016
2	Iraq	432,162	58	0.134
3	Jordan	91,971	26	0.283
4	Sudan	2,376,000	853	0.359
5	Bosnia and Herzegovina	51,197	20	0.391
6	Algeria	2,381,740	998	0.419
7	Republic of the Congo	341,500	169	0.495
8	Mauritania	1,030,400	754	0.732
9	Cameroon	469,440	402	0.856
10	Brazil	8,456,510	7,491	0.886

Source: CIA, *The World Factbook 2010*

There are some 44 landlocked countries in the world. Landlocked countries often suffer through having to rely on their neighbours for trade routes. In times of conflict this makes them especially vulnerable to blockades. Two countries in the world are actually doubly landlocked – completely surrounded by other landlocked countries – so anyone leaving the country would have to cross two borders before reaching a sea coast. They are Liechtenstein, which is surrounded by Austria and Switzerland, and Uzbekistan, surrounded by Afghanistan, Kazakhstan, Kyrgyzstan, Tajikistan and Turkmenistan.

TOP 10 LARGEST LANDLOCKED COUNTRIES

	COUNTRY / NEIGHBOURS	AREA SQ KM	SQ MILES
1	Kazakhstan — China, Kyrgyzstan, Russia, Turkmenistan, Uzbekistan	2,717,300	1,049,156
2	Mongolia — China, Russia	1,564,116	603,908
3	Niger — Algeria, Benin, Burkina Faso, Chad, Libya, Mali, Nigeria	1,266,699	489,075
4	Chad — Cameroon, Central African Republic, Libya, Niger, Nigeria, Sudan	1,259,201	486,180
5	Mali — Algeria, Burkina Faso, Côte d'Ivoire, Guinea, Mauritania, Niger, Senegal	1,219,999	471,044
6	Ethiopia — Djibouti, Eritrea, Kenya, Somalia, Sudan	1,127,127	435,186
7	Bolivia — Argentina, Brazil, Chile, Paraguay, Peru	1,098,580	424,164
8	Zambia — Angola, Dem. Rep. of Congo, Malawi, Mozambique, Namibia, Tanzania, Zimbabwe	752,614	290,585
9	Afghanistan — China, Iran, Pakistan, Tajikistan, Turkmenistan, Uzbekistan	647,500	250,001
10	Central African Republic — Cameroon, Chad, Congo, Dem. Rep. of Congo, Sudan	622,984	240,535

POPULATION PROJECTIONS

TOP 10 MOST DENSELY POPULATED COUNTRIES, 2050

	COUNTRY	AREA (SQ KM)	ESTIMATED POPULATION (2050)	POPULATION PER SQ KM
1	Monaco	2	29,810	14,905
2	Singapore	687	4,635,110	6,747
3	Hong Kong	1,054	6,172,723	5,856
4	Bangladesh	130,168	250,155,274	1,922
5	Maldives	298	444,429	1,491
6	Bahrain	741	980,431	1,323
7	Rwanda	24,668	27,506,207	1,115
8	Burundi	25,680	27,148,888	1,057
9	Malta	316	295,639	936
10	Comoros	2,235	1,837,671	822
	UK	241,930	71,153,797	294

Source (all lists): US Census Bureau, *International Data Base*

▼ **People power**
India has a rapidly growing population as well as an increasingly important economy.

TOP 10 MOST POPULATED COUNTRIES IN 2011

	COUNTRY	ESTIMATED POPULATION (2011)
1	China	1,336,718,015
2	India	1,189,172,906
3	USA	313,232,044
4	Indonesia	245,613,043
5	Brazil	203,429,773
6	Pakistan	187,342,721
7	Bangladesh	158,570,535
8	Nigeria	152,217,341
9	Russia	139,390,205
10	Japan	126,804,433
	UK	*62,698,362*
	Top 10 total	*3,772,611,166*
	World total	*6,929,098,151*

TOP 10 MOST POPULATED COUNTRIES, 2050

	COUNTRY	ESTIMATED POPULATION (2050)
1	India	1,656,553,632
2	China	1,303,723,332
3	USA	439,010,253
4	Indonesia	313,020,847
5	Pakistan	290,847,790
6	Ethiopia	278,283,137
7	Nigeria	264,262,405
8	Brazil	260,692,493
9	Bangladesh	250,155,274
10	Congo (Kinshasa)	189,310,849
	UK	*71,153,797*
	Top 10	*5,245,860,012*
	World	*9,284,107,424*

Estimates of national populations in 2050 present a striking change as long-time world leader China is eclipsed by India, a reversal that is projected to take place around the year 2025.

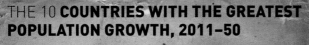

THE 10 **COUNTRIES WITH THE GREATEST POPULATION GROWTH, 2011–50**

COUNTRY / ESTIMATED POPULATION 2010 / ESTIMATED POPULATION 2050 / % GROWTH

1 Uganda
34,612,250 / 128,007,514 / 269.83%

2 Niger
16,468,886 / 55,304,449 / 235.81%

3 Burkina Faso
16,751,455 / 47,429,509 / 183.14%

4 Zambia
13,881,336 / 38,371,544 / 176.43%

5 Congo (Kinshasa)
73,179,859 / 189,310,849 / 158.69%

6 Somalia
10,399,807 / 26,024,500 / 150.24%

7 Rwanda
11,370,425 / 27,506,207 / 141.91%

8 Malawi
15,879,252 / 37,406,745 / 135.57%

9 Liberia
3,786,764 / 8,192,118 / 116.34%

10 Chad
10,758,945 / 20,473,601 / 90.29%

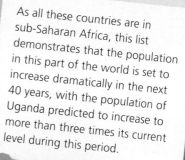

As all these countries are in sub-Saharan Africa, this list demonstrates that the population in this part of the world is set to increase dramatically in the next 40 years, with the population of Uganda predicted to increase to more than three times its current level during this period.

▶ *Greatest growth*
Despite substantial growth in the coming decades, Africa will remain considerably underpopulated compared to Asia.

THE 10 **LEAST DENSELY POPULATED COUNTRIES, 2050**

	COUNTRY	AREA (SQ KM)	ESTIMATED POPULATION (2050)	POPULATION PER SQ KM
1	Namibia	823,290	2,149,815	2.6
2	Mongolia	1,553,556	4,340,496	2.8
3	Iceland	100,250	350,922	3.5
4	Australia	7,682,300	29,012,740	3.8
5	Suriname	156,000	617,249	4.0
6	=Canada	9,093,507	41,135,648	4.5
	=Guyana	196,850	888,494	4.5
8	Botswana	566,730	2,871,345	5.1
9	Kazakhstan	2,669,700	15,099,700	5.6
10	Libya	1,759,540	10,871,760	6.2

▶ *Namibia*
It is estimated that the population of Namibia will increase by a mere 2,230 people by 2050.

PEOPLE ON THE MOVE

TOP 10 ORIGINAL NATIONALITIES OF REFUGEES AND ASYLUM SEEKERS

NATIONALITY / REFUGEES/ASYLUM SEEKERS*

1 Afghanistan
2,805,100

2 Iraq
1,876,000

3 Myanmar
754,100

4 Somalia
530,400

5 Sudan
424,100

6 Columbia
394,700

7 Congo (Kinshasa)
361,100

8 Vietnam
319,300

9 Burundi
256,000

10 Eritrea
224,700

* Latest available year

Source: US Committee for Refugees

TOP 10 ETHNIC GROUPS IN THE UK

GROUP / TOTAL POPULATION

1 White 54,154,000
2 Indian 1,053,000
3 Pakistani 747,000
4 Mixed 677,000
5 Black Caribbean 566,000
6 Black African 485,000
7 Bangladeshi 283,000
8 Other Asian 248,000
9 Chinese 247,000
10 Other ethnic groups 231,000

Source: UK Office for National Statistics

TOP 10 MOST COMMON COUNTRIES OF BIRTH OF UK RESIDENTS

COUNTRY / TOTAL*

1 India 653,000
2 Poland 520,000
3 Pakistan 441,000
4 Republic of Ireland 389,000
5 Germany 293,000
6 South Africa 216,000
7 Bangladesh 200,000
8 USA 187,000
9 Nigeria 156,000
10 Jamaica 142,000

* As of 1 January 2010

Source: UK Office for National Statistics

◀ *Safety in Syria*
A Palestinian boy arrives in one of the Syrian refugee camps.

There are more than 13.5 million refugees and asylum seekers worldwide, the majority of whom are in the Middle East and Africa. In addition to these people, whose country of origin is undisputed, there are an estimated 3.2 million Palestinians in Middle Eastern, African and other countries, but whose homeland lies within Israel, and who thus do not have a country affiliation.

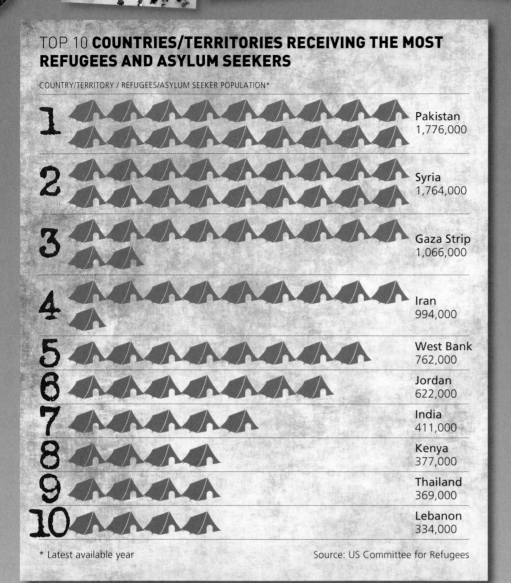

TOP 10 COUNTRIES/TERRITORIES RECEIVING THE MOST REFUGEES AND ASYLUM SEEKERS

COUNTRY/TERRITORY / REFUGEES/ASYLUM SEEKER POPULATION*

1 Pakistan
1,776,000

2 Syria
1,764,000

3 Gaza Strip
1,066,000

4 Iran
994,000

5 West Bank
762,000

6 Jordan
622,000

7 India
411,000

8 Kenya
377,000

9 Thailand
369,000

10 Lebanon
334,000

* Latest available year

Source: US Committee for Refugees

TOP 10 COUNTRIES RECEIVING REMITTANCES FROM MIGRANTS*

COUNTRY / RECEIPTS 2008 (US$)

1 India
52,000,000,000

2 China
40,600,000,000

3 Mexico
26,300,000,000

4 Philippines
18,600,000,000

5 Poland
10,700,000,000

6 Nigeria
10,000,000,000

7 Egypt
9,500,000,000

8 Romania
9,400,000,000

9 Bangladesh
9,000,000,000

10 Vietnam
7,200,000,000

* Nationals working overseas

Source: World Bank

▼ *Iraq's dispossesed*
At least 15% of the Iraqi population have become long-term refugees since 2003.

CITIES

TOP 10 **MOST POPULOUS CITIES**

	CITY / COUNTRY	POPULATION
1	Tokyo, Japan	34,000,000
2	= Guangzhou, China	24,200,000
	= Seoul, South Korea	24,200,000
4	Mexico City, Mexico	23,400,000
5	Delhi, India	23,200,000
6	Mumbai, India	22,800,000
7	New York, USA	22,200,000
8	São Paulo, Brazil	20,900,000
9	Manila, Philippines	19,600,000
10	Shanghai, China	18,400,000
	Top 10 total	*232,900,000*

Source: Th. Brinkhoff: The Principal Agglomerations of the World, www.citypopulation.de © Thomas Brinkhoff 2010-01-23

◀ *Tokyo*
27% of the total population of Japan live in this enormous conurbation.

TOP 10 **COUNTRIES WITH THE MOST MILLION-PLUS CITIES**

	COUNTRY	CITIES WITH POPULATIONS OF OVER 1 MILLION*
1	China	76#
2	USA	53
3	India	48
4	Brazil	21
5	Russia	15
6	= Japan	13
	= Mexico	13
8	Germany	10
9	= Pakistan	8
	= UK	8

* As of 1 January 2011
\# 81 including Taiwan

THE 10 **FIRST CITIES WITH POPULATIONS OF MORE THAN ONE MILLION**

CITY / COUNTRY

Rome's population was reckoned to have exceeded one million some time in the second century BC, and Alexandria soon after. Angkor and Hangchow had both reached this figure by about AD 900 and 1200 respectively, but all subsequently declined. No other city attained one million until London in the early years of the 19th century.

▶ *Ankor*
Prior to industrialization, Angkor was the largest city in the world, and was the centre of the Khmer Empire from the 9th to the 13th centuries.

1	2	3	4	5
Rome Italy	**Alexandria** Egypt	**Angkor** Cambodia	**Hangchow (Hangzhou)** China	**London** UK

TOP 10 **MOST URBANIZED COUNTRIES**

	COUNTRY	% OF POPULATION LIVING IN URBAN AREAS (2010)
1	= Singapore	100.0
	= Hong Kong	100.0
	= Monaco	100.0
	= Nauru	100.0
5	Kuwait	98.4
6	Belgium	97.4
7	Qatar	95.8
8	Malta	94.7
9	= Venezuela	93.4
	= Iceland	93.4
	UK	79.6

Source: United Nations, *Human Development Report 2010*

▲ *Singapore*
This hi-tech city-state has a population density of nearly 7,000 people per sq km.

THE 10 **LEAST URBANIZED COUNTRIES**

	COUNTRY	% OF POPULATION LIVING IN URBAN AREAS (2010)
1	Burundi	11.0
2	Papua New Guinea	12.5
3	Uganda	13.3
4	Trinidad and Tobago	13.9
5	= Liechtenstein	14.3
	= Sri Lanka	14.3
7	Ethiopia	16.7
8	Niger	17.1
9	= Nepal	18.6
	= Solomon Islands	18.6

Source: United Nations, *Human Development Report 2010*

◄ *Burundi*
Despite having the lowest urban population, Burundi claims the highest rate of urbanzation.

6 Paris France	**7** Peking (Beijing) China	**8** Canton Guangzhou) China	**9** Berlin Prussia	**10** New York USA

Skyscrapers

TOP 10 TALLEST HABITABLE BUILDINGS IN 2012

	BUILDING / LOCATION	YEAR COMPLETED	STOREYS	HEIGHT M	FT
1	Burj Khalifa, Dubai, UAE	2010	163	828	2,717
2	Makkah Royal Clock Tower Hotel, Makkah, Saudi Arabia	2011	95	601	1,972
3	Taipei 101, Taipei, Taiwan, China	2004	101	508	1,667
4	Shanghai World Financial Centre, Shanghai, China	2008	101	492	1,614
5	International Commerce Centre, Hong Kong, China	2010	108	484	1,588
6	=Petronas Tower 1, Kuala Lumpur, Malaysia	1998	88	452	1,483
	=Petronas Tower 2, Kuala Lumpur, Malaysia	1998	88	452	1,483
8	Nanjing Greenland Financial Center, Nanjing, China	2010	66	450	1,476
9	Willis (formerly Sears) Tower, Chicago, USA	1974	108	442	1,451
10	Guangzhou International Finance Center, Guangzhou, China	2010	103	438	1,435

Source: Council on Tall Buildings and Urban Habitat

TOP 10 TALLEST BUILDINGS IN 1912

	BUILDING / LOCATION	YEAR COMPLETED	HEIGHT M	FT
1	Eiffel Tower, Paris, France	1889	300	984
2	Metropolitan Life Tower, New York, USA	1909	213	700
3	City Hall, Philadelphia, USA	1901	167	548
4	14 Wall Street, New York, USA	1912	165	540
5	Ulm Minster, Ulm, Germany	1890	162	530
6	Cologne Cathedral, Cologne, Germany	1880	157	516
7	Park Row Building, New York, USA	1898	119	391
8	Domtoren, Utrech, Netherlands	1382	112	369
9	Nieuwe Kerk, Delft, Netherlands	1496	109	358
10	Our Lady Tower, Amersfoort, Netherlands	1444	98	323

Source: Council on Tall Buildings and Urban Habitat

▼ *Onwards and upwards*
For the past 100 years the height of the world's tallest building has grown, on average, by over 6 m per year. In the last decade this figure has risen to nearly 40 m per year.

The Top 10 tallest buildings in the world has undergone drastic change in the last few years. Half of the buildings in the Top 10 have been completed since 2009. Such is the pace of construction that Taipei 101, previously the world's highest, only held the title for six years, whereas previous record-holders, such as the Empire State Building, enjoyed the top spot for over 40 years.

▼ *On top of the world*
Over 3,000 workers spent seven million man-hours constructing the Empire State Building.

STANDING UP TO THE STORMS

The taller a building is, the more prone it is to lightning strikes. The 22-storey television antenna at the top of the Empire State Building acts as a lightning rod, absorbing about 100 lightning strikes a year. Many tall buildings contain tuned mass dampers, which are huge weights near the top of the building that act like pendulums to exert an equal and opposite push to high winds, typhoons and earthquakes.

EMPIRE STATE BUILDING

Containing 10 million bricks, the Empire State Building is one of the American Society of Civil Engineers' Seven Wonders of the Modern World. It held the title of 'World's Tallest Building' from 1931 to 1972, overtaking the Chrysler Building (seen in the background on the right), and was the first structure ever built that was more than 1,000 ft (305 m) high.

SKYSCRAPER FACTS AND FIGURES

Speedy ascent Taipei 101's elevators ascend at 17 m (56 ft) per second, or 1 km (0.62 mile) per minute – faster than a jumbo jet's climb during take-off.

Great weight The concrete, reinforced steel and aluminium alone in the Burj Khalifa weigh over 800,000 tonnes. Yet this is only one-eighth of the weight of the Great Pyramid of Giza.

High climb The Burj Khalifa has 2,909 stairs from the ground floor to the 160th floor, and is expected to hold 35,000 people at any one time.

Windows on the world The Petronas Towers (below) have so many windows that window cleaners take a month to clean each tower.

▲ *Great heights*
The Shanghai World Financial Centre has the world's highest restaurant and observation deck, on the 94th and 100th floors respectively.

SUPERSTRUCTURES

TOP 10 **TALLEST FERRIS WHEELS**

FERRIS WHEEL / LOCATION / YEAR / HEIGHT (M / FT)

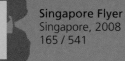

Singapore Flyer
Singapore, 2008
165 / 541

▶ *View from the top*
The 45-km view radius
of the Singapore Flyer
enables visitors to see
as far as Malaysia.

Star of Nanchang
China, 2006
160 / 525

Jeddah Eye
Saudi Arabia,
2012*
150 / 492

* Under construction –
scheduled completion

▼ *Gateway to*
the globe
90 km (56 miles)
of conveyor belts
transport baggage
around the
terminal at Dubai
International Airport.

London Eye
UK, 2000
135 / 443

5
= **Suzhou Ferris Wheel**
China, 2009
120 / 394

= **Southern Star**
Australia, 2008
120 / 394

= **Tianjin Eye**
China, 2008
120 / 394

= **Changsha Ferris Wheel**
China, 2004
120 / 394

= **Zhengzhou Ferris Wheel**
China, 2003
120 / 394

= **Sky Dream**
Fukuoka, Japan, 2002
120 / 394

TOP 10 **LARGEST BUILDINGS**

BUILDING / LOCATION	FLOOR SPACE SQ M	SQ FT
1 Dubai International Airport Terminal 3, Dubai, UAE	1,185,000	12,755,000
2 CentralWorld, Bangkok, Thailand	1,024,000	11,022,000
3 Aalsmeer Flower Auction, Aalsmeer, Netherlands	990,000	10,656,000
4 Beijing Capital International Airport Terminal 3, Beijing, China	986,000	10,613,000
5 The Venetian, Macau, China	980,000	10,549,000
6 The Palazzo, Las Vegas, USA	646,000	6,953,000
7 The Pentagon, Virginia, USA	610,000	6,566,000
8 K-25, Tennessee, USA	609,000	6,555,000
9 Air Force Plant 4, Texas, USA	604,000	6,501,000
10 Marina Bay Sands, Singapore	581,000	6,254,000

TOP 10 **TALLEST CHIMNEYS**

CHIMNEY / LOCATION / YEAR / HEIGHT (M / FT)

1 GRES-2 power station
Ekibastuz, Kazakhstan, 1987
420 / 1,378

2 Inco Superstack
International Nickel Company,
Copper Hill, Sudbury,
Ontario, Canada, 1971
381 / 1,250

3 Homer City Generating
Station Unit 3,
Minersville, Pennsylvania,
USA, 1977
371 / 1,217

4 = Kennecott Copper
Corporation, Magna,
Utah, USA, 1974
370 / 1,214

= Beryozovskaya GRES
Shaypovo, Russia, 1985
370 / 1,214

6 Mitchell Power Plant
Moundsville, West Virginia,
USA, 1971
368 / 1,207

7 Zasavje power station
Trbovlje, Slovenia, 1976
360 / 1,181

8 Endesa Termic
La Coruña, Spain, 1974
356 / 1,168

9 Phoenix Copper Smelter
Baia Mare, Romania, 1995
352 / 1,155

10 Syrdarya Power Plant
Units 5–10, Syrdarya,
Uzbekistan, 1975
350 / 1,148

TOP 10 **LARGEST STADIUMS**

STADIUM / LOCATION / YEAR BUILT / CAPACITY

1 Indianapolis Motor Speedway,
USA, 1909
250,000

2 Tokyo Racecourse*, Japan, 1933
223,000

3 Shanghai International Circuit,
China, 2004
200,000

4 Daytona International
Speedway,
USA, 1959
168,000

5 Lowe's Motor Speedway,
USA, 1959
167,000

6 Nakayama Racecourse*
Japan, 1990
165,000

7 Bristol Motor Speedway
USA, 1961
160,000

8 = Suzuka Circuit, Japan, 1962
155,000

= Istanbul Park, Turkey, 2005
155,000

10 Texas Motor Speedway
USA, 1997
154,000

* Horse racing; all others motor racing

TOP 10 **TALLEST STATUES**

	STATUE / LOCATION	YEAR	HEIGHT M	FT
1	Spring Temple Buddha, Henan, China	2002	128	420
2	Laykyun Setkyar, Sagaing, Myanmar	2008	116	381
3	Ushiku Daibutsu, Ibaraki, Japan	1995	110	361
4	Nanshan Haishang Guanyin, Hainan, China	2005	108	354
5	Emperors Yan and Huang, Henan, China	2007	106	348
6	Sendai Daikannon, Miyagi, Japan	1985	100	328
7	Qianshou Qianyan Guanyin of Weishan, Hunan, China	2009	99	326
8	Peter the Great, Moscow, Russia	1997	96	315
9	Great Buddha, Ang Thong, Thailand	2008	92	300
10	Grand Buddha, Jiangsu, China	1996	88	289

▲ *Ushiku Daibutsu*
The 4,000-tonne depiction of Amitabha Buddha features an 85-m (279-ft) elevator.

TOP 10 LONGEST CABLE-STAYED BRIDGES

BRIDGE / LOCATION	YEAR COMPLETED	LENGTH OF MAIN SPAN	
		M	FT
1 Russky Island Bridge, Primorsky Russia	2012*	1,104	3,622
2 Sutong Bridge, Changshu-Nantong, China	2008	1,088	3,570
3 Stonecutters Bridge, Hong Kong	2008	1,018	3,339
4 Edong Bridge, Hubei, China	2009	926	3,038
5 Tatara Bridge, Onomichi-Imabari, Japan	1999	890	2,920
6 Pont de Normandie, Le Havre, France	1994	856	2,808
7 Jingsha Bridge, Hubei, China	2009	816	2,677
8 Incheon-Yeongjong Bridge, South Korea	2009	800	2,625
9 Zolotoy Roy Bridge, Primorsky, Russia	2011*	737	2,418
10 Chongming North Bridge, Shanghai, China	2010	730	2,395

* Under construction – scheduled completion
Source: Swedish Institute of Steel Construction

▲ *Incheon-Yeongjong*
The 18-km (11-mile) bridge is designed to survive earthquakes and the impact of being hit by a ship.

▼ *Royal Gorge*
For 72 years this was the highest bridge in the world.

THE 10 FIRST THAMES CROSSINGS IN LONDON

CROSSING	YEARS IN OPERATION
1 London Bridge	1st century AD–1014
2 Kingston Bridge	13th century
3 Putney Bridge	1729–1886
4 Westminster Bridge	1750–1857
5 Kew Bridge	1759–89
6 Blackfriars Bridge	1769–1860
7 Battersea Bridge	1772–1890
8 Vauxhall Bridge	1816–98
9 Waterloo Bridge	1817–1934
10 Southwark Bridge	1819–1913

TOP 10 HIGHEST BRIDGES

BRIDGE	LOCATION	YEAR COMPLETED	HEIGHT*	
			M	FT
1 Siduhe River	Hubei, China	2009	472	1,550
2 Baluarte	Sinaloa, Mexico	2012	390	1,280
3 Balinghe River	Guizhou, China	2009	370	1,214
4 Beipanjiang 2003	Guizhou, China	2003	366	1,200
5 =Aizhai	Guizhau, China	2012	330	1,083
=Beipanjiang 2009	Guizhou, China	2009	330	1,083
7 Liuguanghe	Guizhou, China	2001	297	975
8 Zhijinghe River	Hubei, China	2009	294	965
9 Royal Gorge	Colorado, USA	1929	291	955
10 Millau Viaduct	Millau, France	2004	277	909

* Clearance above water

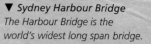
▼ *Sydney Harbour Bridge*
The Harbour Bridge is the world's widest long span bridge.

TOP 10 **LONGEST ARCH BRIDGES**

	BRIDGE / LOCATION	YEAR COMPLETED	LENGTH OF MAIN SPAN M	FT
1	Sheikh Rashid bin Saeed Crossing, Dubai, UAE	2012*	667	1,600
2	Chaotianmen, Chongqing, China	2008	552	1,811
3	Lupu, Shanghai, China	2003	550	1,804
4	New River Gorge, Fayetteville, West Virginia, USA	1977	518	1,699
5	Bayonne, Kill Van Kull, New Jersey/New York, USA	1931	504	1,654
6	Sydney Harbour, Sydney, Australia	1932	503	1,650
7	Chenab, Bakkal, India	2009	480	1,575
8	Wushan, Chongqing, China	2005	460	1,509
9	Xinguang, Guangzhou, China	2008	428	1,405
10 =	Wanxian, Wanxian, China	1997	420	1,378
=	Caiyuanba, Chongqing, China	2007	420	1,378

* Under construction – scheduled completion

Source: Swedish Institute of Steel Construction

► *Lake Pontchartrain*
The two parallel bridges connect New Orleans to Mandeville.

TOP 10 **LONGEST BRIDGES**

	BRIDGE / LOCATION	YEAR COMPLETED	LENGTH M	FT
1	Danyang-Kunshan Grand Bridge, China	2010	164,800	540,700
2	Tianjin Grand Bridge, China	2010	113,700	373,000
3	Weinan Weihe Grand Bridge, China	2008	79,723	261,588
4	Bang Na Expressway, Thailand	2008	54,000	177,000
5	Beijing Grand Bridge, China	2010	48,153	157,982
6	Lake Pontchartrain Causeway, USA	1956	38,442	126,122
7	Manchac Swamp Bridge, USA	1970	36,710	120,440
8	Yangcun Bridge, China	2007	35,812	117,037
9	Hangzhou Bay Bridge, China	2007	35,673	117,037
10	Runyang Bridge, China	2005	35,660	116,990

TUNNELS

TOP 10 **LONGEST SUBSEA TUNNELS**

TUNNEL / LOCATION / YEAR COMPLETED / LENGTH (M / FT)

* Road; all others rail

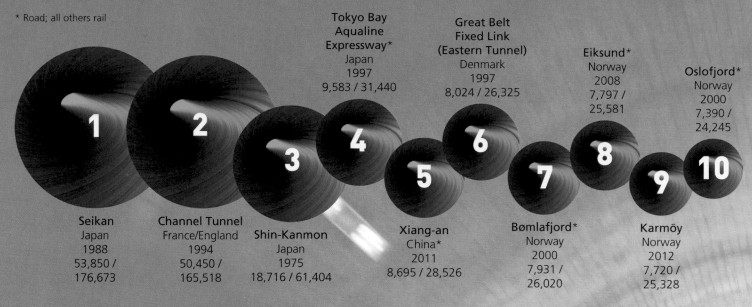

Tokyo Bay Aqualine Expressway*
Japan
1997
9,583 / 31,440

Great Belt Fixed Link (Eastern Tunnel)
Denmark
1997
8,024 / 26,325

Eiksund*
Norway
2008
7,797 / 25,581

Oslofjord*
Norway
2000
7,390 / 24,245

Seikan
Japan
1988
53,850 / 176,673

Channel Tunnel
France/England
1994
50,450 / 165,518

Shin-Kanmon
Japan
1975
18,716 / 61,404

Xiang-an
China*
2011
8,695 / 28,526

Bømlafjord*
Norway
2000
7,931 / 26,020

Karmöy
Norway
2012
7,720 / 25,328

Collision Path

The Large Hadron Collider, operated by CERN near Geneva, Switzerland, is housed in a tunnel with a 27-km (17-mile) circumference. It is roughly the length of the London Underground Circle Line, and required 1.4 million cubic metres of material to be excavated – over half the volume of the Pentagon. By accelerating and colliding particles along its path, scientists are able to study the deepest laws of nature.

TOP 10 LONGEST DISUSED TUNNELS IN THE UK

TUNNEL / LOCATION	YEAR OPENED	YEAR CLOSED	LENGTH FT	M
1 Woodhead II, Yorkshire	1954	1981	16,038	4,888
2 Standedge, Yorkshire	1870	1969	16,026	4,884
3 Woodhead I, Yorkshire	1852	1954	15,906	4,848
4 Rhondda, South Wales	1890	1962	10,329	3,148
5 Catesby, Northamptonshire	1897	1966	8,991	2,740
6 Victoria, Liverpool	1849	1972	8,118	2,474
7 Bolsover, Derbyshire	1897	1951	7,875	2,400
8 Queensbury, Yorkshire	1878	1956	7,503	2,286
9 Merthyr, South Wales	1853	1962	7,491	2,283
10 Gildersome, Yorkshire	1900	1966	6,993	2,131

TOP 10 LONGEST ROAD TUNNELS

TUNNEL / LOCATION	YEAR COMPLETED	LENGTH M	FT
1 Lærdal, Norway	2000	24,510	80,413
2 Zhongnanshan, China	2007	18,040	59,186
3 St Gotthard, Switzerland	1980	16,918	55,505
4 Arlberg, Austria	1978	13,972	45,850
5 Hsuehshan, Taiwan	2006	12,900	42,323
6 Fréjus, France/Italy	1980	12,895	42,306
7 Mont-Blanc, France/Italy	1965	11,611	38,094
8 Gudvangen, Norway	1991	11,428	37,493
9 Baojiashan, China	2009	11,200	36,745
10 Folgefonn, Norway	2001	11,100	36,417

THE 10 LONGEST CANAL TUNNELS

TUNNEL / CANAL / LOCATION	YEAR COMPLETED	LENGTH M	FT
1 Le Rôve, Canal de Marseille au Rhône, France	1927	7,120	23,359
2 Bony ('Le Grand Souterrain'), Canal de St Quentin, France	1810	5,677	18,625
3 Standedge, Huddersfield Narrow, UK	1811	5,210	17,093
4 Mauvages, Canal de la Marne et Rhin, France	1853	4,970	16,305
5 Balesmes, Canal Marne à la Saône, France	1883	4,820	15,813
6 Ruyaulcourt, Canal du Nord, France	1923	4,500	14,763
7 Strood*, Thames and Medway, UK	1924	3,608	11,837
8 Lapal, Birmingham, UK	1798	3,570	11,712
9 Sapperton, Thames and Severn, UK	1789	3,488	11,443
10 Pouilly-en-Auxois, Canal de Bourgogne, France	1832	3,333	10,935

* Later converted to a rail tunnel

◀ Underground waterway
The UK is home to some of oldest canal tunnels in the world.

5
CULTURE & LEARNING

SISTINE CHAPEL ANNIVERSARY

2012 marks the 500th anniversary of Michelangelo completing the painting of his famous frescoes on the ceiling of the Sistine Chapel – a commission he received from Pope Julius II. Work began in 1508, finishing four years later in October 1512. The ceiling is 40 m (131 ft) long by 13 m (43 ft) wide, which means that Michelangelo painted over 523 sq m (5,633 sq ft) of frescoes in total. They are among the most famous in the world, and include nine scenes from the Book of Genesis, of which the Creation of Adam is the best known.

LANGUAGES

TOP 10 **MOST COMMON WORDS IN ENGLISH**

	NOUNS	VERBS	ADJECTIVES	ALL
1	time	be*	good	the
2	person	have	new	be
3	year	do	first	to
4	way	say	last	of
5	day	get	long	and
6	thing	make	great	a
7	man	go	little	in
8	world	know	own	that
9	life	take	other	have
10	hand	see	old	I

* 'be' incorporates 'is', 'was' and 'are', etc.

Source: Oxford English Corpus

◄ **Teaching English**
English is widely spoken in more than 58 countries throughout the world.

The Oxford English Corpus is a tool used by the Oxford Dictionaries to follow the development of the English language. It is a collection of texts presented in electronic format, which provides details of written or spoken language. It represents all different sources, including newspapers, magazines, novels, professional journals, chat rooms, blogs and emails.

TOP 10 **LANGUAGES MOST SPOKEN IN THE UK**

LANGUAGE / APPROX. SPEAKERS*

1	English	58,190,000
2	Welsh	582,000
3	Eastern Panjabi	471,000
4	= Bengali	400,000
	= Urdu	400,000
6	= Chinese (Cantonese)	300,000
	= Sylheti#	300,000
8	= Greek	200,000
	= Italian	200,000
10	Caribbean Creole	170,000

* As primary language
\# Spoken in Bangladesh

TOP 10 **LANGUAGES FROM WHICH MOST BOOKS ARE TRANSLATED**

LANGUAGE	TRANSLATIONS 1979–2009
1 English	1,032,456
2 French	189,064
3 German	172,940
4 Russian	94,714
5 Italian	56,368
6 Spanish	43,883
7 Swedish	31,358
8 Latin	16,831
9 Danish	16,694
10 Dutch	16,350

Source: UNESCO, *Index Translationum* (1979–2009)

TOP 10 **LANGUAGES INTO WHICH MOST BOOKS ARE TRANSLATED**

LANGUAGE	TRANSLATIONS 1979–2009
1 German	271,085
2 Spanish	207,825
3 French	203,633
4 Japanese	124,542
5 English	116,646
6 Dutch	113,964
7 Portuguese	71,287
8 Polish	64,138
9 Russian	63,009
10 Danish	59,008

► Chinese voices
Standard Mandarin is based on the Beijing dialect and is understood throughout mainland China.

TOP 10 MOST-SPOKEN LANGUAGES

	LANGUAGE*	SPEAKERS
1	Chinese (Mandarin)	845,456,760
2	Spanish	328,518,810
3	English	328,008,138
4	Arabic	221,002,544
5	Hindi	181,676,620
6	Bengali	181,272,900
7	Portuguese	177,981,570
8	Russian	143,553,950
9	Japanese	122,080,100
10	German	90,294,110

* Primary speakers only

Source: Ethnologue

TOP 10 ONLINE LANGUAGES

	LANGUAGE	% OF ALL INTERNET USERS	INTERNET USERS*
1	English	27.3	536,564,837
2	Chinese (Mandarin)	22.6	444,948,013
3	Spanish	7.8	153,309,074
4	Japanese	5.0	99,143,700
5	Portuguese	4.2	82,548,200
6	German	3.8	75,158,584
7	Arabic	3.5	65,356,400
8	French	3.0	59,779,525
9	Russian	3.0	59,700,000
10	Korean	2.0	39,440,800
	Top 10 languages	82.2	1,615,957,333
	Rest of world languages	17.8	350,557,483
	World total	100.0	1,996,514,816

* As of 30 June 2010

SCHOOLS & UNIVERSITIES

THE 10 COUNTRIES WITH THE MOST PRIMARY SCHOOLS

COUNTRY / PRIMARY SCHOOLS

	Country	Primary Schools
1	China	628,840
2	India	598,354
3	Brazil	196,479
4	Indonesia	173,893
5	Mexico	95,855
6	Pakistan	77,207
7	USA	72,000
8	Russia	66,235
9	Iran	63,101
10	Colombia	48,933

UK 23,306

Source: UNESCO

▲ *Indonesia*
Despite high primary enrolment, only 75% of Indonesian children go on to senior school.

THE 10 COUNTRIES WITH THE MOST PRIMARY SCHOOL TEACHERS

COUNTRY* / PUPILS PER TEACHER / TEACHERS

	Country	Pupils per teacher	Teachers
1	USA	14	1,775,000
2	Brazil	24	754,000
3	Nigeria	40	566,000
4	Mexico	28	523,000
5	Pakistan	40	450,000
6	Iran	19	373,000
7	Bangladesh	45	364,000
8	Italy	10	273,000
9	UK	18	250,000
10	Germany	14	243,000

World 25 27,871,000

* No data available for China, India, Indonesia or Japan

Source: UNESCO

THE 10 COUNTRIES WITH THE MOST SECONDARY SCHOOL TEACHERS

COUNTRY* / PUPILS PER TEACHER / TEACHERS

	Country	Pupils per teacher	Teachers
1	China	16	6,221,000
2	USA	15	1,698,000
3	Indonesia	13	1,435,000
4	Russia	9	1,284,000
5	Brazil	19	1,263,000
6	Mexico	18	621,000
7	Japan	12	608,000
8	Germany	13	593,000
9	Iran	19	530,000
10	= Egypt	–	491,000
	= France	12	491,000

UK 15 368,000

* No data for India

Source: UNESCO

TOP 10 **COUNTRIES FOR EDUCATION**

	COUNTRY	EDUCATION INDEX*
1	= Australia	0.993
	= Finland	0.993
	= Denmark	0.993
	= New Zealand	0.993
	= Cuba	0.993
6	Canada	0.991
7	Norway	0.989
8	Republic of Korea	0.988
9	= Ireland	0.985
	= Netherlands	0.985
	UK	*0.957*

* The education index takes into account adult literacy and school enrolment rates

Source: United Nations, *Human Development Report*

► *Stanford celebrates*
Stanford is the world's third richest university and teaches 6,800 undergraduates and 3,800 graduate students.

TOP 10 **UNIVERSITIES**

	UNIVERSITY* / COUNTRY	SCORE
1	Harvard University, USA	96.1
2	California Institute of Technology, USA	96.0
3	Massachusetts Institute of Technology, USA	95.6
4	Stanford University, USA	94.3
5	Princeton University, USA	94.2
6	= University of Cambridge, UK	91.2
	= University of Oxford, UK	91.2
8	University of California Berkeley, USA	91.1
9	Imperial College London, UK	90.6
10	Yale University, USA	89.5

* Includes only universities that provided profiling data

Source: *Times Higher Education World University Rankings 2010–11*

The Times Higher Education World University Rankings is compiled with the help of 13,000 academics from all around the world. It gathers opinion on research and teaching, and factual data from the universities themselves.

TOP 10 **LARGEST UNIVERSITIES* IN THE UK**

	UNIVERSITY	UNDERGRADUATES
1	University of Manchester	38,190
2	Manchester Metropolitan University	34,515
3	Sheffield Hallam University	33,830
4	University of Nottingham	32,925
5	Northumbria University	32,665
6	University of Leeds	32,370
7	University of the West of England	31,645
8	University of Plymouth	30,930
9	Cardiff University	30,010
10	University of Birmingham	29,185

* Excluding the Open University (approx. 193,835 students)

LIBRARIES & LOANS

TOP 10 MOST-BORROWED ADULT FICTION TITLES IN THE UK

AUTHOR / TITLE

1 James Patterson
Sail

2 Linwood Barclay,
No Time for Goodbye

3 James Patterson and
Maxine Paetro,
7th Heaven

4 James Patterson and
Howard Roughan
You've Been Warned

5 Sadie Jones
The Outcast

6 Lee Child
Nothing to Lose

7 Patricia Cornwell
The Front

8 Harlan Coben
Hold Tight

9 John Grisham
The Appeal

10 Joanna Trollope
Friday Nights

Source: Public Lending Right

TOP 10 MOST-BORROWED CHILDREN'S FICTION TITLES IN THE UK

AUTHOR / TITLE

1 Francesca Simon*, Horrid Henry and the Football Fiend

2 Francesca Simon*, Horrid Henry and the Abominable Snowman

3 Claire Freedman and Ben Cort, Aliens Love Underpants

4 Jacqueline Wilson#, My Sister Jodie

5 J. K. Rowling, Harry Potter and the Deathly Hallows

6 Francesca Simon*, Horrid Henry Meets the Queen

7 Francesca Simon*, Horrid Henry and the
Bogey Babysitter

8 Francesca Simon*, Horrid Henry's Underpants

9 Francesca Simon*, Horrid Henry Robs the Bank

10 Francesca Simon*, Horrid Henry and the
Mega-Mean Time Machine

* Illustrated by Tony Ross
# Illustrated by Nick Sharratt

Source: Public Lending Right

TOP 10 MOST-BORROWED CLASSIC ADULT TITLES IN THE UK

AUTHOR / TITLE

1 J. D. Salinger, The Catcher in the Rye

2 Daphne du Maurier, Rebecca

3 Daphne du Maurier, Jamaica Inn

4 Harper Lee, To Kill a Mockingbird*

5 Agatha Christie,
Elephants Can Remember

6 Harper Lee, To Kill a Mockingbird*

7 Daphne du Maurier,
Frenchman's Creek

8 Harper Lee, To Kill a Mockingbird*

9 Daphne du Maurier, Hungry Hill

10 Agatha Christie, Sad Cypress

* Various editions

Source: Public Lending Right

There is no official definition of what makes a novel a 'classic'. However, it is usually agreed that these are books that have stood the test of time and that remain widely influential – and widely read – many years after their publication.

► **Library of Congress**
The library houses more than 144 million items, including 33 million books.

◄ **Mother Goose**
Nursery rhymes and fairy stories by Mother Goose have been published since the 18th century.

TOP 10 **LARGEST LIBRARIES**

LIBRARY / LOCATION	FOUNDED	BOOKS
1 Library of Congress Washington DC, USA	1800	32,124,001
2 British Library* London, UK	1753	29,000,000
3 Deutsche Bibliothek# Frankfurt, Germany	1990	22,200,000
4 National Library of China Beijing, China	1909	22,000,000
5 Library of the Russian Academy of Sciences St Petersburg, Russia	1714	20,500,000
6 National Library of Canada Ottawa, Canada	1953	19,500,000
7 Russian State Library† Moscow, Russia	1862	17,000,000
8 Harvard University Library Cambridge, Massachusetts, USA	1638	15,826,570
9 Boston Public Library Boston, Massachusetts, USA	1895	15,760,879
10 Vernadsky National Scientific Library of Ukraine Kiev, Ukraine	1919	15,000,000

* Founded as part of the British Museum, 1753; became an independent body in 1973
# Formed in 1990 through the unification of the Deutsche Bibliothek, Frankfurt (founded 1947) and the Deutsche Bucherei, Leipzig
† Founded 1862 as Rumyantsev Library, formerly State V. I. Lenin Library

TOP 10 **BOOKS FOUND IN MOST LIBRARIES**

BOOK / TOTAL LIBRARY HOLDINGS*

1 Bible 796,882

2 US Census 460,628

3 Mother Goose 67,663

4 Dante Alighieri, The Divine Comedy 62,414

5 Homer, The Odyssey 45,551

6 Homer, The Iliad 44,093

7 Mark Twain, Huckleberry Finn 42,724

8 J. R. R. Tolkien, Lord of the Rings (trilogy) 40,907

9 William Shakespeare, Hamlet 39,521

10 Lewis Carroll, Alice's Adventures in Wonderland 39,277

* Based on WorldCat listings of all editions of books held in 53,000 libraries in 96 countries

Source: Online Computer Library Center (OCLC)

BOOK AWARDS

THE 10 **LATEST CARNEGIE MEDAL WINNERS**

YEAR*   AUTHOR / TITLE

2010 Neil Gaiman, The Graveyard Book

2009 Siobhan Dowd, Bog Child

2008 Philip Reeve, Here Lies Arthur

2007 Meg Rosoff, Just in Case

2005 Mal Peet, Tamar

2004 Frank Cottrell Boyce, Millions

2003 Jennifer Donnelly, A Gathering Light

2002 Sharon Creech, Ruby Holler

2001 Terry Pratchett, Amazing Maurice and his Educated Rodents

2000 Beverley Naidoo, The Other Side of Truth

* Prior to 2007, publication year; since 2007, award year – hence there was no 2006 award

Established in 1937, the Carnegie Medal is named in honour of Scots-born millionaire Andrew Carnegie, who was a notable library benefactor. In its early years, winners included such distinguished authors as Arthur Ransome, Noel Streatfeild, Walter de la Mare and C. S. Lewis, while among notable post-war winners are books such as *Watership Down* by Richard Adams.

◄ *Neil Gaiman*
Gaiman won both the Hugo Award and the Carnegie Medal for the same work.

2010

Freya Blackwood
Harry and Hopper

2009

Catherine Rayner
Harris Finds His Feet

2008

Emily Gravett
Little Mouse's Big Book of Fears

2007

Mini Grey
The Adventures of the Dish and the Spoon

2006

THE 10 **LATEST KATE GREENAWAY MEDAL WINNERS**

YEAR* / ILLUSTRATOR / TITLE

The Kate Greenaway Medal, named after the English illustrator (1846–1901), has been awarded annually since 1956 for the most distinguished work in the illustration of children's books published in the UK.

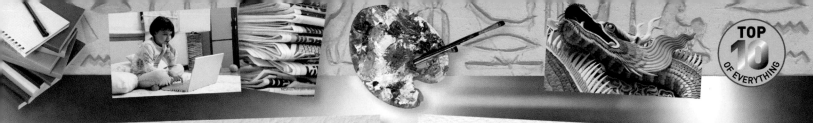

THE 10 **LATEST MAN BOOKER PRIZE WINNERS**

YEAR	AUTHOR	COUNTRY	TITLE
2010	Howard Jacobson	UK	The Finkler Question
2009	Hilary Mantell	UK	Wolf Hall
2008	Aravind Adiga	India	The White Tiger
2007	Anne Enright	Ireland	The Gathering
2006	Kiran Desai	India	The Inheritance of Loss
2005	John Banville	Ireland	The Sea
2004	Alan Hollinghurst	UK	The Line of Beauty
2003	D.B.C. Pierre	Australia	Vernon God Little
2002	Yann Martel	Canada	Life of Pi
2001	Peter Carey	Australia	True History of the Kelly Gang

THE 10 **LATEST WINNERS OF HUGO AWARDS FOR BEST SCIENCE-FICTION NOVEL**

YEAR	AUTHOR / TITLE
2010	China Miéville, The City & The City Paolo Bacigalupi, The Windup Girl
2009	Neil Gaiman, The Graveyard Book
2008	Michael Chabon, The Yiddish Policemen's Union
2007	Vernor Vinge, Rainbows End
2006	Robert Charles Wilson, Spin
2005	Susanna Clarke, Jonathan Strange & Mr Norrell
2004	Lois McMaster Bujold, Paladin of Souls
2003	Robert J. Sawyer, Hominids
2002	Neil Gaiman, American Gods
2001	J. K. Rowling, Harry Potter and the Goblet of Fire

THE 10 **LATEST WINNERS OF THE NOBEL PRIZE FOR LITERATURE**

YEAR / WINNER / COUNTRY

2010 Mario Vargas Llosa, Peru **2009** Herta Müller, Romania **2008** J. M. G. Le Clézio, France
2007 Doris Lessing, UK **2006** Orhan Pamuk, Turkey **2005** Harold Pinter, UK **2004** Elfriede Jelinek, Austria
2003 J. M. Coetzee, South Africa **2002** Imre Kertész, Hungary **2001** Sir V. S. Naipaul, UK

2005
Emily Gravett
Wolves

2004
Chris Riddell
Jonathan
Swift's
Gulliver

2003

2002
Bob Graham
Jethro Byrde,
Fairy Child

2001
Chris Riddell
(text
Richard Platt)
Pirate Diary

2000
Lauren Child
I Will Never
Not Ever
Eat a Tomato

Bestselling Books

TOP 10 BESTSELLING NOVELS*

	AUTHOR / TITLE / FIRST PUBLISHED	ESTIMATED SALES#
1	Charles Dickens A Tale of Two Cities, 1859	>200,000,000
2	J. R. R. Tolkien The Lord of the Rings†, 1954–55	150,000,000
3 =	J. R. R. Tolkien The Hobbit, 1937	>100,000,000
=	Cao Xueqin Dream of the Red Chamber, 18th century	>100,000,000
5	Agatha Christie And Then There Were None, 1939	100,000,000
6	C. S. Lewis The Lion, the Witch and the Wardrobe, 1950	85,000,000
7	H. Rider Haggard She, 1887	83,000,000
8 =	Antoine de Saint-Exupery Le Petit Prince, 1943	80,000,000
=	Dan Brown The Da Vinci Code, 2003	80,000,000
10	J. D. Salinger The Catcher in the Rye, 1951	65,000,000

* Single-volume novels
\# Including translations
† Written as a single book – figure is an estimate of copies of the full story sold, whether published as one volume or three

▲ The Hobbit
A two-part film adaptation of the classic novel is currently in production.

CHARLES DICKENS

2012 marks the 200th anniversary of Charles Dickens' birth, so it is fitting that his most famous work should top the list of bestselling novels, with well over 200 million copies sold. There have been at least five feature films based on the book, and numerous recreations in the form of television mini-series, musicals and even a Monty Python sketch. While first published in Dickens' own weekly literary magazine, *All the Year Round*, in 32 instalments between 30 April and 25 November 1859, *A Tale of Two Cities* has become the bestselling book in the history of fictional literature.

From 1833, when his first story was published, to his death in 1870, Dickens published more than a dozen novels – including *Oliver Twist*, *David Copperfield*, *Bleak House*, *Little Dorrit* and *Great Expectations* – many short stories, and some plays and works of non-fiction. His books and short stories are still so popular that they have never gone out of print.

FICTIONAL FIGURES

True long-term sales figures are difficult to gauge. Although modern sales monitoring has made assessing book sales figures more accurate, it is often jokingly suggested that publishers' claims should be classified as 'fiction', while all-time cumulative sales and those of multiple editions of any book make such assessments round-figure estimates at best.

THE MILLENNIUM TRILOGY

One of the bestselling authors of modern times, Stieg Larsson was a Swedish journalist and writer. He became a bestselling author after his sudden death from a heart attack in 2004. Larsson left behind three completed but unpublished manuscripts – *The Girl With the Dragon Tattoo*, *The Girl Who Played with Fire* and *The Girl Who Kicked the Hornets' Nest* – the first of which was published just months after his death. This series of crime novels, *The Millennium Trilogy*, has sold more than 20 million copies worldwide and has spawned three popular Swedish films.

▼ *Lisbeth Salander*
The heroine of Larsson's books was played by Noomi Rapace in the films.

▲ *The Bard of Avon*
Shakespeare is attributed with writing at least 37 plays and over 150 sonnets.

TOP 10 BESTSELLING ENGLISH-LANGUAGE AUTHORS

AUTHOR / COUNTRY / DATES / MAX. ESTIMATED SALES

1 = Agatha Christie (UK; 1890–1976)
4,000,000,000

= William Shakespeare (UK; 1564–1616)
4,000,000,000

3 Barbara Cartland (UK; 1901–2000)
1,000,000,000

4 Harold Robbins (USA; 1916–97)
750,000,000

5 = Enid Blyton (UK; 1897–1968)
600,000,000

= Sidney Sheldon (USA; 1917–2007)
600,000,000

= Danielle Steel (USA; b. 1947)
600,000,000

8 = Gilbert Patten (USA; 1866–1945)
500,000,000

= Dr Seuss (Theodor Seuss Geisel, USA; 1904–91)
500,000,000

10 J. K. Rowling (UK; b. 1965)
450,000,000

▲ *J. K. Rowling*
Rowling has received seven honorary degrees from universities in the UK and US.

WIZARD WOMAN

Although J. K. Rowling ranks only 10th in the list of English-language authors, her success is extraordinary when one considers the number of works produced – in a book-by-book comparison, she would easily top the list. Her massive sales figure is based on a grand total of only seven books over a relatively short expanse of time. The huge popularity of the Harry Potter series has put Rowling at the very top of the world's richest authors list, and the brand continues to expand. Several of the Harry Potter books would also appear on the Top 10 bestselling novels list if series were included.

THE PRESS

TOP 10 DAILY NEWSPAPERS IN THE UK

NEWSPAPER	AVERAGE NET CIRCULATION*
1 The Sun	2,974,939
2 The Daily Mail	2,123,886
3 The Mirror	1,231,726
4 Daily Star	833,017
5 The Daily Telegraph	673,858
6 Daily Express	660,976
7 The Times	496,732
8 Financial Times	389,834
9 Daily Record (Scotland)	325,214
10 The Guardian	281,670

* May–Oct 2010

Source (all UK lists): Audit Bureau of Circulations Ltd

TOP 10 SUNDAY NEWSPAPERS IN THE UK

NEWSPAPER / AVERAGE CIRCULATION*

1 News of the World
2,869,463

2 The Mail on Sunday
1,957,544

3 Sunday Mirror
1,141,394

4 The Sunday Times
1,081,919

5 Sunday Express
564,927

6 The People
527,173

7 The Sunday Telegraph
507,985

8 Sunday Mail (Scotland)
389,430

9 Daily Star – Sunday
363,176

10 Sunday Post
325,114

* May–Oct 2010

Top Newspapers

An estimated 1.7 billion people read a newspaper every day. Including non dailies, newspapers reach a much greater audience than the Internet. The newspaper with the world's highest circulation is the Japanese *Yomiuri Shinbun*, selling 10,020,000 copies a day. Japan, China and India each have 13, 12 and 11 newspapers respectively that have over one million readers.

TOP 10 OLDEST NEWSPAPERS

NEWSPAPER / COUNTRY / FOUNDED

This list includes only newspapers that have been published continuously since their founding. The former No. 1 on this list, the Swedish *Post-och Inrikes Tidningar*, founded in 1645, ceased publication on paper on 1 January 2007, and is now available only online.

Haarlems Dagblad	Gazzetta di Mantova	The London Gazette	Wiener Zeitung	Hildesheimer Allgemeine Zeitung
Netherlands	Italy	UK	Austria	Germany 1705
1656	1664	1665	1703	

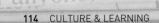

TOP 10 MAGAZINES IN THE UK

MAGAZINE / AVERAGE NET CIRCULATION*

1 Sky Magazine
7,041,602

2 Sky Sports Magazine
4,200,369

3 Sky Movies Magazine
3,478,534

4 Tesco Magazine
1,998,767

5 Asda Magazine
1,947,567

6 Sainsbury's Fresh Ideas
1,487,850

7 TV Choice
1,309,469

8 Tesco Real Food
1,250,000

9 What's on TV
1,209,018

10 Morrisons Magazine
1,030,186

* Up to June 2010

TOP 10 COUNTRIES WHERE MOST REPORTERS HAVE DIED

	COUNTRY	DEATHS (2010)
1	Mexico	10
2	=Honduras	8
	=Pakistan	8
4	Iraq	6
5	=Nigeria	3
	=Philippines	3
7	=Angola	2
	=Indonesia	2
	=Nepal	2
	=Somalia	2
	=Thailand	2
	=Uganda	2

▲ Mexican war zone
In 2010, some 15,273 deaths were attributed to Mexico's drug wars. After incidents of reporters being kidnapped and murdered, many newspapers stopped coverage.

Berrow's Worcester Journal
UK
1709

Newcastle Journal
UK
1711

Stamford Mercury
UK
1712

Northampton Mercury
UK
1720

Hanauer Anzeiger
Germany
1725

CULTURE & LEARNING 115

MUSEUMS & GALLERIES

TOP 10 BEST-ATTENDED ART EXHIBITIONS, 2010

EXHIBITION*	VENUE / CITY / DATES	ATTENDANCE# DAILY AVERAGE	TOTAL
1 Texture of Night: James McNeill Whistler	Freer and Sackler Galleries, Washington DC, 6 Jun 2009–25 Jul 2010	2,514	1,043,246
2 Rising Currents: Projects for NY's Waterfront	Museum of Modern Art, New York, 24 Mar–11 Oct 2010	4,358	881,520
3 Abstract America: New Painting and Sculpture	Saatchi Gallery, London, 29 May–17 Jan 2010	4,006	837,200
4 Tim Burton	Museum of Modern Art, New York, 22 Nov 2009–26 Apr 2010	5,200	810,511
5 Post-Impressionism: from the Musée d'Orsay	National Art Center, Tokyo, 26 May–16 Aug 2010	10,757	777,551
6 The Original Copy: Photography of Sculpture	Museum of Modern Art, New York, 1 Aug–1 Nov 2010	8,073	749,638
7 Picasso in the Metropolitan Museum of Art	Metropolitan Museum of Art, New York, 27 Apr–15 Aug 2010	7,380	703,256
8 India: the Art of the Temple	Shanghai Museum, Shanghai, 5 Aug–15 Nov 2010	6,630	682,867
9 Doug & Mike Starn on the Roof: Big Bambú	Metropolitan Museum of Art, New York, 27 Apr–31 Oct 2010	3,913	631,064
10 Hans Memling	Galleria degli Uffizi, Florence, 22 Jun–10 Oct 2010	6,469	616,411

* With longest part of run in 2010
# Approximate totals provided by museums

Source: *The Art Newspaper*

▲ **The Louvre**
One of the largest museums in the world, the Louvre has over 35,000 exhibits.

TOP 10 MOST-VISITED GALLERIES AND MUSEUMS, 2010

GALLERY / LOCATION	TOTAL ATTENDANCE
1 Louvre Museum, Paris, France	8,500,000
2 British Museum, London, UK	5,842,138
3 Metropolitan Museum of Art, New York, USA	5,216,988
4 Tate Modern, London, UK	5,061,172
5 National Gallery, London, UK	4,954,914
6 National Gallery of Art, Washington, DC, USA	4,775,114
7 Museum of Modern Art, New York, USA	3,131,238
8 Centre Pompidou, Paris, France	3,130,000
9 National Museum of Korea, Seoul, South Korea	3,067,909
10 Musée d'Orsay, Paris, France	2,985,510

Source: *The Art Newspaper*

TOP 10 **MOST-VISITED ART GALLERIES AND MUSEUMS IN THE UK, 2010**

GALLERY / LOCATION / VISITORS

1 British Museum
London
5,842,138

2 Tate Modern
London
5,061,172

3 National Gallery
London
4,954,914

4 Victoria & Albert Museum
London
2,629,065

5 National Portrait Gallery
London
1,819,442

6 Tate Britain
London
1,665,291

7 National Galleries of Scotland
Edinburgh
1,281,465

8 Saatchi Gallery
London
1,271,301

9 Kelvingrove Art Gallery
Glasgow
1,070,521

10 Ashmoleum Museum
Oxford
1,041,310

Source: ALVA

TOP 10 **BEST-ATTENDED EXHIBITIONS AT THE TATE MODERN, LONDON**

EXHIBITION / YEAR / ATTENDANCE

1 Matisse/Picasso
2002
467,166

2 Edward Hopper
2004–05
429,909

3 Frida Kahlo
2005
369,249

4 Rothko
2008–09
327,244

5 Kandinsky: The Path to Abstraction
2006
282,439

6 Andy Warhol
2002
218,801

7 Between Cinema and a Hard Place
2000
200,937

8 Pop Life: Art in a Material World
2009–10
192,754

9 Henri Rousseau: Jungles in Paris
2005–06
190,795

10 Surrealism: Desire Unbound
2001–02
168,825

▶ **Paul Gauguin**
Beginning in 2010, the Paul Gauguin exhibition at Tate Modern proved one of the year's most popular art attractions.

TOP 10 **BEST-ATTENDED EXHIBITIONS AT THE MUSEUM OF MODERN ART, NEW YORK***

EXHIBITION / YEAR / ATTENDANCE

1 Rising Currents: Projects for NY's Waterfront
2010 / 881,520

2 Tim Burton
2010 / 810,511

3 The Original Copy: Photography of Sculpture
2010 / 749,638

4 Richard Serra Sculpture: 40 Years
2007 / 737,074

5 Matisse: Radical Invention, 1913–17
2010 / 602,524

6 Superheroes: Fashion and Fantasy
2008 / 576,901

7 Marina Abramovic: The Artist is Present
2010 / 561,471

8 Home Delivery
2008 / 521,871

9 William Kentridge: Five Themes
2010 / 492,196

10 Dalí: Painting and Film
2008 / 449,483

* 20th century only

◀ **The Starry Night**
Since 1941, Van Gogh's best-loved work has hung in the Museum of Modern Art, New York.

▲ **Bal au Moulin de la Galette**
Renoir's 1876 masterpiece was bought at auction in May 1990 by the same Japanese businessman who bought Portrait du Dr Gachet.

TOP 10 MOST EXPENSIVE PAINTINGS EVER SOLD AT AUCTION

PAINTING / ARTIST / SALE	PRICE (US$)
1 Nude, Green Leaves and Bust, Pablo Picasso (Spanish; 1881–1973) Christie's, New York, 4 May 2010	106,482,500
2 Garçon à la pipe, Pablo Picasso Sotheby's, New York, 5 May 2004	104,168,000
3 Dora Maar au chat, Pablo Picasso Sotheby's, New York, 3 May 2006	95,216,000
4 Portrait of Adele Bloch-Bauer II, Gustav Klimt (Austrian; 1862–1918) Christie's, New York, 8 Nov 2006	87,936,000
5 Triptych, Francis Bacon (Irish; 1909–92) Sotheby's, New York, 14 May 2008	86,281,000
6 Portrait du Dr Gachet, Vincent van Gogh (Dutch; 1853–90) Christie's, New York, 15 May 1990	82,500,000
7 Le Bassin aux Nymphéas, Claude Monet (French; 1840–1926) Christie's, London, 24 Jun 2008	80,643,507 (£40,921,250)
8 Bal au Moulin de la Galette, Montmartre Pierre-Auguste Renoir (French; 1841–1919) Sotheby's, New York, 17 May 1990	78,100,000
9 The Massacre of the Innocents, Sir Peter Paul Rubens (Flemish; 1577–1640) Sotheby's, London, 10 Jul 2002	75,930,440 (£49,506,648)
10 White Center (Yellow, pink and lavender on rose), Mark Rothko (American; 1903–70) Sotheby's, New York, 15 May 2007	72,840,000

Old Masters at Auction

A previously unknown painting by Sir Peter Paul Rubens, 'The Massacre of the Innocents', made history when it sold at Sotheby's London for £49,506,648. Painted between 1609 and 1611, the work had been incorrectly attributed to an assistant of Rubens, Jan van den Hoeck, and had hung unnoticed in an Austrian monastery for many years, until it was brought to the attention of Sotheby's just a few months before the sale. The record-breaking sale is still more than double the amount paid for the second most expensive Old Master painting. That title goes to Raphael's 'Portrait of Lorenzo de' Medici, Duke of Urbino', which was sold by Christie's in London for £18,500,000 in 2007.

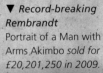

▼ *Record-breaking Rembrandt*
Portrait of a Man with Arms Akimbo *sold for £20,201,250 in 2009.*

TOP 10 **MOST EXPENSIVE WORKS OF ART BY LIVING ARTISTS**

PAINTING / ARTIST / SALE	PRICE (US$)
1 Benefits Supervisor Sleeping, Lucian Freud (British; b.1922) Christie's, New York, 13 May 2008	33,641,000
2 Flag, Jasper Johns (American; b.1930) Christie's, New York, 11 May 2010	28,642,500
3 Balloon Flower – Magenta, Jeff Koons (American; b.1955) Christie's, London, 30 Jun 2008	25,765,204 (£12,921,250)
4 Hanging Heart – Magenta/Gold, Jeff Koons Sotheby's, New York, 14 Nov 2007	23,561,000
5 Naked Portrait with Reflection, Lucian Freud Christie's, London, 30 Jun 2008	23,531,904 (£11,801,250)
6 IB and Her Husband, Lucian Freud Christie's, New York, 13 Nov 2007	19,361,000
7 Lullaby Spring, Damien Hirst (British; b.1965) Sotheby's, London, 21 Jun 2007	19,230,922 (£9,652,000)
8 The Golden Calf, Damien Hirst Sotheby's, London, 15 Sep 2008	18,603,218 (£10,345,250)
9 Figure 4, Jasper Johns Christie's, New York, 16 May 2007	17,400,000
10 The Kingdom, Damien Hirst Sotheby's, London, 15 Sep 2008	17,193,400 (£9,561,250)

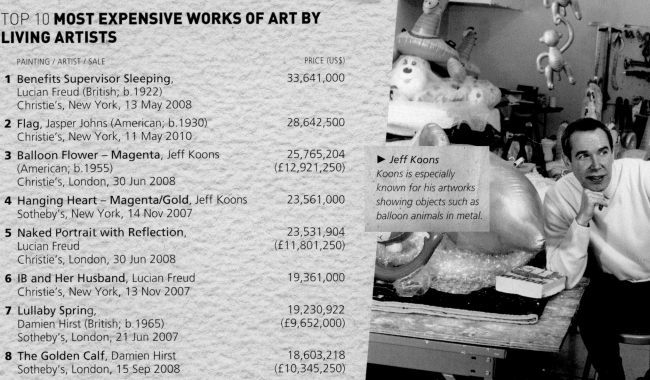

▶ *Jeff Koons*
Koons is especially known for his artworks showing objects such as balloon animals in metal.

TOP 10 **MOST EXPENSIVE PHOTOGRAPHS**

PHOTOGRAPH* / PHOTOGRAPHER / SALE	PRICE (US$)
1 Untitled (Cowboy)# (2001–02) Richard Prince (American; b.1949), Sotheby's, New York, 14 Nov 2007	3,401,000
2 99 Cent II# (2001), Andreas Gursky (German; b.1955), Sotheby's, London, 7 Feb 2007	3,346,456 (£1,700,000)
3 Los Angeles (1998), Andreas Gursky, Sotheby's, London, 27 Feb 2008	2,941,483 (£1,476,500)
4 The Pond – Moonlight (1904), Edward Steichen (American; 1879–1973), Sotheby's, New York, 14 Feb 2006	2,928,000
5 Untitled No. 153 (1985), Cindy Sherman (American; b. 1954), Phillips de Pury & Company, New York, 8 Nov 2010	2,770,500
6 Pyongyang IV (2007), Andreas Gursky, Sotheby's, London, 15 Oct 2010	2,125,736 (£1,329,250)
7 Untitled, No. 92 (1981), Cindy Sherman, Christie's, New York, 16 May 2007	2,112,000
8 Frankfurt (2007), Andreas Gursky, Sotheby's, New York, 9 Nov 2010	2,098,500
9 Black Sea. Ozuluce, Yellow Sea. Cheju, Red Sea (1991), Hiroshi Sugimoto (Japanese; b.1948), Christie's, New York, 16 May 2007	1,888,000
10 Madonna I (2001), Andreas Gursky, Sotheby's, London, 10 Feb 2010	1,684,280 (£1,077,250)

* Single prints only
# Other versions of same photograph also sold for lesser amounts

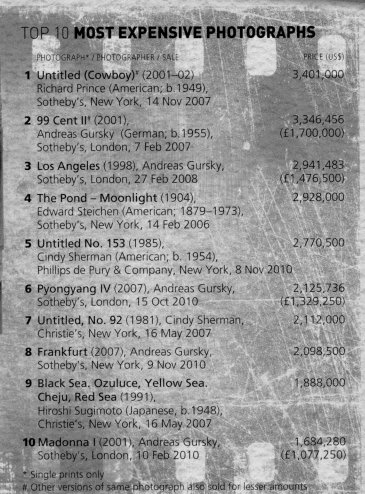

6
MUSIC

'THRILLER' ANNIVERSARY

The bestselling album of all time, Michael Jackson's *Thriller* was recorded and released in 1982. Still earning accolades 30 years later, *Thriller* has broken record after record in the music industry, and is estimated to have sold approximately 65–110 million copies worldwide. 'Billie Jean', 'Beat It' and 'Thriller' were just three of its seven Top 10 singles on the *Billboard* Hot 100 – the first album to ever accomplish such a feat. *Thriller* also solidified Jackson's influence on music videos and pop culture, with the 14-minute-long 'Thriller' epic still consistently being named the best music video ever.

TOP 10 SINGLES OF ALL TIME

	TITLE / ARTIST	YEAR OF ENTRY	SALES EXCEED
1	'White Christmas', Bing Crosby	1942	50,000,000
2	'Candle in the Wind (1997)'/ 'Something About the Way You Look Tonight', Elton John	1997	33,000,000
3	= 'Rock Around the Clock', Bill Haley and His Comets	1954	25,000,000
	= 'Little Drummer Boy', The Harry Simeone Chorale	1958	25,000,000
5	= 'It's Now or Never', Elvis Presley	1960	20,000,000
	= 'We Are the World', USA for Africa	1985	20,000,000
7	'Yes Sir, I Can Boogie', Baccara	1977	18,000,000
8	'Wind of Change', The Scorpions	1991	14,000,000
9	'Sukiyaki', Kyu Sakamoto	1963	13,000,000
10	= 'I Want to Hold Your Hand', The Beatles	1963	12,000,000
	= 'I Will Always Love You', Whitney Houston	1992	12,000,000

Source: Music Information Database

TOP 10 SINGLES THAT STAYED LONGEST IN THE UK CHARTS

	TITLE / ARTIST	CHART ENTRY	WEEKS IN IN CHART
1	'My Way', Frank Sinatra (42)	1969	124
2	'Chasing Cars', Snow Patrol (48)	2006	98
3	'Rule the World', Take That (30)	2007	73
4	'I Gotta Feeling', Black Eyed Peas (63)	2009	69
5	'Amazing Grace', Judy Collins (32)	1970	66
6	'Don't Stop Believin'', Journey (48)	1982	62
7	'Relax', Frankie Goes to Hollywood (48)	1983	59
8	'Rehab', Amy Winehouse (34)	2006	58
9	= 'Rock Around the Clock', Bill Haley and His Comets (17)	1955	57
	= 'Release Me', Engelbert Humperdinck (56)	1967	57

Source: Music Information Database

These include reissues and remixes. Numbers in parentheses denote the longest consecutive run on the charts.

TOP 10 ARTISTS WITH THE MOST NO. 1 SINGLES IN THE UK

	ARTIST (TOTAL CHART HITS) / NO. 1 SINGLES	
1	Elvis Presley (174)	21
2	The Beatles (58)	17
3	= Cliff Richard (136)	14
	= Westlife (25)	14
5	Madonna (66)	13
6	Take That (21)	10
7	= Abba (28)	9
	= Spice Girls (11)	9
9	= Rolling Stones (55)	8
	= Oasis (26)	8

Source: Music Information Database

◀ *King of the charts*
Although Elvis died 35 years ago, he has had four No. 1 singles in the UK in the past decade.

TOP 10 **SINGLES IN THE UK IN 2010**

TITLE / ARTIST

1 'Love The Way You Lie'
Eminem feat. Rihanna

2 'When We Collide'
Matt Cardle

3 'Just the Way You Are (Amazing)'
Bruno Mars

4 'Only Girl (In the World)'
Rihanna

5 'OMG'
Usher feat. will.i.am

6 'Fireflies'
Owl City

7 'Airplanes'
Bob feat. Hayley Williams

8 'California Gurls'
Katy Perry

9 'We No Speak Americano'
Yolanda Be Cool Vs. D Cup

10 'Pass Out'
Tinie Tempah

▲ *Black Eyed Peas*
'I Gotta Feeling' was the first single to sell more than one million downloads in the UK.

▼ *Katy Perry*
Katy Perry became the ninth artist to have four No. 1 Hot 100 singles from one album.

TOP 10 **SINGLES IN THE UK IN THE PAST 10 YEARS**

YEAR / TITLE / ARTIST

2010 'Love the Way You Lie'
Eminem feat. Rihanna

2009 'Poker Face'
Lady Gaga

2008 'Hallelujah'
Alexandra Burke

2007 'Bleeding Love'
Leona Lewis

2006 'Crazy'
Gnarls Barkley

2005 '(Is This the Way to) Amarillo'
Tony Christie feat. Peter Kay

2004 'Do They Know It's Christmas?'
Band Aid 20

2003 'Where is the Love'
Black Eyed Peas

2002 'Anything is Possible'/ 'Evergreen'
Will Young

2001 'It Wasn't Me'
Shaggy feat. Rikrok

Source: Music Information Database

ALBUMS

TOP 10 ALBUMS OF ALL TIME IN THE UK

	TITLE / ARTIST	YEAR
1	Greatest Hits, Queen	1981
2	Sgt. Pepper's Lonely Hearts Club Band, The Beatles	1967
3	= Abba Golzqrms, Dire Straits	1985
	= The Dark Side of the Moon, Pink Floyd	1973
	= Thriller, Michael Jackson	1982
	= Greatest Hits II, Queen	1991
9	Bad, Michael Jackson	1987
10	The Immaculate Collection, Madonna	1990

TOP 10 ALBUMS OF ALL TIME

TITLE / ARTIST / YEAR OF ENTRY

1 Thriller
Michael Jackson 1982

2 Back in Black
AC/DC 1980

3 Dark Side of the Moon,
Pink Floyd 1973

4 The Bodyguard
Soundtrack 1992

5 Bat out of Hell
Meat Loaf 1977

6 Their Greatest Hits 1971–1975,
The Eagles 1976

7 Dirty Dancing
Various Artists 1987

8 Millennium
The Backstreet Boys 1999

9 Saturday Night Fever,
Soundtrack 1977

10 Rumours
Fleetwood Mac 1977

▲ *Rock school*
Angus Young,
founding member
of AC/DC, is famous
for his stage antics,
which include
wearing a schoolboy
uniform and the
'duck walk'.

▼ *In the pink*
Founded in 1965,
Pink Floyd have
sold more than
200 million
albums worldwide.

TOP 10 ALBUMS THAT STAYED LONGEST IN THE UK CHARTS

	TITLE / ARTIST	FIRST CHART ENTRY	WEEKS IN CHART
1	Rumours, Fleetwood Mac (120)	1977	478
2	Bat Out of Hell, Meat Loaf (329)	1978	473
3	Greatest Hits, Queen (222)	1981	472
4	Gold – Greatest Hits, Abba (101)	1992	445
5	The Sound of Music, Soundtrack (318)	1965	383
6	Dark Side of the Moon, Pink Floyd (135)	1973	370
7	South Pacific, Soundtrack (153)	1960	319
8	Bridge Over Troubled Water, Simon & Garfunkel (244)	1970	307
9	Greatest Hits, Simon & Garfunkel (195)	1972	283
10	Tubular Bells, Mike Oldfield (128)	1973	276

Source: Music Information Database

Numbers in parentheses denote the longest consecutive run on the charts.

Total worldwide sales of albums have traditionally been notoriously hard to gauge, but even with the huge expansion of the album market during the 1980s, and multiple million sales of many major releases, this Top 10 is still élite territory.

TOP 10 ALBUMS IN THE UK IN 2010

TITLE / ARTIST

1 Progress
Take That

2 Crazy Love
Michael Buble

3 The Fame
Lady Gaga

4 Loud
Rihanna

5 The Defamation of Strickland Banks
Plan B

6 Sunny Side Up
Paolo Nutini

7 The Element of Freedom
Alicia Keys

8 Lungs
Florence + the Machine

9 Recovery
Eminem

10 Sigh No More
Mumford & Sons

TOP 10 ALBUMS IN THE UK IN THE PAST 10 YEARS

YEAR / TITLE / ARTIST

2010 Progress
Take That

2009 I Dreamed a Dream
Susan Boyle

2008 Rockferry
Duffy

2007 Back to Black
Amy Winehouse

2006 Eyes Open
Snow Patrol

2005 Back to Bedlam
James Blunt

2004 Scissor Sisters
Scissor Sisters

2003 Life for Rent
Dido

2002 Escapology
Robbie Williams

2001 No Angel
Dido

▶ *Going Gaga*
The Fame *was the debut studio album for the singer/songwriter, whose real name is Stefani Germanotta.*

MALE SINGERS

Elton John
Sir Elton John has had more than 50 Top 40 hits and has won 6 Grammy Awards, an Academy Award and a Golden Globe.

TOP 10 BESTSELLING SINGLES BY MALE SOLO SINGERS IN THE UK

	TITLE / ARTIST	YEAR
1	'Candle in the Wind (1997)'/'Something About the Way You Look Tonight', Elton John	1997
2	'I Just Called to Say I Love You', Stevie Wonder	1984
3	'Anything is Possible'/'Evergreen', Will Young	2002
4	'(Everything I Do) I Do It for You', Bryan Adams	1991
5	'Imagine', John Lennon	1975
6	'Tears', Ken Dodd	1965
7	'Careless Whisper', George Michael	1984
8	'Release Me', Engelbert Humperdinck	1967
9	'Unchained Melody', Gareth Gates	2002
10	'It's Now or Never', Elvis Presley	1960

TOP 10 OLDEST MALE SOLO SINGERS TO HAVE A NO. 1 SINGLE IN THE UK

	ARTIST / TITLE	YEAR	YRS	AGE MTHS	DAYS
1	Louis Armstrong, 'What a Wonderful World'	1968	66	9	11
2	Tony Christie, '(Is This the Way To) Amarillo'	2005	62	0	12
3	Cliff Richard, 'The Millennium Prayer'	1999	59	2	4
4	Elton John, 'Are You Ready for Love?'	2003	56	5	12
5	Isaac Hayes*, 'Chocolate Salty Balls'	1999	56	4	13
6	Elton John, 'Candle in the Wind (1997)'/'Something About the Way You Look Tonight'	1997	51	6	23
7	Telly Savalas, 'If'	1975	51	1	22
8	Frank Sinatra, 'Strangers in the Night'	1967	50	6	4
9	Charles Aznavour, 'She'	1974	50	1	28
10	Clive Dunn, 'Grandad'	1971	49	0	14

* Credited as 'Chef'

Source (all lists): Music Information Database

The ages listed are those of the artists during the final week of their last (to date) No. 1 hit. Six of the 10 are still alive, so there is room for further improvement.

Youngest No. 1 Male Achievers

Little Jimmy Osmond has held the title for the youngest performer to have a No. 1 single in the UK singles chart since 1972. When 'Long Haired Lover from Liverpool' made it to the top of the charts, he was a mere 9 years, 8 months and 7 days old. His big brother, Donny Osmond, had a No. 1 hit with 'Puppy Love' in the same year and – at 14 years, 6 months and 30 days old – was the second youngest male soloist to do so. Gareth Gates is the youngest British male artist to make it solo to No. 1, and did so three times before his 19th birthday.

TOP 10 BESTSELLING ALBUMS BY MALE SOLO ARTISTS IN THE UK IN THE PAST 10 YEARS

YEAR / TITLE / ARTIST

2010 Crazy Love
Michael Buble

2009 Crazy Love
Michael Buble

2008 Home Before Dark
Neil Diamond

2007 Life in Cartoon Motion
Mika

2006 Undiscovered
James Morrison

2005 Back to Bedlam
James Blunt

2004 Greatest Hits
Robbie Williams

2003 Justified
Justin Timberlake

2002 Escapology
Robbie Williams

2001 Swing When
You're Winning,
Robbie Williams

TOP 10 MALE ARTISTS WITH THE MOST PLATINUM ALBUMS IN THE UK

ARTIST / GOLD TOTAL	PLATINUM ALBUMS
1 Robbie Williams (11)	58
2 Michael Jackson (17)	51
3 Phil Collins (13)	34
4 Elton John (25)	29
5 George Michael (8)	27
6 Rod Stewart (29)	21
7 = Meat Loaf (10)	18
= Eminem (8)	18
9 Michael Buble (9)	17
10 = Chris Rea (10)	15
= Cliff Richard (26)	15

Michael Jackson's *Thriller* and *Bad* have both sold in excess of 3.5 million copies, meaning that approximately one in every six British households, or one in every 15 inhabitants, owns a copy of one or both of these mega-sellers.

TOP 10 BESTSELLING ALBUMS BY A MALE SOLO ARTIST IN THE UK

TITLE / ARTIST / YEAR

1 Thriller, Michael Jackson 1982
2 Bad, Michael Jackson 1987
3 Back to Bedlam, James Blunt 2006
4 Bat Out of Hell, Meat Loaf 1978
5 White Ladder, David Gray 2000
6 But Seriously..., Phil Collins 1989
7 Tubular Bells, Mike Oldfield 1974
8 I've Been Expecting You, Robbie Williams 1998
9 Ladies Gentlemen – The Best of, George Michael 1998
10 The Marshall Mathers LP, Eminem 2000

◀ *Eminem*
Eminem released his seventh studio album, Recovery, in June 2010.

FEMALE SINGERS

TOP 10 **FEMALE ARTISTS WITH THE MOST PLATINUM ALBUMS IN THE UK**

ARTIST / PLATINUM ALBUMS

1	Madonna (17)*	59
2	Kylie Minogue (11)	27
3	= Celine Dion (12)	23
	= Tina Turner (10)	23
5	Whitney Houston (7)	19
6	Dido (2)	16
7	Shania Twain (4)	15
8	= Mariah Carey (13)	13
	= Enya (8)	13
	= Katie Melua (6)	13

* Gold totals listed in brackets

Source: BPI

▶ *Queen of reinvention*
Madonna was inducted into the Rock and Roll Hall of Fame in 2008.

TOP 10 **BESTSELLING ALBUMS BY A FEMALE ARTIST IN THE UK**

TITLE / ARTIST / YEAR

1 The Immaculate Collection, Madonna 1990

2 Come on Over, Shania Twain 1998

3 No Angel, Dido 2000

4 Back to Black, Amy Winehouse 2006

5 Life for Rent, Dido 2003

6 Spirit, Leona Lewis 2008

7 Jagged Little Pill, Alanis Morissette 1995

8 Come Away With Me, Norah Jones 2002

9 Tracy Chapman, Tracy Chapman 1998

10 I Dreamed a Dream, Susan Boyle 2010

Source: Music Information Database

The top three albums listed here have all sold in excess of three million copies – in fact, Dido's first two releases have a combined sale of almost 5.8 million. Although not featured in this Top 10, Celine Dion has six million-plus selling albums.

TOP 10 **FEMALE SOLO SINGERS IN THE UK**

SINGER / TOTAL CHART HITS

1 Madonna 68

2 Diana Ross 61

3 Kylie Minogue 46

4 Mariah Carey 40

5 = Donna Summer 39
= Janet Jackson 39

7 Tina Turner 36

8 Whitney Houston 34

9 Shirley Bassey 33

10 = Cher 31
= Gloria Estefan 31

Source: Music Information Database

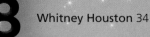

TOP 10 **BESTSELLING SINGLES BY FEMALE SOLO SINGERS IN THE UK**

TITLE / ARTIST / YEAR

1 'Believe', Cher 1998
2 '… Baby One More Time', Britney Spears 1999
3 'I Will Always Love You', Whitney Houston 1992
4 'My Heart Will Go On', Celine Dion 1998
5 'The Power of Love', Jennifer Rush 1985
6 'Think Twice', Celine Dion 1994
7 'Hallelujah', Alexandra Burke 2008
8 'Can't Get You Out of My Head', Kylie Minogue 2001
9 'Saturday Night', Whigfield 1994
10 'Torn', Natalie Imbruglia 1997

Source: Music Information Database

TOP 10 **OLDEST FEMALE SOLO SINGERS TO HAVE A NO. 1 SINGLE IN THE UK**

ARTIST / TITLE	YEAR	YRS	AGE MTHS	DAYS
1 Cher, 'Believe'	1998	52	5	12
2 Madonna, '4 Minutes'	2008	49	8	11
3 Barbra Streisand, 'Woman in Love'	1980	38	6	1
4 Vera Lynn, 'My Son My Son'	1954	37	7	25
5 Kylie Minogue, 'Slow'	2003	35	5	18
6 Jennifer Lopez, 'Get Right'	2005	34	7	3
7 Nicole Kidman, 'Something Stupid'	2001	34	6	2
8 Tammy Wynette, 'Stand By Your Man'	1975	33	0	12
9 Kitty Kallen, 'Little Things Mean a Lot'	1954	32	3	16
10 Robin Beck, 'First Time'	1988	32	2	12

Source: Music Information Database

Youngest Female No. 1 Solo Artists in the UK

Helen Shapiro was only 14 years, 10 months and 13 days old when she made it to No. 1 with 'You Don't Know' in 1961. The youngest female solo singer to accomplish such a feat in the UK, the height of Shapiro's career came and went before she was out of her teens. Billie's single 'Because We Want To' went to No. 1 in 1998, making her the second youngest to do so – at 15 years, 9 months and 13 days. The most recent of the Top 10 youngsters is Pixie Lott, who was 18 years, 5 months and 2 days old when she took the No. 1 spot in 2009 with 'Mama Do (Uh Oh, Uh Oh)'.

▲ Celine Dion
The French-Canadian singer performs 70 shows a year at Caesar's Palace in Las Vegas.

GROUPS & DUOS

TOP 10 ALBUMS BY GROUPS AND DUOS IN THE UK

TITLE / ARTIST / YEAR

1 Greatest Hits (Volume One)
Queen 1981

2 Sgt. Pepper's Lonely Hearts Club Band The Beatles 1967

3 Abba Gold – Greatest Hits
Abba 1992

4 (What's the Story) Morning Glory, Oasis 1995

5 Brothers in Arms
Dire Straits 1985

6 The Dark Side of the Moon
Pink Floyd 1973

7 Greatest Hits Volume II
Queen 1991

8 Stars
Simply Red 1991

9 Rumours
Fleetwood Mac 1977

10 Urban Hymns
The Verve 1997

TOP 10 GROUPS AND DUOS WITH THE MOST NO. 1 ALBUMS IN THE UK

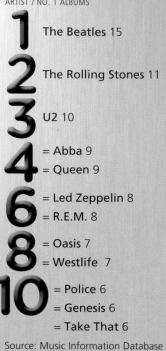

ARTIST / NO. 1 ALBUMS

1 The Beatles 15

2 The Rolling Stones 11

3 U2 10

4 = Abba 9
= Queen 9

6 = Led Zeppelin 8
= R.E.M. 8

8 = Oasis 7
= Westlife 7

10 = Police 6
= Genesis 6
= Take That 6

Source: Music Information Database

▲ *Fleetwood Mac*
A year after Stevie Nicks joined, the band found success with its eponymous 1975 album.

▼ *Luck of the Irish*
Originally from Dublin, Ireland, U2 have been together for more than three and a half decades.

TOP 10 GROUPS AND DUOS WITH THE MOST NO. 1 SINGLES IN THE UK

ARTIST / NO. 1 SINGLES

1 The Beatles 17

2 Westlife* 14

3 Take That# 11

4 = Abba 9
= Spice Girls 9

6 = Oasis 8
= The Rolling Stones 8

8 = U2 7
= McFly 7

10 = Blondie 6
= Boyzone 6
= Queen† 6
= Slade 6
= Sugababes 6

* Including one with Mariah Carey
\# Including one with Lulu
† Including ones with David Bowie, George Michael and Five

Source: Music Information Database

▲ The Fab Four
The bestselling Beatles' single in the UK is 1963's 'She Loves You'.

More than one poll has ranked Queen's 'Bohemian Rhapsody' in the Top 10 of a list of '100 Greatest Singles' of all time. Its total sales in the UK alone are over 2.13 million.

TOP 10 SINGLES OF ALL TIME BY GROUPS AND DUOS IN THE UK

TITLE / ARTIST / YEAR

1 'Bohemian Rhapsody', Queen 1975

2 'Mull of Kintyre'/'Girls' School', Wings 1977

3 'Rivers of Babylon'/'Brown Girl in the Ring', Boney M 1978

4 'You're the One That I Want', John Travolta and Olivia Newton-John 1978

5 'Relax', Frankie Goes to Hollywood 1984

6 'She Loves You', The Beatles 1963

7 'Unchained Melody'/'(There'll Be Bluebirds Over the) White Cliffs of Dover', Robson Green and Jerome Flynn 1995

8 'Mary's Boy Child'/'Oh My Lord', Boney M 1978

9 'Love Is All Around', Wet Wet Wet 1994

10 'I Want to Hold Your Hand', The Beatles 1963

TOP 10 GROUPS AND DUOS WITH THE LONGEST SINGLES CHART CAREERS IN THE UK

	ARTIST	CHART SPAN	YRS	MTHS	DAYS
1	Cliff Richard and the Shadows	25 Oct 1958–26 Sep 2009	50	11	1
2	The Beatles	13 Oct 1962–25 Dec 2010	48	2	12
3	Gerry and the Pacemakers	16 Mar 1963–1 May 2010	47	1	14
4	The Four Seasons	6 Oct 1962–14 Mar 2009	46	5	8
5	Moody Blues	12 Dec 1964–11 Dec 2010	45	11	29
6	The Rolling Stones	27 Jul 1963–2 Jun 2007	43	10	6
7	Spencer Davis Group	7 Nov 1964–12 Apr 2008	43	5	6
8	Status Quo	27 Jan 1968–16 Oct 2010	42	8	20
9	The Kinks	15 Aug 1964–25 Sep 2004	40	1	10
10	Slade	19 Jun 1971–25 Dec 2010	39	6	6

Source: Music Information Database

This is a constantly changing list, as just one release of a classic single will move the positions around. After not being on this list for some years, the Beatles go back in at No. 2 on the strength of their catalogue being issued through iTunes.

Rolling Stones at 50

Rock gods
Mick Jagger, Charlie Watts and Keith Richards have been together since the band was formed in 1962, and continue to tour internationally despite a combined age of 206.

TOP 10 **ROLLING STONES ALBUMS IN THE UK**

	ALBUM	YEAR
1	Forty Licks	2002
2	Jump Back – The Best of The Rolling Stones	1993
3	Hot Rocks 1964–1971	1990
4	Let It Bleed	1969
5	The Rolling Stones No. 2	1965
6	Aftermath	1966
7	Rolled Gold – The Very Best of The Rolling Stones	1975
8	Sticky Fingers	1971
9	Some Girls	1978
10	Emotional Rescue	1980

Source: Music Information Database

TOP 10 **ROLLING STONES SINGLES IN THE UK**

	SINGLE	YEAR
1	'The Last Time'	1965
2	'(I Can't Get No) Satisfaction'	1965
3	'19th Nervous Breakdown'	1966
4	'Honky Tonk Women'	1969
5	'Jumping Jack Flash'	1968
6	'Little Red Rooster'	1964
7	'Brown Sugar'	1971
8	'Paint It, Black'	1966
9	'It's All Over Now'	1964
10	'Get Off Of My Cloud'	1965

Source: Music Information Database

As with the Beatles' albums, the long-stay scores of some early Rolling Stones albums were inhibited by the shorter chart of their day. The 1965 album *Out Of Our Heads*, which just missed this Top 10 with a 24-week stay, was issued when only a UK Top 20 LP chart existed, but in reality it continued to sell for longer than *Tattoo You*, *Some Girls* and certain other albums.

► **Bill Wyman**
Wyman was bass player for the first 30 years but left in 1992 to play with his own band, Bill Wyman's Rhythm Kings.

◄ **Brian Jones**
A founding member of the Rolling Stones, Jones left the group in June 1969 and soon afterwards drowned in his own swimming pool.

THE CHANGING FACE OF THE ROLLING STONES

There have been 10 members of the Rolling Stones over the past 50 years – some more enduring than others. Jagger, Richards and Watts are the only ones to claim a full half-century's membership.

Name	Dates	Instrument
Mick Jagger	1962–2012	Vocals
Keith Richards	1962–2012	Guitar
Charlie Watts	1962–2012	Drums
Bill Wyman	1962–92	Bass
Brian Jones	1962–69	Guitar
Ian Stewart	1962–63	Keyboards
Dick Taylor	1962	Bass
Tony Chapman	1962	Drums
Mick Taylor	1969–74	Guitar
Ronnie Wood	1975–2012	Guitar

ROLLING STONES TIMELINE

Apr 1962 Rolling Stones form

Jul 1962 First official gig at the Marquee, London

Jun 1963 First single released in the UK: 'Come On'

May 1963 Stewart leaves the line-up to become the band's manager

Sep–Nov 1963 First UK tour

April 1964 First album released in the UK: *The Rolling Stones*

Jun 1964 First UK No. 1 single 'It's All Over Now'

Jun 1964 First US tour

May 1965 First US No.1 single '(I Can't Get No) Satisfaction'

Feb–Mar 1966 First tour of Australasia

Jul 1969 Brian Jones dies; Stones perform free concert in Hyde Park, London

Apr 1971 Stones sign with Atlantic Records

Jun–Jul 1972 Tour of North America

Dec 1974 Mick Taylor leaves the group

Mar 1975 Wood joins for *Black and Blue* recording sessions

Jun–Aug 1975 46-show tour of the Americas

Apr–June 1976 Nine-country tour of Europe

Jan 1989 Stones inducted into the Rock & Roll Hall of Fame

Aug 1989–Aug 1990 Steel Wheels/Urban Jungle tour

Dec 1992 Wyman leaves the band

Aug 1994–Aug 1995 Voodoo Lounge tour

Sep 1997–Sep 1998 Bridges to Babylon tour

Jan-Apr 1999 No Security tour

Sep 2002–Nov 2003 Licks tour

Aug 2005–Aug 2007 Bigger Bang tour

Apr 2012 Stones celebrate 50 years of rock 'n' roll success

◄ **Ronnie Wood**
Beginning his career as a guitarist with The Birds, Wood joined the Stones in 1975, and still plays with the band as its fourth member.

MUSIC AWARDS

THE 10 ARTISTS WITH MOST MTV AWARDS

	ARTIST	AWARDS
1	Madonna	20
2	Peter Gabriel	13
3	= R.E.M.	12
	= Eminem	12
5	= Green Day	11
	= Aerosmith	11
	= Lady Gaga	11
8	Beyonce	10
9	= Fatboy Slim	9
	= Janet Jackson	9

THE 10 LATEST RECIPIENTS OF THE MERCURY MUSIC PRIZE

YEAR	ARTIST / ALBUM
2010	The xx, xx
2009	Speech Debelle, Speech Therapy
2008	Elbow, The Seldom Seen Kid
2007	Klaxons, Myths of The Near Future
2006	Arctic Monkeys, Whatever People Say I Am, That's What I'm Not
2005	Antony & the Johnsons, I Am a Bird Now
2004	Franz Ferdinand, Franz Ferdinand
2003	Dizzee Rascal, Boy In Da Corner
2002	Ms Dynamite, A Little Deeper
2001	PJ Harvey, Stories from the City, Stories from the Sea

Source: Barclaycard Mercury Prize

▶ **Green Day**
The punk rockers' third album, Dookie, achieved diamond status after selling over 16 million copies worldwide.

THE 10 ARTISTS WITH THE MOST BRIT NOMINATIONS WHO HAVE NEVER WON

	ARTIST	NOMINATIONS
1	= Radiohead	15
	= Jamiroqui	15
3	Craig David	12
4	Jamelia	9
5	Gorillaz	8
6	= Eternal	7
	= PJ Harvey	7
8	= Suede	6
	= Kasabian	6
	= Leona Lewis	6
	= Alicia Keys	6
	= Snow Patrol	6

Source: BRITS

THE 10 **LATEST BRIT RECORDS OF THE YEAR**

YEAR / RECORD / ARTIST

2011
'Pass Out', Tinie Tempah

2010
'Beat Again', JLS

2009
'The Promise', Girls Aloud

2008
'Shine', Take That

2007
'Patience', Take That

2006
'Speed of Sound', Coldplay

2005
'Your Game', Will Young

2004
'White Flag', Dido

2003
'Just a Little', Liberty X

2002
'Don't Stop Movin'', S Club 7

Source: BRITS

► *Georg Solti*
The conductor of the Chicago Symphony Orchestra for 22 years, Solti was nominated for 74 Grammy Awards.

TOP 10 **GROUPS WITH MOST GRAMMY AWARDS**

	GROUP	AWARDS
1	U2	22
2	= Alison Krauss and Union Station	13
	= The Beatles	13
	= Dixie Chicks	13
5	Pat Metheny Group	10
6	Metallica	9
7	= Santana	8
	= Take 6	8
9	= Coldplay	7
	= Simon and Garfunkel	7

Source: NARAS

TOP 10 **ARTISTS WITH MOST GRAMMY AWARDS**

	ARTIST	AWARDS
1	Georg Solti	31
2	Quincy Jones	27
3	= Pierre Boulez	26
	= Alison Krauss	26
5	Vladimir Horowitz	25
6	= Stevie Wonder	22
	= U2	22
8	John Williams	21
9	= Vince Gill	20
	= Henry Mancini	20
	= Bruce Springsteen	20

Source: NARAS

◄ *Alison Krauss*
The multi-platinum selling musician first picked up a fiddle at the age of five.

CLASSICAL & OPERA

◄ The Three Tenors
The tenors first performed together at a concert on the eve of the 1990 World Cup final.

TOP 10 CLASSICAL ALBUMS IN THE UK

TITLE	PERFORMER / ORCHESTRA	YEAR
1 The Three Tenors in Concert	José Carreras, Placido Domingo, Luciano Pavarotti	1990
2 The Essential Pavarotti	Luciano Pavarotti	1990
3 Vivaldi: The Four Seasons	Nigel Kennedy/English Chamber Orchestra	1989
4 The Three Tenors in Concert 1994	José Carreras, Placido Domingo, Luciano Pavarotti, Zubin Mehta	1994
5 The Voice	Russell Watson	2000
6 Voice of an Angel	Charlotte Church	1998
7 Pure	Hayley Westenra	2003
8 Encore	Russell Watson	2002
9 The Essential Pavarotti, 2	Luciano Pavarotti	1991
10 The Pavarotti Collection	Luciano Pavarotti	1986

Source: Music Information Database

Sales of classical music boomed to unprecedented heights at the end of the 1980s and in the early 1990s. One major reason for this was the success of records by a select band of superstars – tenors José Carreras, Placido Domingo and Luciano Pavarotti (particularly the latter, who even had a Top 3 single with 'Nessun Dorma'), and violinist Nigel Kennedy – that soared way ahead of the field as a whole.

TOP 10 OPERAS MOST FREQUENTLY PERFORMED AT THE GLYNDEBOURNE OPERA

OPERA	COMPOSER	YEARS PERFORMED*
1 Cosi Fan Tutte	Wolfgang Amadeus Mozart	30
2 Le Nozze di Figaro	Wolfgang Amadeus Mozart	28
3 Don Giovanni	Wolfgang Amadeus Mozart	23
4 Die Zauberflote	Wolfgang Amadeus Mozart	17
5 Die Entfuhrung aus dem Serail	Wolfgang Amadeus Mozart	15
6 The Rake's Progress	Igor Stravinsky	13
7 Falstaff	Giuseppe Verdi	12
8 Idomeneo	Wolfgang Amadeus Mozart	11
9 =La Cenerentola	Gioachino Rossini	10
=Ariadne auf Naxos	Richard Strauss	10

* As of end of the 2010 season

Source: Glyndebourne Festival Opera

▼ *Andrea Bocelli*
Blind since childhood, Bocelli is one of the world's most popular opera singers.

▶ *Alan Gilbert*
Gilbert was the first native New Yorker to be made music director of the New York Philharmonic.

TOP 10 **BESTSELLING CLASSICAL ARTISTS IN THE UK**

1 Luciano Pavarotti

2 Placido Domingo

3 José Carreras

4 Andrea Bocelli

5 Russell Watson

6 Charlotte Church

7 Katherine Jenkins

8 Nigel Kennedy

9 Hayley Westenra

10 Aled Jones

Source: Music Information Database

THE 10 **LATEST WINNERS OF THE BRIT AWARD FOR BEST CLASSICAL ALBUM**

YEAR	COMPOSER / TITLE
2010	Only Men Aloud! Band of Brothers
2009	Royal Scots Dragoon Guards Spirit of the Glen-Journey
2008	Blake Blake
2007	Paul McCartney Ecce Cor Meum
2006	Katherine Jenkins Living a Dream
2005	Katherine Jenkins Second Nature
2004	Bryn Terfel Bryn
2003	Andrea Bocelli Sentimento
2002	Russell Watson Encore
2001	Russell Watson The Voice

Source: BPI

THE 10 **LATEST CONDUCTORS OF THE NEW YORK PHILHARMONIC ORCHESTRA**

	CONDUCTOR	YEARS
1	Alan Gilbert	2009–
2	Lorin Maazel	2002–09
3	Kurt Masur	1991–2002
4	Zubin Mehta	1978–91
5	Pierre Boulez	1971–77
6	George Szell*	1969–70
7	Leonard Bernstein	1958–69
8	Dimitri Mitropoulos	1949–58
9	Leopold Stokowski#	1949–50
10	Bruno Walter*	1947–49

* Music advisor
# Co-principal conductor

The New York Philharmonic Orchestra was founded in 1842 by conductor Ureli Corelli Hill, giving its first performance – of Beethoven's Symphony No. 5 – at the Apollo Rooms. In 1909 Gustav Mahler was appointed the orchestra's principal conductor. During the 1930s the orchestra, under the baton of Arturo Toscanini, began Sunday afternoon concerts from Carnegie Hall, which were broadcast on CBS radio for 38 years.

MOVIE MUSIC

▲ **Mamma Mia!**
Based on songs by Abba, the film was shot on the Greek island of Skopelos.

In recent years, animated films with an important musical content have taken over from traditional musicals (in which the cast actually sing), with *Beauty and the Beast*, *Aladdin*, *The Lion King*, *Pocahontas*, *The Prince of Egypt*, *Tarzan* and *Monsters, Inc.* all winning 'Best Original Song' Oscars.

TOP 10 BESTSELLING MUSICAL ALBUMS IN THE UK

ALBUM / YEAR OF RELEASE

1 The Sound of Music
1965

2 Grease
1978

3 South Pacific
1958

4 West Side Story
1962

5 Oklahoma
1955

6 The King and I
1956

7 Oliver
1968

8 Mary Poppins
1965

9 Evita
1996

10 My Fair Lady
1964

Source: Music Information Database

TOP 10 MUSICAL FILMS

FILM / YEAR

1 Mamma Mia!
2008

2 Grease
1978

3 Chicago
2002

4 The Sound of Music
1965

5 The Rocky Horror Picture Show
1975

6 High School Musical 3: Senior Year
2008

7 Saturday Night Fever
1977

8 Hairspray
2007

9 Moulin Rouge!
2001

10 Dreamgirls
2006

TOP 10 ORIGINAL SOUNDTRACK ALBUMS IN THE UK

	TITLE	YEAR OF RELEASE
1	The Sound of Music	1965
2	Dirty Dancing	1998
3	Grease	1978
4	Saturday Night Fever	1977
5	The Bodyguard	1992
6	South Pacific	1958
7	Titanic	1997
8	Bridget Jones's Diary	2001
9	Trainspotting	1996
10	The Commitments	1991

Source: Music Information Database

▲ The Bodyguard
Madonna was originally considered for the role eventually played by Whitney Houston.

▼ Grease
Set in a US high school in the 1950s, the film shot John Travoltxa and Olivia Newton-John to stardom.

TOP 10 BESTSELLING 'BEST SONG' OSCAR-WINNING SINGLES IN THE UK

	TITLE / ARTIST / FILM (IF DIFFERENT)	YEAR
1	'I Just Called to Say I Love You', Stevie Wonder (The Woman in Red)	1984
2	'My Heart Will Go On', Celine Dion (Titanic)	1997
3	'Fame', Irene Cara	1980
4	'Take My Breath Away', Berlin (Top Gun)	1986
5	'Flashdance... What a Feeling', Irene Cara (Flashdance)	1983
6	'Evergreen', Barbra Streisand (A Star is Born)	1976
7	'Lose Yourself', Eminem (8 Mile)	2002
8	'Streets of Philadelphia', Bruce Springsteen (Philadelphia)	1994
9	'Moon River', Danny Williams (Breakfast at Tiffany's)	1961
10	'Whatever Will Be, Will Be', Doris Day (The Man Who Knew Too Much)	1956

Source: Music Information Database

THE 10 LATEST WINNERS OF THE OSCAR FOR BEST ORIGINAL SONG

YEAR	TITLE	FILM
2010	'We Belong Together'	Toy Story 3
2009	'The Weary Kind'	Crazy Heart
2008	'Jai Ho'	Slumdog Millionaire
2007	'Falling Slowly'	Once
2006	'I Need To Wake Up'	An Inconvenient Truth
2005	'It's Hard Out Here for a Pimp'	Hustle & Flow
2004	'Al Otro Lado Del Rio'	The Motorcycle Diaries
2003	'Into The West'	The Lord of the Rings: The Return of the King
2002	'Lose Yourself'	8 Mile
2001	'If I Didn't Have You'	Monsters, Inc.

* Of release; awards made the following year

7
ENTERTAINMENT

50 YEARS OF JAMES BOND

Sixty years ago, whilst at his Jamaican estate Goldeneye, Ian Fleming started work on the first of his 12 James Bond novels. Published in 1953, *Casino Royale* gained widespread popularity and was adapted for the screen three times. In 1962, EON Productions produced its first Bond film, *Dr. No*, starring Sean Connery. Despite not being Fleming's first choice of actor, Connery went on to star in six of the James Bond movies. Since then, George Lazenby, Roger Moore, Timothy Dalton, Pierce Brosnan and, most recently, Daniel Craig have portrayed 007 in one of the longest-running film franchises of all time.

YEAR	MUSICAL
2011	Legally Blonde – The Musical
2010	Spring Awakening
2009	Jersey Boys
2008	Hairspray
2007	Caroline, Or Change
2006	Billy Elliot – The Musical
2005	The Producers
2004	Jerry Springer – The Opera
2003#	Our House
2001†	Merrily We Roll Along

* Awards are for previous season
\# The Hilton Award for Best New Musical in 2003
† No award in 2002

◄ *Hakuna Matata*
Based on the 1994 Disney film, The Lion King *musical features songs by Elton John and Tim Rice.*

TOP 10 **LONGEST-RUNNING MUSICALS ON BROADWAY**

	SHOW	RUN	PERFORMANCES
1	The Phantom of the Opera	26 Jan 1988–	9,547*
2	Cats	7 Oct 1982–10 Sep 2000	7,485
3	Les Misérables	12 Mar 1987–18 May 2003	6,680
4	A Chorus Line	25 Jul 1975–28 Apr 1990	6,137
5	Chicago	14 Nov 1996–	5,876*
6	=Beauty and the Beast	18 Apr 1994–29 Jul 2007	5,461
	=The Lion King	13 Nov 1997–	5,461*
8	Rent	29 Apr 1996–7 Sep 2008	5,123
9	Miss Saigon	11 Apr 1991–28 Jan 2001	4,092
10	Mamma Mia!	18 Oct 2001–	3,824*

* Still running, total as of 17 January 2011

All the longest-running musicals date from the past 40 years. Prior to these record-breakers, the longest runner of the 1940s was *Oklahoma!*, which debuted in 1943 and ran for 2,212 performances up to 1948, and from the 1950s *My Fair Lady*, which opened in 1956 and closed in 1962 after 2,717 performances.

TOP 10 **MOST PRODUCED PLAYS BY SHAKESPEARE, 1878–2010**

	PLAY	PRODUCTIONS
1	As You Like It	83
2	=Hamlet	81
	=Twelfth Night	81
4	The Taming of the Shrew	80
5	A Midsummer Night's Dream	77
6	Much Ado About Nothing	72
7	The Merchant of Venice	70
8	Macbeth	67
9	=The Merry Wives of Windsor	62
	=Romeo and Juliet	62

Source: Shakespeare Centre

This list is based on an analysis of Shakespearean productions (rather than individual performances) from 31 December 1878 to 31 December 2010 at Stratford-upon-Avon and by the Royal Shakespeare Company in London and on tour.

TOP 10 LONGEST SHAKESPEAREAN ROLES

	ROLE	PLAY	LINES
1	Hamlet	Hamlet	1,422
2	Falstaff	Henry IV, Parts I and II	1,178
3	Richard III	Richard III	1,124
4	Iago	Othello	1,097
5	Henry V	Henry V	1,025
6	Othello	Othello	860
7	Vincentio	Measure for Measure	820
8	Coriolanus	Coriolanus	809
9	Timon	Timon of Athens	795
10	Antony	Antony and Cleopatra	766

If more than one play (or parts of a play) are taken into account, some would increase their tallies, among them Richard III, who appears (as Richard, Duke of Gloucester) in *Henry VI*, Part III, and Henry V who appears (as Prince Hal) in *Henry IV*, where he speaks 117 lines, making his total 1,142. Rosalind's 668-line role in *As You Like It* is the longest female part in the works of Shakespeare.

▼ *Hamlet Who?*
The 10th Doctor in Dr Who, actor David Tennant also played Hamlet in a 2008–09 production.

THE 10 LATEST WINNERS OF THE LAURENCE OLIVIER AWARD FOR BEST NEW PLAY*

YEAR / PLAY / PLAYWRIGHT

2011 Clybourne Park / Bruce Norris

2010 The Mountaintop / Katori Hall

2009 National Theatre of Scotland's Black Watch / Gregory Burke

2008 A Disappearing Number / Simon McBurney and Complicite

2007 Blackbird / David Harrower

2006 On the Shore of the Wide World / Simon Stephens

2005 The History Boys / Alan Bennett

2004 The Pillowman / Martin McDonagh

2003 Vincent in Brixton / Nicholas Wright

2002 Jitney / August Wilson

* 'The BBC Award for Best New Play' until 2004; awards are for previous season

MOVIE WORLD

TOP 10 FILMS OF THE SILENT ERA

FILM / YEAR

1 The Birth of a Nation 1915
2 The Big Parade 1925
3 Ben-Hur 1926
4 The Ten Commandments 1923
5 = The Covered Wagon 1923
= What Price Glory? 1926
7 = Hearts of the World 1918
= Way Down East 1921
9 = The Four Horsemen of the Apocalypse 1921
= Wings 1927

★ ★ ★ ★ ★
▲ Ben-Hur
The most expensive silent movie ever made changed director and location in the middle of filming.

TOP 10 FILM FRANCHISES OF ALL TIME

FRANCHISE / NO. OF FILMS / YEARS	TOTAL WORLDGROSS (US$)
1 Harry Potter 7 / 2001–10	6,361,655,490
2 James Bond 23 / 1963–2008	5,074,402,453
3 Star Wars 6 / 1977–2005	4,441,410,761
4 Shrek 4 / 2001–10	2,955,741,576
5 The Lord of the Rings 3 / 2001–03	2,913,933,388
6 Pirates of the Caribbean 3 / 2003–07	2,681,667,528
7 Batman 6 / 1989–2008	2,648,834,002
8 Spider-Man 3 / 2002–07	2,496,285,178
9 Indiana Jones 4 / 1981–2008	1,980,610,580
10 Toy Story 3 / 1995–2020	1,946,968,297

Source: boxofficemojo.com/IBMD Pro/the-numbers

★ ★ ★ ★ ★
▲ Harry Potter and friends
The three young Harry Potter stars top the list of average takings per film starred in.

TOP 10 BLACK AND WHITE FILMS

FILM / YEAR

1 Young Frankenstein (1974)
2 Schindler's List (1993)
3 Paper Moon (1973)
4 Manhattan (1979)
5 Mom and Dad (1944)
6 Who's Afraid of Virginia Woolf? (1966)
7 Easy Money (1983)
8 The Last Picture Show (1971)
9 From Here to Eternity (1953)
10 Dead Men Don't Wear Plaid (1982)

★ ★ ★ ★ ★

▲ Young Frankenstein
The affectionate parody used many of the same props from the original Frankenstein.

TOP 10 FILMS OF ALL TIME

FILM / YEAR	USA	GROSS INCOME (US$) OVERSEAS	WORLD TOTAL
1 Avatar 2009	760,307,594	2,009,924,355	2,770,231,949
2 Titanic* 1997	600,788,188	1,242,413,080	1,843,201,268
3 The Lord of the Rings: The Return of the King* 2003	377,027,325	742,083,616	1,119,110,941
4 Pirates of the Caribbean: Dead Man's Chest 2006	423,315,812	642,863,913	1,066,179,725
5 Toy Story 3 2010	412,031,733	644,400,000	1,056,431,733
6 Alice in Wonderland 2010	334,191,110	690,108,181	1,024,299,291
7 The Dark Knight 2008	533,345,358	468,576,467	1,001,921,825
8 Harry Potter and the Philospher's Stone 2001	317,575,550	657,158,000	974,733,550
9 Pirates of the Caribbean: At World's End 2007	309,420,425	651,576,067	960,996,492
10 Harry Potter and the Deathly Hallows: Part I 2010	295,001,070	657,240,000	952,241,070

* Won Best Picture Oscar

TOP 10 COUNTRIES WITH THE MOST CINEMA SCREENS

COUNTRY	NO. OF CINEMA SCREENS*
1 USA	39,476
2 China	36,112
3 India	10,189
4 France	5,426
5 Germany	4,810
6 Spain	4,140
7 Mexico	3,920
8 UK	3,661
9 Italy	3,410
10 Japan	3,359

* Latest available year for which data available; excluding drive-in screens

★ ★ ★ ★ ★

▶ Avatar
The equivalent of 13 years worth of HD video was used for data storage on the film.

OPENING WEEKENDS

◀ Sherlock Holmes
Since his creation by Sir Arthur Conan Doyle, Holmes has been portrayed in over 200 films.

TOP 10 **CHRISTMAS OPENING WEEKENDS***

FILM	YEAR	OPENING WEEKEND GROSS (US$)
1 Sherlock Holmes	2009	24,608,941
2 Marley and Me	2008	14,380,980
3 The Curious Case of Benjamin Button	2008	11,871,831
4 Bedtime Stories	2008	10,578,817
5 Ali	2001	10,216,625
6 Catch Me If You Can	2002	9,882,063
7 Aliens Vs. Predator – Requiem	2007	9,515,615
8 Dreamgirls	2006	8,726,095
9 Valkyrie	2008	8,493,972
10 Patch Adams	1998	8,081,760

* First release anywhere in the world on Christmas weekend

TOP 10 **BIGGEST SECOND-WEEKEND DROPS**

FILM* / YEAR	SECOND WEEKEND DROP (%)
1 Friday the 13th 2009	80.4
2 Jonas Brothers: The 3D Concert Experience 2009	77.4
3 Star Trek: Nemesis 2002	76.2
4 George A. Romero's Land of the Dead 2005	73.4
5 Bruno 2009	72.8
6 Doom 2005	72.7
7 A Nightmare on Elm Street 2010	72.3
8 Notorious 2009	71.8
9 Predators 2010	71.7
10 Hellboy II: The Golden Army 2008	70.7

* Earning over US$10 million in opening weekend

TOP 10 **HALLOWEEN OPENERS**

FILM / YEAR	OPENING WEEKEND GROSS (US$)
1 Saw III 2006	33,610,391
2 Saw IV 2007	32,110,000
3 Saw II 2005	31,725,652
4 Jackass: The Movie 2002	22,763,437
5 Ray 2004	20,039,730
6 Brother Bear 2003	19,404,492
7 Saw 2004	18,276,468
8 K-PAX 2001	17,215,275
9 Stargate 1994	16,651,018
10 The Legend of Zorro 2005	16,328,506

TOP 10 U-RATED OPENING WEEKENDS

	FILM / YEAR	OPENING WEEKEND GROSS (US$)
1	Toy Story 3 2010	110,307,189
2	Finding Nemo 2003	70,251,710
3	WALL-E 2008	63,087,526
4	Monsters, Inc. 2001	62,577,067
5	Cars 2006	60,119,509
6	Toy Story 2 1999	57,388,839
7	Ratatouille 2007	47,027,395
8	Horton Hears a Who! 2008	45,012,998
9	High School Musical 3: Senior Year 2008	42,030,184
10	The Lion King 1994	40,888,194

A U rating denotes a film that is suitable for everyone, even young children.

TOP 10 FILMS THAT SPENT THE LONGEST AT NO. 1

	FILM / YEAR	CONSECUTIVE NO. 1 WEEKENDS
1	Titanic 1997	15
2 =	Beverly Hills Cop 1984	13
=	Tootsie 1982	13
4	Home Alone 1990	12
5 =	Crocodile Dundee 1986	9
=	Good Morning, Vietnam 1987	9
7 =	Back to the Future 1985	8
=	Fatal Attraction 1987	8
=	Porky's 1982	8
10 =	Avatar 2009	7
=	Ghostbusters 1984	7
=	On Golden Pond 1981	7

▲ Home Alone
Earning US$477 million worldwide, Home Alone is the highest-grossing live-action comedy of all time.

TOP 10 15-RATED OPENING WEEKENDS

	FILM / YEAR	OPENING WEEKEND GROSS (US$)
1	The Matrix Reloaded 2003	91,774,413
2	The Passion of the Christ 2004	83,848,082
3	300 2007	70,885,301
4	Hannibal 2001	58,003,121
5	Sex and the City 2008	57,038,404
6	Watchmen 2009	55,214,334
7	8 Mile 2002	51,240,555
8	Wanted 2008	50,927,641
9	Jackass 3D 2010	50,353,641
10	The Matrix Revolutions 2003	48,475,154

▶ 300
The adaptation of Frank Miller's graphic novel was shot almost entirely on blue screen, using 1,300 visual effects.

FILMS OF THE DECADES

TOP 10 FILMS OF THE 1920s

FILM / YEAR

1 The Big Parade 1925
2 The Four Horsemen of the Apocalypse 1921
3 Ben-Hur 1926
4 The Ten Commandments 1923
5 What Price Glory? 1926
6 The Covered Wagon 1923
7 Way Down East 1921
8 The Singing Fool 1928
9 Wings 1927
10 The Gold Rush 1925

Earnings data for early films are unreliable, but if this list were extended back to the first decade of the 20th century, *The Birth of a Nation* (1915) would be a contender as the highest-earning film of the silent era. *The Broadway Melody* (1929), which just fails to make the list, was the first ever winner of a Best Picture Oscar.

TOP 10 FILMS OF THE 1930s

FILM / YEAR

1 Gone With the Wind* 1939
2 Snow White and the Seven Dwarfs 1937
3 The Wizard of Oz 1939
4 Frankenstein 1931
5 King Kong 1933
6 San Francisco 1936
7 = Hell's Angels 1930
  = Lost Horizon 1937
  = Mr. Smith Goes to Washington 1939
10 Maytime 1937

* Winner of Best Picture Academy Award

If the income of *Gone With the Wind* is adjusted to allow for inflation in the period since its release, it could be regarded as the most successful film ever.

▼ The Wizard of Oz
Toto, Dorothy's dog, was paid more than twice the weekly wage of the actors portraying the Munchkins.

TOP 10 FILMS OF THE 1940s

FILM / YEAR

1 Bambi* 1942
2 Pinocchio* 1940
3 Fantasia* 1940
4 Song of the South# 1946
5 Mom and Dad 1944
6 Samson and Delilah 1949
7 The Best Years of Our Lives† 1946
8 The Bells of St. Mary's 1945
9 Duel in the Sun 1946
10 This is the Army 1943

* Animated
# Part animated/part live-action
† Winner of Best Picture Academy Award

▶ Bambi
The feature lost money on its first run, but was re-released six times.

TOP 10 FILMS OF THE 1970s

FILM / YEAR

1 Star Wars* 1977
2 Jaws 1975
3 Grease 1978
4 Close Encounters of the Third Kind 1977
5 The Exorcist 1973
6 Superman 1978
7 Saturday Night Fever 1977
8 Jaws 2 1978
9 Moonraker 1979
10 The Spy Who Loved Me 1977

* Later retitled *Star Wars: Episode IV – A New Hope*

The first nine films in the list exemplify the upward trend of box-office blockbusters, each earning in excess of $200 million worldwide, with *Star Wars* reaping a total global take approaching $800 million.

TOP 10 **FILMS OF THE** 1950s

FILM / YEAR

1 Lady and the Tramp* 1955
2 Peter Pan* 1953
3 Cinderella* 1950
4 The Ten Commandments 1956
5 Ben-Hur# 1959
6 Sleeping Beauty* 1959
7 Around the World in 80 Days 1956
8 This is Cinerama 1952
9 South Pacific 1958
10 The Robe 1953

* Animated
# Winner of Best Picture Academy Award

While the popularity of animated films continued, the 1950s was outstanding as the decade of the 'big' picture: many of the most successful films were enormous in terms of cast numbers.

TOP 10 **FILMS OF THE** 1960s

FILM / YEAR

1 One Hundred and One Dalmatians* 1961
2 The Jungle Book* 1967
3 The Sound of Music# 1965
4 Thunderball 1965
5 Goldfinger 1964
6 Doctor Zhivago 1965
7 You Only Live Twice 1967
8 The Graduate 1968
9 Butch Cassidy and the Sundance Kid 1969
10 Mary Poppins 1964

* Animated
# Winner of Best Picture Academy Award

▶ *Bond begins*
Fifty years of Bond has seen seven actors in the leading role, 14 directors, 114 drinks and 240 kills.

TOP 10 **FILMS OF THE** 1980s

FILM / YEAR

1 E.T.: The Extra-Terrestrial 1982
2 Return of the Jedi* 1983
3 The Empire Strikes Back# 1980
4 Indiana Jones and the Last Crusade 1989
5 Rain Man† 1988
6 Raiders of the Lost Ark 1981
7 Batman 1989
8 Back to the Future 1985
9 Who Framed Roger Rabbit 1988
10 Top Gun 1986

* Later retitled Star Wars: Episode VI – Return of the Jedi
# Later retitled Star Wars: Episode V – The Empire Strikes Back
† Winner of Best Picture Academy Award

The 1980s was clearly the decade of the adventure film, with George Lucas and Steven Spielberg continuing to assert their control of Hollywood, carving up the Top 10 between them.

TOP 10 **FILMS OF THE** 1990s

FILM / YEAR

1 Titanic* 1997
2 Star Wars: Episode I – The Phantom Menace 1999
3 Jurassic Park 1993
4 Independence Day 1996
5 The Lion King# 1994
6 Forrest Gump* 1994
7 The Sixth Sense 1999
8 The Lost World: Jurassic Park 1997
9 Men in Black 1997
10 Armageddon 1998

* Winner of Best Picture Academy Award
# Animated

Each of the Top 10 films of the 1990s has earned more than US$550 million around the world, a total of more than $8.4 billion between them.

TOP 10 **FILMS OF THE** 2000s

FILM / YEAR

1 Avatar 2009*
2 The Lord of the Rings: The Return of the King 2003
3 Pirates of the Caribbean: Dead Man's Chest 2006
4 Toy Story 3 2010
5 Alice in Wonderland 2010
6 The Dark Knight 2008
7 Harry Potter and the Philosopher's Stone 2001
8 Pirates of the Caribbean: At World's End 2007
9 Harry Potter and the Deathly Hallows: Part I 2010
10 Harry Potter and the Order of the Phoenix 2007

* Multiple releases

FILM GENRES

TOP 10 **GANGSTER FILMS***

FILM / YEAR

1 The Departed
2006

2 American Gangster
2007

3 The Godfather
1972

4 Public Enemies
2009

5 Pulp Fiction
1994

6 Gangs of New York
2002

7 The Godfather Part II
1974

8 Heat
1995

9 Road to Perdition
2002

10 Analyze This
1999

* Based on US gross box office

▲ **Public Enemy**
Johnny Depp trained with the FBI for his role as Depression Era gangster John Dillinger.

TOP 10 **HORROR FILMS**

FILM / YEAR

The Exorcist
1973

What Lies Beneath
2000

The Blair Witch Project
1999

The Ring
2002

The Grudge
2004

Paranormal Activity
2009

Scream
1996

Scream 2
1997

The Haunting
1999

Scream 3
2000

This list encompasses classic supernatural and 'slasher' horror films, but not those featuring monster creatures or historical horror flicks.

TOP 10 **SUPERHERO FILMS***

FILM	YEAR
1 The Dark Knight	2008
2 Spider-Man 3	2007
3 Spider-Man	2002
4 Spider-Man 2	2004
5 The Incredibles	2004
6 Hancock	2008
7 Iron Man 2	2010
8 Iron Man	2008
9 X-Men: The Last Stand	2006
10 Batman	1989

* Based on US gross box office

▲ **The Dark Knight**
Heath Ledger's final film was the fastest to earn US$400 million, doing so in just 18 days.

TOP 10 **3D FILMS IN THE USA**

FILM / YEAR / GROSS INCOME USA (US$)*

1 Avatar
2009
$760,507,624

2 Toy Story 3
2010
$415,004,880

3 Alice in Wonderland
2010
$334,191,110

4 Up
2009
$293,004,164

5 Despicable Me
2010
$251,513,985

6 Shrek Forever After
2010
$238,395,990

7 How to Train Your Dragon
2010
$217,581,231

8 Tangled
2010
$199,441,791

9 Monsters Vs. Aliens
2009
$198,351,526

10 Ice Age: Dawn of the Dinosaurs
2009
$196,573,705

* Includes box-office takings from non-3D screenings

▲ How the Grinch Stole Christmas
Three hours of make-up transformed Jim Carrey into Dr Suess's Grinch.

TOP 10 **CHRISTMAS FILMS**

FILM	YEAR	US GROSS (US$)
1 How the Grinch Stole Christmas	2000	260,044,825
2 The Polar Express	2004	181,320,482
3 Elf	2003	173,398,518
4 The Santa Clause	1994	144,833,357
5 The Santa Clause 2: The Mrs. Clause	2002	139,236,327
6 A Christmas Carol	2009	137,855,863
7 Four Christmases	2008	120,146,040
8 The Santa Clause 3: The Escape Clause	2006	84,500,112
9 Tim Burton's The Nightmare before Christmas	1993	75,082,668
10 Christmas with the Kranks	2004	73,780,539

This list only includes films in which Christmas and/or Santa Claus provide the principal theme, rather than those containing Christmas or holiday scenes.

TOP 10 **SPORT FILMS***

FILM / YEAR / SPORT

1 The Blind Side 2009
American Football

2 Cars 2006
Car racing

3 The Karate Kid 2010
Martial arts

4 The Waterboy 1998
American football

5 The Longest Yard 2005
American football

6 Jerry Maguire 1996
American football

7 Talladega Nights 2006
Car racing

8 Rocky IV 1985
Boxing

9 Rocky III 1982
Boxing

10 Seabiscuit 2003
Horse racing

* Based on US gross box office

Animated Hits

◀ Toy Story 3
Fifteen years after the original, Toy Story 3 – the first feature film created entirely in CGI – was the highest-grossing film of 2010.

TOP 10 **ANIMATED FILMS OF ALL TIME**

FILM / YEAR / WORLD GROSS (US$)

1 Toy Story 3
2010
$1,058,144,168

2 Ice Age: Dawn of the Dinosaurs
2009
$887,773,705

3 Shrek 2
2004
$880,871,036

4 Finding Nemo
2003
$864,625,978

5 Shrek the Third
2007
$791,106,665

6 The Lion King
1994
$783,841,776

7 Shrek Forever After
2010
$731,071,987

8 Up
2009
$727,079,556

9 Kung Fu Panda
2008
$633,395,021

10 The Incredibles
2004
$624,037,578

THE 10 **FIRST MICKEY MOUSE CARTOONS**

FILM	DISNEY DELIVERY DATE
1 Plane Crazy	15 May 1928
2 Steamboat Willie	29 Jul 1928
3 Gallopin' Gaucho	2 Aug 1928
4 The Barn Dance	14 Mar 1929
5 The Opry House	20 Mar 1929
6 When the Cat's Away	3 May 1929
7 The Plow Boy	28 Jun 1929
8 The Barnyard Battle	2 Jul 1929
9 The Karnival Kid	31 Jul 1929
10 Mickey's Follies	28 Aug 1929

Walt Disney's iconic Mickey Mouse first appeared in *Plane Crazy*, a silent film in which he copies the exploits of aviator Charles Lindbergh in an attempt to impress Minnie Mouse. *Steamboat Willie* was the first Mickey Mouse cartoon with sound. He went on to appear in some 130 films, including a starring role in *Fantasia* (1940), while *Lend a Paw* won an Oscar in 1941. He made only occasional appearances after the 1950s, but guested in *Who Framed Roger Rabbit* (1988), *A Goofy Movie* (1995) and *Fantasia/2000* (2000).

JAPANESE SPIRIT

Japanese anime *Spirited Away* (2001) is the only non-English speaking animated movie ever to have won an Oscar. More than a decade after its release, it remains the top-grossing film in its native country's history. Global bestseller *Avatar* racked up only half of *Spirited Away*'s takings at the Japanese box office. The film was only the second recipient of the Best Animated Feature award, which was introduced to the Oscars in 2001, when it was won by the first *Shrek* film.

▲ *Hanks gets animated*
Motion-capture technology revolutionized the realism in animated features.

CAPTIVATING PERFORMANCE

Christmas favourite *The Polar Express* (2004) was the first fully animated feature to use motion (or performance) capture technology, a process in which the movements of live actors are recorded and then turned into an animated image. The technique has its roots in rotoscoping, in which animators traced individual frames from live-action sequences by hand. Performance capture is now a common movie technique, especially in films that combine CGI with live-action sequences, such as *The Lord of the Rings* trilogy and *Avatar*.

ANNIE ANNIVERSARY

The Annie Awards have been presented by the International Animated Film Society since 1972, and celebrate their 40th birthday in 2012. Since its inaugural year, the Winsor McKay award has been given to honour individual contributions to animation. The first of these awards went to animation pioneer brothers Max and Dave Fleischer, who brought characters such as Betty Boop and Popeye the Sailor to the big screen. More recent winners of the award have included Tim Burton, Nick Park and Matt Groening.

▶ *Wallace and Gromit*
2.8 tonnes of plasticine were used in Nick Park's The Curse of the Were-Rabbit.

ACTORS

TOP 10 GEORGE CLOONEY FILMS

FILM / YEAR

1 Ocean's Eleven 2001
2 Ocean's Twelve 2004
3 The Perfect Storm 2000
4 Ocean's Thirteen 2007
5 Batman & Robin 1997
6 Up in the Air 2009
7 Burn After Reading 2008
8 Spy Kids 2001
9 Intolerable Cruelty 2003
10 The Peacemaker 1997

TOP 10 MATT DAMON FILMS

FILM / YEAR

1 The Bourne Ultimatum 2007
2 Saving Private Ryan 1998
3 Ocean's Eleven 2001
4 The Bourne Supremacy 2004
5 True Grit 2010
6 Good Will Hunting 1997
7 The Departed 2006
8 Ocean's Twelve 2004
9 The Bourne Identity 2002
10 Ocean's Thirteen 2007

▲ The Bourne Ultimatum
The third film starring Damon as Jason Bourne won all three of its Oscar nominations.

► *Stones' Sparrow Depp based his characterization of Jack Sparrow on Stones' guitarist Keith Richards.*

TOP 10 JOHNNY DEPP FILMS

FILM / YEAR

1 Pirates of the Caribbean: Dead Man's Chest 2006
2 Alice in Wonderland 2010
3 Pirates of the Caribbean: At World's End 2007
4 Pirates of the Caribbean: The Curse of the Black Pearl 2003
5 Charlie and the Chocolate Factory 2004
6 The Tourist 2010
7 Rango 2011
8 Public Enemies 2009
9 Sleepy Hollow 1999
10 Platoon 1986

TOP 10 **WILL SMITH FILMS**

FILM / YEAR

1 Independence Day 1996
2 I Am Legend 2007
3 Men in Black 1997
4 Hancock 2008
5 Men in Black II 2002
6 Hitch 2005
7 The Pursuit of Happyness 2006
8 Shark Tale* 2004
9 I, Robot 2004
10 Bad Boys II 2003

* Voice

TOP 10 **LEONARDO DICAPRIO FILMS**

FILM / YEAR

1 Titanic 1997
2 Inception 2010
3 Catch Me If You Can 2002
4 The Departed 2006
5 Shutter Island 2010
6 The Aviator 2004
7 Gangs of New York 2002
8 The Man in the Iron Mask 1998
9 Blood Diamond 2006
10 The Beach 2000

TOP 10 **BEN STILLER FILMS**

FILM / YEAR

1 Meet the Fockers 2004
2 Night at the Museum 2006
3 Night at the Museum: Battle of the Smithsonian 2009
4 There's something about Mary 2000
5 Little Fokkers 2010
6 Meet the Parents 2000
7 Dodgeball: A True Underdog Story 2004
8 Tropic Thunder 2008
9 Starsky & Hutch 2004
10 Along Came Polly 2004

▶ **Inception**
DiCaprio was the first actor that writer, producer and director Christopher Nolan cast.

◀ **Night at the Museum**
Visitor numbers rose 20% at the American Museum of Natural History after the release of the movie.

ACTRESSES

TOP 10 **JULIA ROBERTS FILMS**

FILM / YEAR

1 Ocean's Eleven 2001
2 Pretty Woman 1990
3 Runaway Bride 1999
4 My Best Friend's Wedding 1997
5 Erin Brockovich 2000
6 Ocean's Twelve 2004
7 Hook 1991
8 Notting Hill 1999
9 Valentine's Day 2010
10 Sleeping with the Enemy 1991

▲ *Julia Roberts*
Roberts was the first actress to command a $20 million paycheck for a single movie.

TOP 10 **CATE BLANCHETT FILMS**

FILM / YEAR

1 The Lord of the Rings: The Return of the King 2003
2 The Lord of the Rings: The Two Towers 2002
3 The Lord of the Rings: The Fellowship of the Ring 2001
4 Indiana Jones and the Kingdom of the Crystal Skull 2008
5 The Curious Case of Benjamin Button 2008
6 Robin Hood 2010
7 The Aviator 2004
8 The Talented Mr Ripley 1999
9 Babel 2006
10 Elizabeth 1998

TOP 10 **RACHEL WEISZ FILMS**

FILM / YEAR

1 The Mummy Returns 2001
2 The Mummy 1999
3 Constantine 2005
4 About a Boy 2002
5 Fred Claus 2007
6 The Lovely Bones 2009
7 Chain Reaction 1996
8 Definitely, Maybe 2008
9 Enemy at the Gates 2001
10 Runaway Jury 2003

▶ *Rachel Weisz*
The former model founded a theatrical group while a student at Cambridge.

TOP 10 **CAMERON DIAZ FILMS**

FILM / YEAR

1 Shrek 2* 2004
2 Shrek the Third* 2007
3 Shrek Forever After* 2010
4 Shrek* 2001
5 There's Something About Mary 1998
6 The Mask 1994
7 My Best Friend's Wedding 1997
8 Charlie's Angels 2000
9 Charlie's Angels: Full Throttle 2003
10 The Green Hornet 2011

* Voice

◄ *Cameron Diaz*
The actress's films have earned a combined $2.6 billion in the US alone.

TOP 10 **ANGELINA JOLIE FILMS**

FILM / YEAR

1 Kung Fu Panda* 2008
2 Mr & Mrs Smith 2005
3 Wanted 2008
4 Shark Tale* 2004
5 Salt 2010
6 The Tourist 2010
7 Lara Croft: Tomb Raider 2001
8 Gone in 60 Seconds 2000
9 Beowulf 2007
10 Alexander 2004

* Voice

TOP 10 **KEIRA KNIGHTLEY FILMS**

FILM / YEAR

1 Pirates of the Caribbean: Dead Man's Chest 2006
2 Pirates of the Caribbean: At World's End 2007
3 Star Wars: Episode I – The Phantom Menace 1999
4 Pirates of the Caribbean: The Curse of the Black Pearl 2003
5 Love Actually 2003
6 King Arthur 2004
7 Atonement 2007
8 Pride and Prejudice 2005
9 Bend it Like Beckham 2003
10 The Duchess 2008

► *Keira Knightley*
Atonement featured all eight surviving World War II ambulances, and Knightley and the rest of the cast wore genuine uniforms.

157

DIRECTORS

▲ **Explosive success**
With The Hurt Locker, *Kathryn Bigelow* became the first woman to take the Best Director Oscar.

THE 10 **LATEST BEST DIRECTOR OSCAR-WINNERS**

YEAR / DIRECTOR / FILM

Year	Director	Film
2011	Tom Hooper	The King's Speech*
2010	Kathryn Bigelow	The Hurt Locker*
2009	Danny Boyle	Slumdog Millionaire*
2008	Joel and Ethan Coen	No Country for Old Men*
2007	Martin Scorsese	The Departed*
2006	Ang Lee	Brokeback Mountain
2005	Clint Eastwood	Million Dollar Baby*
2004	Peter Jackson	The Lord of the Rings: The Return of the King*
2003	Roman Polanski	The Pianist
2002	Ron Howard	A Beautiful Mind*

* Won Best Picture Oscar

TOP 10 **MOST BANKABLE DIRECTORS**

DIRECTOR / FILMS / TOP GROSSING / AVERAGE PER FILM (US$)

#	Director	Films	Top Grossing	Average per film
1	Lee Unkrich	4	Toy Story 3	$314,100,000
2	David Yates	3	Harry Potter 6	$296,300,000
3	Andrew Adamson	4	Shrek 2	$285,600,000
4	George Lucas	6	Star Wars	$283,400,000
5	Andrew Stanton	2	Finding Nemo	$281,800,000
6	Pete Docter	2	Up	$274,400,000
7	Kelly Asbury	2	Shrek 2	$257,300,000
8	James Cameron	9	Avatar	$212,900,000
9	John Lasseter	4	Toy Story 2	$211,100,000
10	J. J. Abrams	2	Star Trek	$195,900,000

▶ Spider-Man 3
One visual effect in the film – the birth of Sandman – took almost three years to create.

TOP 10 **DIRECTORS BY TOTAL**

	DIRECTOR	FILMS	US BOX OFFICE ($)
1	Steven Spielberg	25	3,824,973,778
2	Robert Zemeckis	15	1,939,038,112
3	James Cameron	9	1,915,765,570
4	Ron Howard	19	1,747,233,886
5	George Lucas	6	1,698,038,621
6	Chris Columbus	14	1,670,878,041
7	Tim Burton	15	1,634,284,737
8	Michael Bay	8	1,495,552,807
9	Gore Verbinski	8	1,426,086,704
10	Peter Jackson	8	1,315,538,479

TOP 10 **DIRECTORS BY BIGGEST BUDGET**

	DIRECTOR	FILM	BUDGET (US$)
1	Gore Verbinski	Pirates of the Caribbean: At Worlds End	300,000,000
2	= Nathan Greno	Tangled	260,000,000
	= Byron Howard	Tangled	260,000,000
4	Sam Raimi	Spider-Man 3	258,000,000
5	David Yates	Harry Potter and the Half-Blood Prince	250,000,000
6	James Cameron	Avatar	237,000,000
7	Bryan Singer	Superman Returns	232,000,000
8	Marc Forster	Quantum of Solace	230,000,000
9	Andrew Adamson	The Chronicles of Narnia: Prince Caspian	225,000,000
10	= Ridley Scott	Robin Hood	210,000,000
	= Michael Bay	Transformers: Revenge of the Fallen	210,000,000

Prolific Producer

Already a self-made billionaire before he started producing, Arnon Milchan has been involved in 104 movies. He has collaborated with many celebrated directors including Sergio Leone, Martin Scorsese, Ridley Scott and Oliver Stone, and produced hits such as JFK, Pretty Woman, Free Willy, Heat and Fight Club. His net worth is estimated at around $3.6 billion and he owns an extensive art collection.

◀ Mr. and Mrs. Smith
Arnon Milchan's top-grossing film starred Angelina Jolie and Brad Pitt as married assassins.

ACADEMY AWARDS

TOP 10 MOST NOMINATED FILMS WITH NO WINS

	FILM	YEAR*	NOMINATIONS
1	= The Turning Point	1977	11
	= The Colour Purple	1985	11
3	= Gangs of New York	2002	10
	= True Grit	2010	10
5	= The Little Foxes	1941	9
	= Peyton Place	1957	9
7	= Quo Vadis	1951	8
	= The Nun's Story	1959	8
	= The Sand Pebbles	1966	8
	= The Elephant Man	1980	8
	= Ragtime	1981	8
	= The Remains of the Day	1993	8

* Of release; awards made the following year

TOP 10 FILMS WINNING MOST AWARDS WITHOUT THE BEST PICTURE AWARD

	FILM	YEAR*	AWARDS
1	Cabaret	1972	8
2	= A Place in the Sun	1951	6
	= Star Wars	1977	6
4	= Wilson	1944	5
	= The Bad and the Beautiful	1952	5
	= The King and I	1956	5
	= Mary Poppins	1964	5
	= Doctor Zhivago	1965	5
	= Who's Afraid of Virginia Woolf?	1966	5
	= Saving Private Ryan	1998	5
	= The Aviator	2004	5

* Of release; awards made the following year

▶ **Million Dollar Baby**
Clint Eastwood became the oldest recipient of the Best Director Oscar, at 74 years of age.

TOP 10 BEST PICTURE WIN BOX-OFFICE BOOSTS*

	FILM	YEAR#	BOX-OFFICE RECEIPTS POST NOMINATION (%)
1	Million Dollar Baby	2004	56.1
2	Gandhi	1982	51.2
3	The King's Speech	2010	49.4
4	Platoon	1986	46.7
5	Chicago	2002	40.7
6	Driving Miss Daisy	1989	39.0
7	Slumdog Millionaire	2008	38.0
8	Shakespeare in Love	1998	36.5
9	Rain Man	1988	35.2
10	Schindler's List	1993	31.9

* Since 1982
# Of release; awards made the following year

THE 10 **LATEST FILMS TO WIN THE 'BIG THREE'***

FILM / YEAR#

1 The King's Speech 2010
2 The Hurt Locker 2009
3 Slumdog Millionaire 2008
4 No Country for Old Men 2007
5 The Departed 2006
6 The Lord of the Rings: The Return of the King 2003
7 A Beautiful Mind 2001
8 American Beauty 1999
9 Forrest Gump 1994
10 Schindler's List 1993

* Best Picture, Director and Screenplay
# Of release; awards made the following year

▲ The King's Speech
Writer David Seidler, who suffered from a stammer in his youth, is the oldest winner of the Best Original Screenplay Oscar.

THE 10 **LATEST STARS NOMINATED IN TWO ACTING CATEGORIES IN THE SAME YEAR**

ACTOR / ACTRESS	YEAR*	LEADING ROLE	SUPPORTING ROLE
1 Cate Blanchett	2007	Elizabeth: The Golden Age	I'm Not There
2 Jamie Foxx	2004	Ray#	Collateral
3 Julianne Moore	2002	Far From Heaven	The Hours
4 Emma Thompson	1993	The Remains of the Day	In the Name of the Father
5 Holly Hunter	1992	The Piano#	The Firm
6 Al Pacino	1992	Scent of a Woman#	Glengarry Glen Ross
7 Sigourney Weaver	1988	Gorillas in the Mist	Working Girl
8 Jessica Lange	1982	Frances	Tootsie#
9 Barry Fitzgerald	1944	Going My Way	Going My Way#†
10 Teresa Wright	1942	The Pride of the Yankees	Mrs. Miniver#

* Of release; awards made the following year
# Winner
† Rules have since been changed to disallow double nomination for the same performance

▶ *Cate Blanchett*
Blanchett is the only actress to be nominated for an Oscar for the same role in two separate films, as Elizabeth I.

THE 10 **FIRST COUNTRIES TO HAVE TELEVISION***

COUNTRY / FIRST BROADCAST

1 UK
2 Nov 1936

2 USSR
31 Dec 1938

3 USA
30 Apr 1939

4 France
29 Jun 1949

5 Mexico
31 Aug 1950

6 Brazil
18 Sep 1950

7 Cuba
24 Oct 1950

8 = Denmark
2 Oct 1951

= Netherlands
2 Oct 1951

10 Argentina
17 Oct 1951

▲ *Early broadcast*
NBC's first regularly scheduled broadcast featured the opening of the 1939 New York World's Fair.

* High-definition regular public broadcasting service

TOP 10 **TV-BUYING COUNTRIES**

COUNTRY / TVS BOUGHT PER HOUSEHOLD*

1 United Arab Emirates 4.14

2 Singapore 3.34

3 UK 2.96

4 USA 2.74

5 Australia 2.64

6 Japan 2.60

7 France 2.58

8 Chile 2.49

9 Spain 2.48

10 Greece 2.14

* In last decade   *World average 1.44*

Source: Euromonitor International

THE 10 **TOP-EARNING TV STARS**

NAME / PAY (US$)

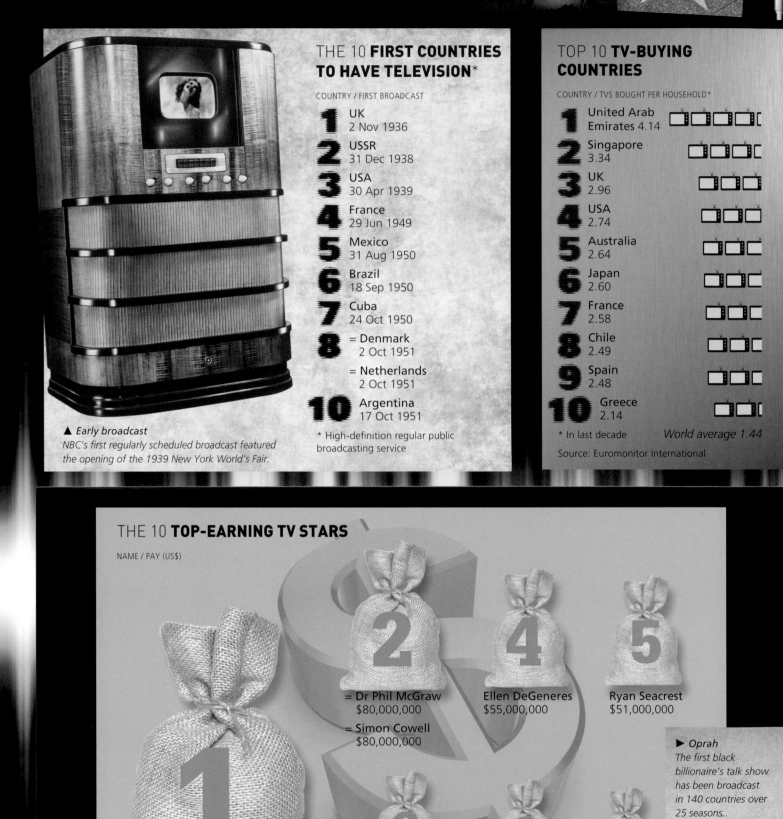

1 Oprah Winfrey
$315,000,000

2 = Dr Phil McGraw
$80,000,000

= Simon Cowell
$80,000,000

4 Ellen DeGeneres
$55,000,000

5 Ryan Seacrest
$51,000,000

6 = Judge Judy Sheindlin
$45,000,000

= David Letterman
$45,000,000

8 Conan O'Brien
$38,000,000

10 = Jay Leno
$35,000,000

= Ray Romano
$35,000,000

Source: Forbes

▶ *Oprah*
The first black billionaire's talk show has been broadcast in 140 countries over 25 seasons..

TOP 10 **TV COUNTRIES**

	COUNTRY	TV HOUSEHOLDS*
1	China	401,264,000
2	India	233,029,000
3	USA	122,463,000
4	Indonesia	72,581,000
5	Brazil	57,503,000
6	Russia	52,432,000
7	Japan	51,328,000
8	Germany	40,017,000
9	Mexico	29,770,000
10	UK	27,854,000
	Top 10 total	1,088,241,000
	World total	1,884,509,000

* 2012 forecast

Source: Euromonitor International

▲ *Family viewing*
India's 600 million viewers watch an average of 2.5 hours of television a day.

TOP 10 **GENRES BROADCAST ON BBC TELEVISION***

	GENRE	HOURS	%
1	Factual	6,395	27.0
2	News and weather	3,347	14.1
3	Entertainment	2,393	10.1
4	Drama	2,371	10.0
5	Children's	2,142	9.0
6	Music and arts	1,765	7.5
7	Sport	1,695	7.2
8	Film	1,547	6.5
9	Current affairs	842	3.6
10	Continuity	726	3.1

* BBC 1, 2, 3 and 4

Source: BBC Trust

TOP 10 **DOWNLOADED PODCASTS ON BBC RADIO**

	PODCAST	MONTHLY DOWNLOADS*
1	Global News	2,088,770
2	A History of the World in 100 Objects	1,987,404
3	Documentaries	1,860,028
4	Best of Chris Moyles	946,945
5	Best of Today	855,783
6	Friday Night Comedy from BBC Radio 4	852,440
7	NewsPod	811,594
8	The Archers	768,778
9	Scott Mills Daily	636,295
10	Mark Kermode and Simon Mayo's Film Review	485,685

* As of September 2010

Source: BBC

DVDS & GAMING

TOP 10 **DVDS, 2010**

	DVD	SALES
1	Avatar	10,156,458
2	Toy Story 3	9,935,368
3	The Twilight Saga: New Moon	7,829,939
4	The Blind Side	7,266,726
5	The Twilight Saga: Eclipse	7,133,878
6	How to Train Your Dragon	5,344,798
7	Despicable Me	5,167,066
8	Iron Man 2	5,065,079
9	The Princess and the Frog	4,514,936
10	The Hangover	4,356,314

◀ *How to Train Your Dragon*
Elephants, tigers, horses and chihuahuas were used to record the noises of dragons.

TOP 10 **BESTSELLING DVDS OF ALL TIME**

	DVD / YEAR	SALES
1	Finding Nemo, 2003	18,500,000
2	Shrek 2, 2004	18,200,000
3	The Incredibles, 2004	15,600,000
4	Star Wars: Episode III – Revenge of the Sith, 2005	15,100,000
5	The Lord of the Rings: The Two Towers, 2002	14,750,000
6	Pirates of the Caribbean: Dead Man's Chest, 2006	14,450,000
7	Pirates of the Caribbean: At World's End, 2007	13,700,000
8	Pirates of the Caribbean: The Curse of the Black Pearl, 2003	13,300,000
9	Transformers, 2007	13,250,000
10	Cars, 2006	13,200,000

TOP 10 **VIDEO PIRACY COUNTRIES**

	COUNTRY / LOSS TO FILM INDUSTRY* (US$)
1	USA $2,724,000,000
2	China $2,689,000,000
3	France $1,547,000,000
4	Mexico $1,115,000,000
5	UK $1,007,000,000
6	Russia $900,000,000
7	Japan $742,000,000
8	Spain $670,000,000
9	Germany $490,000,000
10	Thailand $465,000,000

TOP 10 **CONSOLES OF ALL TIME**

CONSOLE / RELEASE YEAR / UNITS SOLD

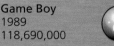

	CONSOLE / RELEASE YEAR / UNITS SOLD		CONSOLE / RELEASE YEAR / UNITS SOLD
1	PlayStation 2, 2000, 141,706,748	6	Wii, 2006, 75,900,000
2	Nintendo DS, 2004, 135,580,000	7	PlayStation Portable 2004, 65,660,000
3	Game Boy, 1989, 118,690,000	8	Nintendo Entertainment System 1983, 61,910,000
4	PlayStation, 1994, 102,500,000	9	Xbox 360, 2005, 51,275,500
5	Game Boy Advance 2001, 81,510,000	10	Super Nintendo Entertainment System 1990, 49,100,000

▲ **Call of Duty**
The latest instalment of the franchise made $360 million in its first 24 hours of release.

TOP 10 **FASTEST-SELLING VIDEO GAMES**

GAME / PLATFORM	WEEKS TO REACH 5 MILLION SALES
1 Call of Duty: Black Ops Xbox 360	1
2 = Call of Duty: Modern Warfare 2 Xbox 360	2
= Grand Theft Auto: San Andreas PlayStation 2	2
= Call of Duty: Black Ops PlayStation 3	2
5 = Pokémon Diamond / Pearl Nintendo DS	3
= Halo: Reach Xbox 360	3
= New Super Mario Bros. Wii	3
8 = Pokémon Heart Gold / Soul Silver Nintendo DS	4
= Halo 3 Xbox 360	4
= Grand Theft Auto IV Xbox 360	4

TOP 10 **PC GAMES**

	TITLE	YEAR	SALES
1	The Sims	2000	16,080,000
2	World of Warcraft	2004	11,990,000
3	Starcraft	1998	11,320,000
4	Myst	1993	8,030,000
5	Half-Life	1998	7,850,000
6	World of Warcraft: The Burning Crusade	2007	7,420,000
7	World of Warcraft: Wrath of the Lich King	2008	6,940,000
8	RollerCoaster Tycoon	1999	5,340,000
9	Diablo II	2000	5,330,000
10	The Sims 2	2004	5,210,000

▶ **Followers of Warcraft**
Blizzard Entertainment's annual convention, Blizzcon, is attended by nearly 30,000 fans (of the Warcraft, Starcraft and Diablo series).

DOWNLOADS

TOP 10 **COUNTRIES WITH THE FASTEST BROADBAND**

	COUNTRY	AVERAGE MBPS*
1	South Korea	14.0
2	Japan	8.5
3	Romania	7.0
4	Netherlands	6.3
5	Latvia	6.0
6	Czech Republic	5.4
7	Switzerland	5.3
8 =	Denmark	5.0
=	Sweden	5.0
=	Canada	5.0
=	USA	5.0
	UK	*4.0*
	World average	*1.9*

* Megabytes per second

▲ *South Korea*
The top 11 fastest cities for broadband are all in South Korea, with an average peak speed of 39 megabytes per second.

TOP 10 **MOST DOWNLOADED PAID APPS***

1 Crash Bandicoot Nitro Kart 3D
2 Moto Chaser
3 Virtual Pool Online
5 Cro-Mag Rally
4 Koi Pond
6 Flick Fishing
7 Monopoly: World Edition
8 Super Monkey Ball
9 Pocket Guitar
10 iCopter

* Since launch in July 2008; all devices

TOP 10 **MOST DOWNLOADED FREE APPS***

1 Facebook
2 iPint
3 Google Earth
5 PAC-MAN Lite
4 Touch Hockey: FS5
6 Labyrinth Lite
7 Lightsaber Unleashed
8 Tap Tap Revenge
9 Flashlight
10 Shazam

* Since launch in July 2008; all devices

TOP 10 **DOWNLOADED ARTISTS, 2010**

ARTIST / SALES

1 Eminem 15,673,000
2 Ke$ha 13,497,000
3 Lady Gaga 11,891,000
4 Katy Perry 11,837,000
5 Black Eyed Peas 11,337,000
6 Usher 10,717,000
7 Glee Cast 10,654,000
8 Rihanna 10,099,000
9 Taylor Swift 9,912,000
10 B.o.B 9,118,000

▶ **Ke$ha**
Ke$ha's debut single, 'Tik Tok' reached No. 1 in 11 countries and sold nearly 13 million copies.

TOP 10 **DOWNLOADED SINGLES**

SONG / ARTIST / SALES*

1 I Gotta Feeling Black Eyed Peas 6,627,000
2 Just Dance Lady Gaga 5,911,000
3 Poker Face Lady Gaga 5,840,000
4 Low Flo Rider 5,781,000
5 Boom Boom Pow Black Eyed Peas 5,754,000
6 Tik Tok Ke$ha 5,483,000
7 I'm Yours Jason Mraz 5,470,000
8 Hey, Soul Sister Train 5,001,000
9 Apologize Timberland 4,880,000
10 Love Story Taylor Swift 4,853,000

* 2004–2011

▲ **Kick-Ass**
After being turned down by major studios, director Matthew Vaughn independently funded the movie.

TOP 10 **PIRATED FILMS, 2010**

FILM / DOWNLOADS (2010) / % OF BOX-OFFICE GROSS*

1 Avatar 16,580,000 / 4.5
2 Kick-Ass 11,400,000 / 88.9
3 Inception 9,720,000 / 8.8
4 Shutter Island 9,490,000 / 24.2
5 Iron Man 2 8,810,000 / 10.6
6 Clash of the Titans 8,040,000 / 12.2
7 Green Zone 7,730,000 / 61.1
8 Sherlock Holmes 7,160,000 / 10.3
9 The Hurt Locker 6,850,000 / 105.7
10 Salt 6,700,000 / 28.7

* Based on ticket price of US$7.50

8

THE COMMERCIAL WORLD

BIRTH OF THE SUPERSTORE

Walmart Stores, Inc. was the world's largest corporation by revenue in 2010 according to the Forbes Global 2000. The chain of discount department and warehouse stores was founded by Sam Walton, who opened the first Walmart store in 1962. Ten years later, Walmart stock was offered for the first time on the New York Stock Exchange. Today – 50 years after the birth of Walmart in Rogers, Arkansas – there are some 8,900 store and club locations in 15 countries, employing 2.1 million 'associates', and bringing in over US$400 billion in annual revenue. Thanks to Walmart, the Walton family is one of the richest in the world.

EMPLOYMENT

TOP 10 COUNTRIES WITH THE LARGEST LABOUR FORCES

COUNTRY	LABOUR FORCE
1 China	776,880,961
2 India	449,888,200
3 USA	158,374,588
4 Indonesia	112,803,749
5 Brazil	99,945,055
6 Bangladesh	76,765,042
7 Russia	76,025,809
8 Japan	66,876,995
9 Pakistan	55,836,770
10 Nigeria	48,620,127
UK	31,494,938

Source: World Bank

TOP 10 COUNTRIES WITH THE HIGHEST GDP PER PERSON EMPLOYED

COUNTRY	GDP PER PERSON EMPLOYED (US$)
1 USA	65,480
2 Hong Kong	58,605
3 Ireland	56,701
4 Belgium	55,448
5 France	55,052
6 Luxembourg	54,511
7 Trinidad and Tobago	53,012
8 Norway	51,736
9 UK	51,697
10 Finland	50,560
World	16,964

Source: World Bank

▼ China's force
China's manufacturing workforce is twice the size of the entire G7 group of countries.

TOP 10 INDUSTRIES IN THE UK

INDUSTRY	NO. EMPLOYED
1 Wholesale and retail trade	4,237,400
2 Manufacturing	3,754,400
3 Healthcare	3,582,800
4 Real estate	3,328,300
5 Education	2,672,800
6 Construction	2,331,700
7 Public administration	2,044,800
8 Transport and telecoms	1,940,000
9 Other service activities	1,632,200
10 Hotels and restaurants	1,270,000

Source: World Bank

THE 10 COUNTRIES WITH THE HIGHEST PROPORTION OF CHILD WORKERS

COUNTRY	10–14 YEAR-OLDS AT WORK IN 2000* TOTAL	%
1 Mali	726,000	51.14
2 Bhutan	136,000	51.10
3 Burundi	445,000	48.50
4 Uganda	1,343,000	43.79
5 Niger	609,000	43.62
6 Burkina Faso	686,000	43.45
7 Ethiopia	3,277,000	42.45
8 Nepal	1,154,000	42.05
9 Rwanda	413,000	41.35
10 Kenya	1,699,000	39.15
World average	67,444	11.24

* Excludes unpaid work

Source: World Bank

TOP 10 COMPANIES WITH THE MOST EMPLOYEES

COMPANY* / COUNTRY / INDUSTRY / EMPLOYEES

1 Wal-Mart Stores / USA / Retail / 2,100,000
2 China National Petroleum / China / Oil and gas / 1,649,992
3 State Grid / China / Electricity / 1,533,800
4 US Postal Service / USA / Mail / 667,605
5 Sinopec / China / Oil and gas / 633,383
6 Hon Hai Precision Industries / Taiwan, China / Electronics / 611,000
7 China Telecommunications / China / Telecoms / 495,239
8 Carrefour / France / Retail / 475,976
9 Tesco / UK / Retail / 468,508
10 Agricultural Bank of China / China / Banking / 441,144

* Excludes state-owned

Source: *Financial Times FT 500 2009/Fortune Global 500 2009*

◄ *Lost childhood*
It is estimated that one in six children aged 5–14 are engaged in child labour.

TRADE

TOP 10 MOST TRADED GOODS

CATEGORY	VALUE OF GOODS (US$)	SHARE (%)
1 Fuels	1,808	14.3
2 Chemicals	1,447	11.4
3 Telecoms equipment	1,323	10.4
4 Food	987	7.8
5 Automotive products	847	6.7
6 Mining products	455	4.3
7 Iron and steel	326	2.6
8 Clothing	316	2.5
9 Textiles	211	1.7
10 Other agriculture	182	1.4

Source: World Trade Organization

TOP 10 BIGGEST PRICE INCREASES IN COMMODITIES

COMMODITY	PRICE INCREASE* (%)
1 Iron ore	292
2 Rubber	274
3 Crude petroleum	243
4 Uranium	237
5 Copper	225
6 Natural gas	205
7 Coal	202
8 Nickel	198
9 Lead	194
10 Tin	178

* 2000–10

Source: World Trade Organization

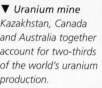

▼ **Uranium mine**
Kazakhstan, Canada and Australia together account for two-thirds of the world's uranium production.

TOP 10 UK IMPORTS

PRODUCT	ANNUAL VALUE OF GOODS (£)
1 Nuclear reactors	35,751,000,000
2 Fuels	31,977,000,000
3 Automobiles	29,208,000,000
4 Electronics	28,568,000,000
5 Pharmaceuticals	12,521,000,000
6 Precious metals	10,330,000,000
7 Aircraft and spacecraft	9,687,000,000
8 Plastics	8,810,000,000
9 Organic chemicals	7,945,000,000
10 Medical equipment	7,922,000,000

Source: HM Revenue and Customs

TOP 10 LEADING EXPORTERS OF COMMERCIAL SERVICES

COUNTRY	VALUE OF SERVICES (US$)	SHARE (%)
1 USA	474,000,000,000	14.1
2 UK	233,000,000,000	7.0
3 Germany	227,000,000,000	6.8
4 France	143,000,000,000	4.3
5 China	129,000,000,000	3.8
6 Japan	126,000,000,000	3.8
7 Spain	122,000,000,000	3.6
8 Italy	101,000,000,000	3.0
9 Ireland	97,000,000,000	2.9
10 Netherlands	91,000,000,000	2.7
World	3,350,000,000,000	100.0

Source: World Trade Organization

TOP 10 LEADING IMPORTERS OF GOODS

COUNTRY / VALUE OF GOODS (US$) / SHARE (%)

1 USA 1,605,000,000,000 12.7
2 China 1,358,000,000,000 10.7
3 Germany 938,000,000,000 7.4
4 France 560,000,000,000 4.4
5 Japan 552,000,000,000 4.4
6 UK 482,000,000,000 3.8
7 Netherlands 445,000,000,000 3.5
8 Italy 413,000,000,000 3.3
9 Belgium 352,000,000,000 2.8
10 Canada 330,000,000,000 2.6

World / 12,682,000,000,000 / 100.0

Source: World Trade Organization

179

Personal Wealth

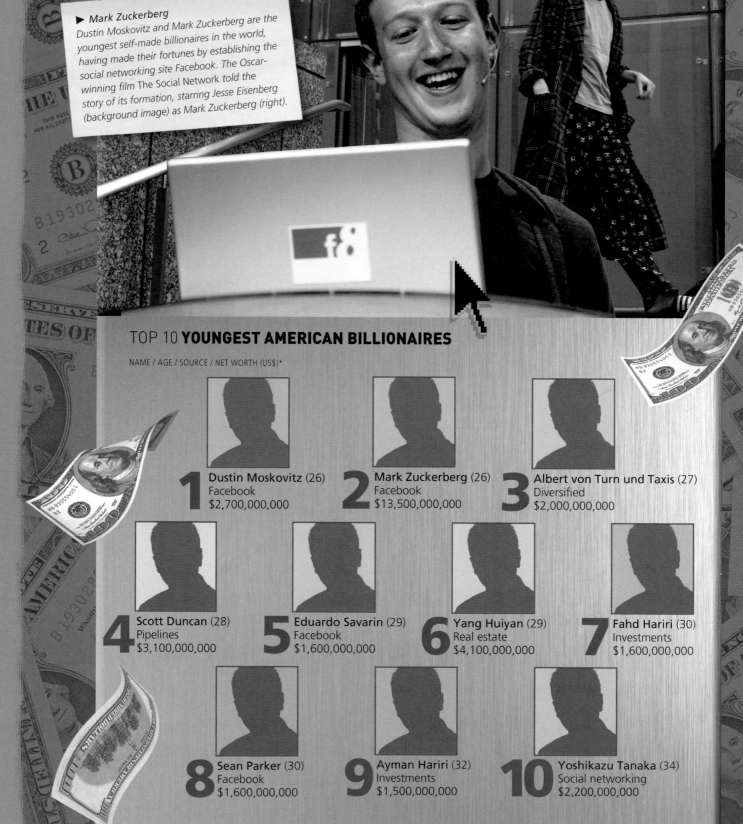

▶ **Mark Zuckerberg**
Dustin Moskovitz and Mark Zuckerberg are the youngest self-made billionaires in the world, having made their fortunes by establishing the social networking site Facebook. The Oscar-winning film The Social Network told the story of its formation, starring Jesse Eisenberg (background image) as Mark Zuckerberg (right).

TOP 10 YOUNGEST AMERICAN BILLIONAIRES

NAME / AGE / SOURCE / NET WORTH (US$)*

1 Dustin Moskovitz (26)
Facebook
$2,700,000,000

2 Mark Zuckerberg (26)
Facebook
$13,500,000,000

3 Albert von Turn und Taxis (27)
Diversified
$2,000,000,000

4 Scott Duncan (28)
Pipelines
$3,100,000,000

5 Eduardo Savarin (29)
Facebook
$1,600,000,000

6 Yang Huiyan (29)
Real estate
$4,100,000,000

7 Fahd Hariri (30)
Investments
$1,600,000,000

8 Sean Parker (30)
Facebook
$1,600,000,000

9 Ayman Hariri (32)
Investments
$1,500,000,000

10 Yoshikazu Tanaka (34)
Social networking
$2,200,000,000

* Wealth calculated as of March 2011

Source: Forbes magazine, The World's Billionaires 2011

THE WORLD'S RICHEST MEN AND WOMEN

NAME / COUNTRY / COMPANY / NET WORTH (US$)

MEN

1 Carlos Slim Helu, Mexico
Grupo Carso
$74,000,000,000

2 William Gates III, USA
Microsoft
$56,000,000,000

3 Warren Buffett, USA
Berkshire Hathaway
$50,000,000,000

4 Bernard Arnault, France
LVMH
$41,000,000,000

5 Lawrence Ellison, USA
Oracle
$39,500,000,000

WOMEN

1 Christy Walton, USA
Wal-Mart
$26,500,000,000

2 Liliane Bettencourt, France
L'Oreal
$23,500,000,000

3 Alice L. Walton, USA
Wal-Mart
$21,200,000,000

4 Iris Fontbona, Chile
Copper
$19,200,000,000

5 Birgit Rausing, Sweden
Tetra Laval
$14,000,000,000

Source: *Forbes* magazine, *The World's Billionaires 2011*

▲ *Liliane Bettencourt*
In 1987 the heiress established a foundation for medical, cultural and humanitarian support.

ROCKEFELLER'S RICHES

John D. Rockefeller embodied the American dream with his rags-to-riches story. He was the founder of Standard Oil Company, which was the origin of his enormous fortune, and in 1916 he became America's first billionaire. By the time of his death his net worth had grown to $1.4 billion – an astonishing 1.53% of total American GDP. In today's terms Rockefeller's fortune is estimated to be between $400 and $600 billion, making him the wealthiest American in history.

CITIES WITH THE MOST BILLIONAIRES

The three cities in the world with most billionaires are New York (below), Moscow and London. New York has 60 billionaires and its wealthiest resident is Michael Blomberg, who combines being mayor of the city with running his eponymous media empire, Blomberg LP. Other well-known billionaire residents include Ralph Lauren, Rupert Murdoch and Donald Trump. Moscow is home to 50 billionaires, the wealthiest being Vladimir Lisin, chairman of Novolipetsk Steel, while London boasts 32 billionaires, including Richard Branson, Bernie Ecclestone and Philip Green.

FOOD & DRINK

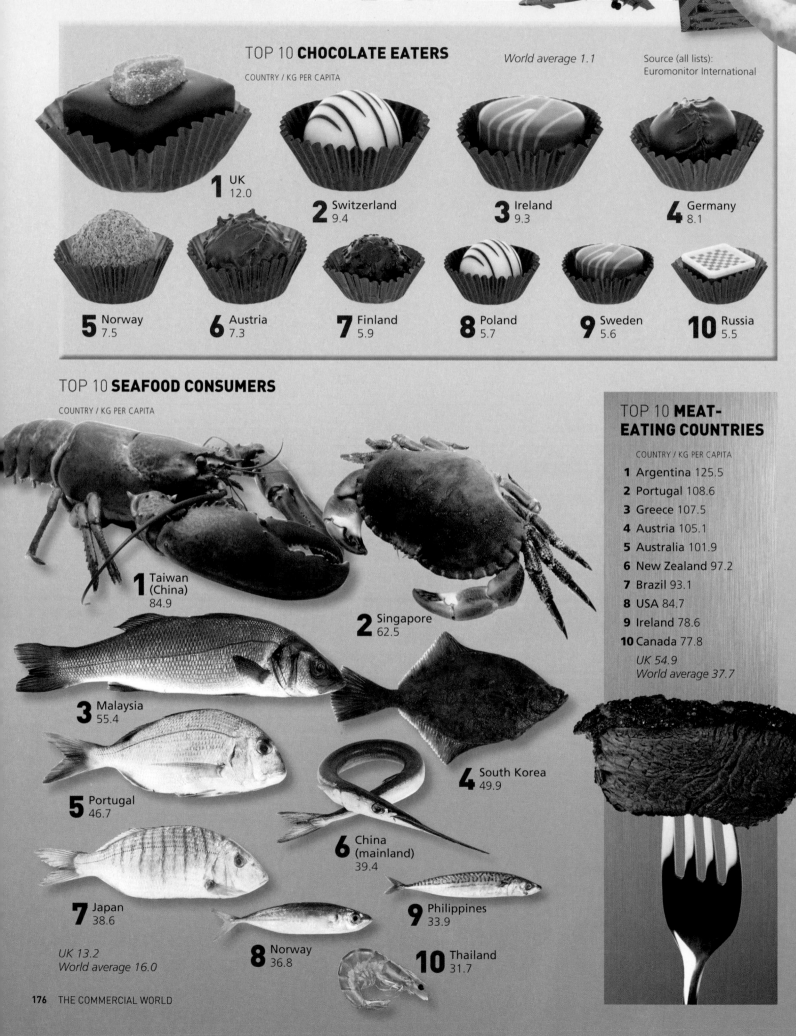

TOP 10 CHOCOLATE EATERS

COUNTRY / KG PER CAPITA

World average 1.1

Source (all lists):
Euromonitor International

1 UK
12.0

2 Switzerland
9.4

3 Ireland
9.3

4 Germany
8.1

5 Norway
7.5

6 Austria
7.3

7 Finland
5.9

8 Poland
5.7

9 Sweden
5.6

10 Russia
5.5

TOP 10 SEAFOOD CONSUMERS

COUNTRY / KG PER CAPITA

1 Taiwan
(China)
84.9

2 Singapore
62.5

3 Malaysia
55.4

4 South Korea
49.9

5 Portugal
46.7

6 China
(mainland)
39.4

7 Japan
38.6

8 Norway
36.8

9 Philippines
33.9

10 Thailand
31.7

UK 13.2
World average 16.0

TOP 10 MEAT-EATING COUNTRIES

COUNTRY / KG PER CAPITA

1 Argentina 125.5

2 Portugal 108.6

3 Greece 107.5

4 Austria 105.1

5 Australia 101.9

6 New Zealand 97.2

7 Brazil 93.1

8 USA 84.7

9 Ireland 78.6

10 Canada 77.8

UK 54.9
World average 37.7

TOP 10 FRUIT JUICE DRINKERS

COUNTRY / LITRES PER CAPITA

1 Canada 60.3
2 Netherlands 48.2
3 UAE 46.5
4 Poland 37.7
5 Finland 37.4
6 Germany 34.7
7 Australia 31.0
8 Norway 29.9
9 USA 29.7
10 UK 28.7

World average 9.3

TOP 10 TEA DRINKERS

COUNTRY / CUPS PER CAPITA

1 Turkey 1,690
2 Morocco 1,160
3 Uzbekistan 998
4 Kazakhstan 924
5 Russia 888
6 Ireland 868
7 New Zealand 806
8 Iran 759
9 Egypt 689
10 UK 633

World average 191

► **Tea time**
Green tea with mint leaves is widely consumed throughout Morocco.

TOP 10 TAKE-AWAY ORDERING COUNTRIES

COUNTRY	TAKE-AWAY ORDERS	% CHANGE IN LAST DECADE
1 Japan	2,704,738,500	-17.8
2 Italy	1,953,728,900	26.6
3 USA	1,056,722,400	4.3
4 UK	623,998,600	22.6
5 Egypt	333,837,700	29.6
6 South Korea	258,740,300	127.3
7 Thailand	185,039,000	48.8
8 Canada	157,168,800	12.9
9 Mexico	96,059,600	46.9
10 Brazil	87,498,400	11.1
World total	7,996,500,300	10.9

TOP 10 SPORTS AND ENERGY DRINK CONSUMERS

COUNTRY / LITRES PER CAPITA

1 USA 19.0
2 Denmark 15.1
3 Japan 12.2
4 Ireland 10.8
5 Australia 9.1
6 UK 8.9
7 Taiwan (China) 7.4
8 Malaysia 7.0
9 New Zealand 6.9
10 Thailand 6.6

World average 2.0

RESOURCES & ENERGY

TOP 10 ELECTRICITY-PRODUCING COUNTRIES

COUNTRY / KW/HR (2008)

1 USA
4,344,000,000,000

2 China
3,457,000,000,000

3 Japan
1,075,000,000,000

4 Russia
1,038,000,000,000

5 India
830,000,000,000

6 Canada
651,000,000,000

7 Germany
631,000,000,000

8 France
570,000,000,000

9 Brazil
463,000,000,000

10 Korea
444,000,000,000

UK 389,000,000,000
World total 20,181,000,000,000

TOP 10 DIAMOND PRODUCERS

COUNTRY / VOLUME (CARATS)

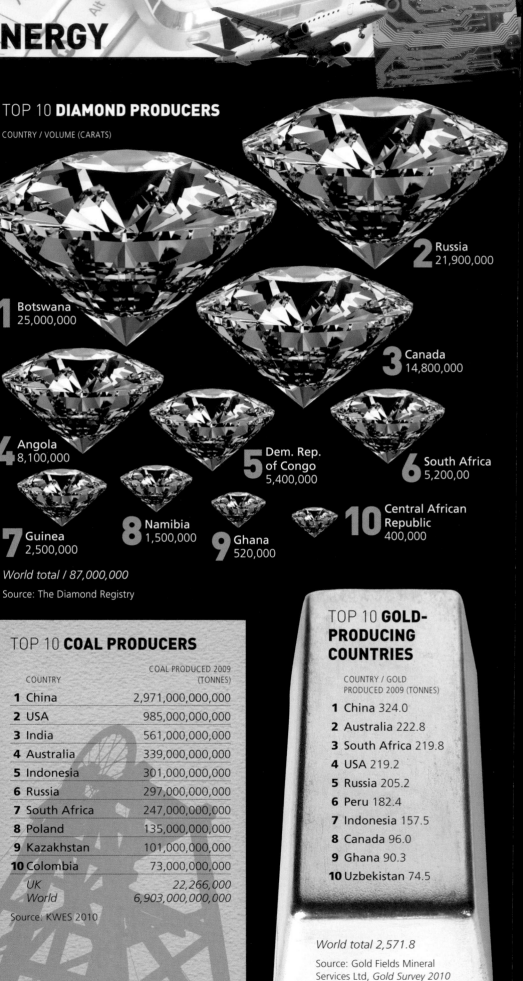

1 Botswana
25,000,000

2 Russia
21,900,000

3 Canada
14,800,000

4 Angola
8,100,000

5 Dem. Rep. of Congo
5,400,000

6 South Africa
5,200,00

7 Guinea
2,500,000

8 Namibia
1,500,000

9 Ghana
520,000

10 Central African Republic
400,000

World total / 87,000,000

Source: The Diamond Registry

TOP 10 COAL PRODUCERS

COUNTRY	COAL PRODUCED 2009 (TONNES)
1 China	2,971,000,000,000
2 USA	985,000,000,000
3 India	561,000,000,000
4 Australia	339,000,000,000
5 Indonesia	301,000,000,000
6 Russia	297,000,000,000
7 South Africa	247,000,000,000
8 Poland	135,000,000,000
9 Kazakhstan	101,000,000,000
10 Colombia	73,000,000,000
UK	*22,266,000*
World	*6,903,000,000,000*

Source: KWES 2010

TOP 10 GOLD-PRODUCING COUNTRIES

COUNTRY / GOLD PRODUCED 2009 (TONNES)

1 China 324.0

2 Australia 222.8

3 South Africa 219.8

4 USA 219.2

5 Russia 205.2

6 Peru 182.4

7 Indonesia 157.5

8 Canada 96.0

9 Ghana 90.3

10 Uzbekistan 74.5

World total 2,571.8

Source: Gold Fields Mineral Services Ltd, *Gold Survey 2010*

TOP 10 **COUNTRIES MOST RELIANT ON NUCLEAR ENERGY**

	COUNTRY	% NUCLEAR (2008)
1	France	77.1
2	Belgium	49.0
3	Ukraine	46.7
4	Switzerland	43.8
5	Sweden	42.6
6	Hungary	40.1
7	Korea	34.0
8	Czech Republic	30.9
9	Finland	28.8
10	Japan	24.0
	UK	*17.7*

Source: International Energy Agency

▶ *French power*
France is the world's largest exporter of electric power, with 58 nuclear reactors.

TOP 10 **COUNTRIES WITH THE GREATEST OIL RESERVES**

COUNTRY / PROVED RESERVES (2009): TONNES / % OF WORLD TOTAL

While world oil consumption has increased, new reserves have been progressively discovered: in 1999 the total stood at 148,500,000,000 tonnes, or 87% of the present level.

1
Saudi Arabia
36,300,000,000
19.8%

UK 400,000,000
0.2%

World 181,700,000,000
100.0%

Source: *BP Statistical Review of World Energy 2010*

2
Venezuela
24,800,000,000
12.9%

3
Iran
18,900,000,000
10.3%

4
Iraq
15,500,000,000
8.6%

5
Kuwait
14,000,000,000
7.6%

6
United Arab Emirates
13,000,000,000
7.3%

7
Russia
10,200,000,000
5.6%

8
Libya
5,800,000,000
3.3%

9
Kazakhstan
5,300,000,000
3.0%

10
Nigeria
5,000,000,000
2.8%

ENVIRONMENT

THE 10 **COUNTRIES WITH THE WORST AIR POLLUTION**

	COUNTRY	PARTICULATE MATTER*
1	Uruguay	174.7
2	Sudan	165.0
3	Mali	151.9
4	Bangladesh	135.4
5	Niger	132.2
6	United Arab Emirates	127.1
7	Pakistan	120.3
8	Egypt	119.2
9	Iraq	115.2
10	Saudi Arabia	112.9
	UK	15.5

* Micrograms per cubic metre

Source: Environmental Performance Index

◀ *Pollution in Pakistan*
As urbanization in Pakistan increases, so does the level of air pollution in the cities.

THE 10 **LARGEST OIL SPILLS**

SPILL / LOCATION /
YEAR / BARRELS SPILT

Source: International
Tanker Owners
Pollution Federation,
United Nations

1
Gulf War, Persian Gulf
1991 / 5–10,000,000

2
Deepwater Horizon,
Gulf of Mexico
2010 / 5,000,000

3
Ixtoc I, Gulf of Mexico
1979–80 / 3,300,000

4
Atlantic Express,
Trinidad and Tobago /
1979 / 2,100,000

5
= **ABT Summer**, Angola
1991 / 1,900,000
= **Nowruz oilfield**,
Uzbekistan
1992 / 1,900,000

7
Castillo de Bellver,
South Africa
1983 / 1,800,000

8
Amoco Cadiz, France
1978 / 1,600,000

9
MT Haven, Italy
1991 / 1,100,000

10
Odyssey, Canada /
1988 / 1,000,000

TOP 10 **COUNTRIES WITH THE MOST PROTECTED AREAS**

COUNTRY / TERRESTRIAL PROTECTED AREA (%)

Venezuela / 71.3

Brunei / 59.3

Germany / 56.2

Seychelles / 55.6

Kiribati / 55.0

Estonia / 47.8

Belize / 44.5

Zambia / 41.1

Liechtenstein / 40.1

Tanzania / 38.8

UK / 22.3

Source: United Nations Environmental Program

TOP 10 **CAPITAL CITIES WITH THE CLEANEST AIR**

CITY / COUNTRY	PARTICULATE MATTER*
1 Minsk, Belarus	9
2 = Paris, France	12
= Stockholm, Sweden	12
= Wellington, New Zealand	12
5 Cape Town, South Africa	15
6 = St Johns, Antigua and Barbuda	16
= Kampala, Uganda	16
8 = Luxembourg, Luxembourg	18
= Ottawa, Canada	18
= Caracas, Venezuela	18

* Micrograms per cubic metre

Source: World Bank

▼ *Heating Helsinki*
Around 90% of Helsinki's buildings are warmed by its district heating system, which uses excess heat from power plants, data centres and even sewage.

TOP 10 **ECO-CITIES**

	CITY	ECO-CITY INDEX
1	Calgary, Canada	145.7
2	Honolulu, USA	145.1
3	= Ottawa, Canada	139.9
	= Helsinki, Finland	139.9
5	Wellington, New Zealand	138.9
6	Minneapolis, USA	137.8
7	Adelaide, Australia	137.5
8	Copenhagen, Denmark	137.4
9	= Kobe, Japan	135.6
	= Oslo, Norway	135.6
	= Stockholm, Sweden	135.6

Source: Mercer Quality of Living Survey

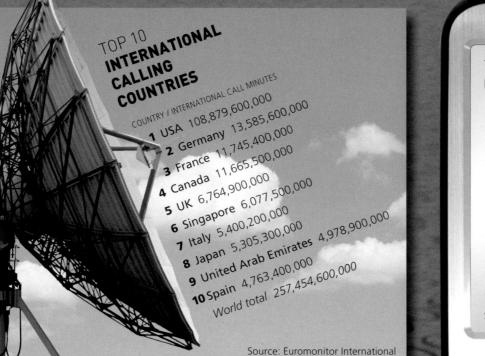

TOP 10 INTERNATIONAL CALLING COUNTRIES

COUNTRY / INTERNATIONAL CALL MINUTES

1 USA 108,879,600,000
2 Germany 13,585,600,000
3 France 11,745,400,000
4 Canada 11,665,500,000
5 UK 6,764,900,000
6 Singapore 6,077,500,000
7 Italy 5,400,200,000
8 Japan 5,305,300,000
9 United Arab Emirates 4,978,900,000
10 Spain 4,763,400,000
World total 257,454,600,000

Source: Euromonitor International

TOP 10 MOBILE-PHONE USERS

COUNTRY / MINUTES PER CAPITA

1 Cyprus 3,751
2 Columbia 3,708
3 Finland 3,095
4 Austria 2,871
5 Norway 2,792
6 Iceland 2,674
7 Greece 2,618
8 UK 2,543
9 Ireland 2,461
10 South Korea 2,391

Source: Euromonitor International

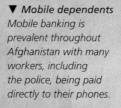

▼ **Mobile dependents**
Mobile banking is prevalent throughout Afghanistan with many workers, including the police, being paid directly to their phones.

TOP 10 MOBILE-DEPENDENT COUNTRIES

COUNTRY / MOBILE PROPORTION OF TELECOM REVENUE (%)

1 Dem. Rep. of Congo 97.3
2 Mali 97.2
3 Mauritania 95.7
4 Sudan 93.7
5 Cameroon 93:4
6 Algeria 91.3
7 Albania 90.9
8 Afghanistan 90.7
9 Czech Republic 89.7
10 South Africa 84.8
   UK 24.9

Source: Euromonitor International

TOP 10 **YOUTUBE VIEWING COUNTRIES**

COUNTRY / AVERAGE HOURS PER MONTH

1	Germany	5.2	**6**	= USA	4.3
2	Singapore	5.0		= Japan	4.3
3	Hong Kong	4.7	**8**	France	2.9
4	UK	4.5	**9**	Austria	2.7
5	Canada	4.4	**10**	Malaysia	2.3

Source: Comscore

TOP 10 **3G NETWORK COUNTRIES**

COUNTRY / % 3G*

1	South Korea	91.0
2	= Japan	75.0
	= Malaysia	75.0
4	Portugal	74.3
5	Singapore	73.5
6	Saudi Arabia	70.0
7	USA	65.0
8	= Australia	60.0
	= Canada	60.0
	= United Arab Emirates	60.0

Source: Euromonitor International

TOP 10 **COUNTRIES ON FACEBOOK**

	COUNTRY	USERS*
1	USA	146,591,880
2	Indonesia	33,920,020
3	UK	27,545,920
4	Turkey	24,788,400
5	Philippines	20,802,540
6	France	20,271,860
7	Mexico	18,830,960
8	India	18,818,720
9	Italy	17,753,040
10	Canada	16,636,880
	World total	585,184,940

* As of January 2011

Source: Facebook

TOP 10 **FASTEST ROLLER COASTERS**

ROLLER COASTER / THEME PARK / COUNTRY / BUILT / MAX. SPEED (KM/H / MPH)

1 Formula Rossa
Ferrari World Abu Dhabi, UAE, 2010
240.0 / 149.1

2 Kingda Ka
Six Flags Great Adventure, USA, 2005
206.0 / 128.0

3 Top Thrill Dragster
Cedar Point, USA, 2003
193.1 / 120.0

4 Dodonpa
Fiji-Q Highland, Japan, 2001
172.0 / 106.9

5 Tower of Terror II
Dreamworld, Australia, 1997
160.9 / 100.0

6 Steel Dragon 2000
Nagashima Spa Land, Japan, 2000
152.9 / 95.0

7 Millennium Force
Cedar Point, USA, 2000
149.7 / 93.0

8 Intimidator 305
Kings Dominion, USA, 2010
144.8 / 90.0

9 = Goliath
Six Flags Magic Mountain, USA, 2000
136.8 / 85.0

= Phantom's Revenge
Kennywood, USA, 1991
136.8 / 85.0

= Titan
Six Flags Over Texas, USA, 2001
136.8 / 85.0

Source: Roller Coaster Database

▼ *G-Force*
The Millennium Force roller coaster reaches a top speed of 150 km/h (93 mph).

TOP 10 MOST-VISITED THEME PARKS

	NAME	LOCATION	VISITORS
1	Magic Kingdom*	Florida, USA	17,233,000
2	Disneyland	California, USA	15,900,000
3	Tokyo Disneyland	Tokyo, Japan	13,646,000
4	Disneyland Paris	Paris, France	12,740,000
5	Tokyo Disney Sea	Tokyo, Japan	12,004,000
6	Epcot*	Florida, USA	10,990,000
7	Disney's Hollywood Studios*	Florida, USA	9,700,000
8	Disney's Animal Kingdom*	Florida, USA	9,590,000
9	Universal Studios Japan	Osaka, Japan	8,000,000
10	Everland	Gyeonggi-Do, South Korea	6,169,000

* At Walt Disney World   Source: Themed Entertainment Association

▲ *Magic Kingdom*
Based on Disneyland in Anaheim, California, the Magic Kingdom opened in 1971.

TOP 10 COUNTRIES SPENDING THE MOST ON TOURISM

COUNTRY / TOURISM SPENDING, 2009

1 Germany $81,200,000,000
2 USA $73,200,000,000
3 UK $50,300,000,000
4 China $43,700,000,000
5 France $38,500,000,000
6 Italy $27,900,000,000
7 Japan $25,100,000,000
8 Canada $24,200,000,000
9 Russia $20,800,000,000
10 Netherlands $20,700,000,000

Source: World Tourism Organization

TOP 10 MOST VISITED ALVA ATTRACTIONS IN THE UK

	ATTRACTION	VISITORS (2009)
1	British Museum	5,569,981
2	National Gallery	4,780,030
3	Tate Modern	4,747,537
4	Natural History Museum	4,105,106
5	Science Museum	2,793,930
6	Tower of London	2,389,548
7	National Maritime Museum	2,367,904
8	Victoria and Albert Museum	2,269,880
9	National Portrait Gallery	1,961,843
10	St Paul's Cathedral	1,821,321

Source: Association of Leading Visitor Attractions

The Association of Leading Visitor Attractions is a UK organization made up of leading museums and galleries as well as some heritage sites, covering more than 1,500 attractions. The sites covered by the ALVA are visited by more than 100 million people a year from both the UK and overseas.

TOP 10 MOST-VISITED COUNTRIES

COUNTRY / INTERNATIONAL VISITORS*

1 France 74,200,000
2 USA 54,900,000
3 Spain 52,200,000
4 China 50,900,000
5 Italy 43,200,000
6 UK 28,000,000
7
8 Germany 24,200,000
9 Malaysia 23,600,000
10 Mexico 21,500,000

* 2009 or later   Source: World Tourism Organization

9

ON THE MOVE

BLOODHOUND SSC

This year, RAF pilot Andy Green will attempt to break his current land speed record by driving *Bloodhound SSC* at over 1,610 km/h (1,000 mph). Reaching speeds faster than a bullet from a Magnum .357, the car will be powered by both a Eurofighter Typhoon jet engine and a hybrid rocket. The 46-cm (18-in) rocket will use synthetic rubber fuel with nearly one tonne of concentrated hydrogen peroxide as an oxidiser. Combined, these give a total thrust of 212 kilonewtons – equivalent to the power of over 1,000 family saloon cars. Air brakes, parachutes and friction brakes will decelerate the car, exposing Andy Green to forces similar to that of a Space Shuttle during launch and re-entry.

FASTEST O LAND

THE 10 FIRST HOLDERS OF THE LAND SPEED RECORD

DRIVER / COUNTRY / CAR	LOCATION	DATE	SPEED* KM/H	MPH
1 Gaston de Chasseloup-Laubat (France), Jeantaud	Achères, France	18 Dec 1898	62.78	39.24
2 Camille Jenatzy (Belgium), Jenatzy	Achères, France	17 Jan 1899	66.27	41.42
3 Gaston de Chasseloup-Laubat, Jeantaud	Achères, France	17 Jan 1899	69.90	43.69
4 Camille Jenatzy, Jenatzy	Achères, France	27 Jan 1899	79.37	49.92
5 Gaston de Chasseloup-Laubat, Jeantaud	Achères, France	4 Mar 1899	92.16	57.60
6 Camille Jenatzy, Jenatzy	Achères, France	29 Apr 1899	105.26	65.79
7 Leon Serpollet (France), Serpollet	Nice, France	13 Apr 1902	120.09	75.06
8 William Vanderbilt (USA), Mors	Albis, France	5 Aug 1902	121.72	76.08
9 Henri Fournier (France), Mors	Dourdan, France	5 Nov 1902	122.56	76.60
10 M. Augières (France), Mors	Dourdan, France	17 Nov 1902	123.40	77.13

* Measured over 1 km (0.6 mile)

The official Land Speed Record was set and broken five times within a year. The first six holders were rival racers Comte Gaston de Chasseloup-Laubat (France) and Camille Jenatzy (Belgium). Both the *Jeantaud* and the *Jenatzy* (nicknamed *La Jamais Contente* – 'Never Satisfied') were electrically powered.

THE 10 LATEST HOLDERS OF THE LAND SPEED RECORD

DRIVER / CAR / DATE / SPEED (KM/H / MPH)

1 Andy Green (UK)
ThrustSSC*
15 Oct 1997
1,227.99 / 763.04

2 Richard Noble (UK)
Thrust2*
4 Oct 1983
1,019.47 / 633.47

3 Gary Gabelich (USA)
The Blue Flame
23 Oct 1970
995.85 / 622.41

4 Craig Breedlove (USA)
Spirit of America – Sonic 1
15 Nov 1965
960.96 / 600.60

5 Art Arfons (USA)
Green Monster
7 Nov 1965
922.48 / 576.55

6 Craig Breedlove (USA)
Spirit of America – Sonic 1
2 Nov 1965
888.76 / 555.48

7 Art Arfons (USA)
Green Monster
27 Oct 1964
858.73 / 536.71

8 Craig Breedlove (USA)
Spirit of America
15 Oct 1964
842.04 / 526.28

9 Craig Breedlove (USA)
Spirit of America
13 Oct 1964
749.95 / 468.7

10 Art Arfons (USA)
Green Monster
5 Oct 1964
694.43 / 434.02

* Location = Black Rock Desert, Nevada, USA; all other speeds were achieved at Bonneville Salt Flats, Utah, USA; speed averaged over a measured mile in two directions

▼ Green Monster
Arfons' world record-holding Green Monster was actually painted red and blue.

Fastest Train Journeys

Though the Japanese JR-Maglev has achieved a speed of 581 km/h (361 mph) on a magnetic-levitation track, the fastest conventional wheeled train record goes to the French TGV. A modified TGV test unit broke the world record in April 2007 with a speed of 574.8 km/h (357.2 mph). The fastest unmodified conventional train is the Chinese CRH380A, which set a record speed of 486.1 km/h (302.0 mph) in December 2010. With an average speed of 312.5 km/h (194.2 mph), the world's fastest scheduled rail journey is the Chinese CRH Wuhan-Guangzhou High-Speed Railway.

▲ CHR2 Express train
The China Railway High-speed (CRH) trains currently offer the fastest daily commercial train services in the world.

THE 10 LATEST HOLDERS OF THE MOTORCYCLE SPEED RECORD

	RIDER*	MOTORCYCLE	DATE	SPEED KM/H	MPH
1	Rocky Robinson	Ack Attack, dual-Suzuki-Hayabusa	25 Sep 2010	605.70	376.36
2	Chris Carr	BUB Seven Streamliner	24 Sep 2009	591.24	367.38
3	Rocky Robinson	Ack Attack, dual-Suzuki-Hayabusa	26 Sep 2008	580.83	360.91
4	Chris Carr	BUB Seven Streamliner	5 Sep 2006	564.69	350.88
5	Rocky Robinson	Ack Attack, dual-Suzuki-Hayabusa	3 Sep 2006	551.68	342.80
6	Dave Campos	Twin 91 cu in/1,491 cc Ruxton Harley-Davidson Easyriders	14 Jul 1990	518.45	322.15
7	Donald A. Vesco	Twin 1,016 cc Kawasaki Lightning Bolt	25 Aug 1978	512.73	318.60
8	Donald A. Vesco	Twin 1,016 cc Kawasaki Lightning Bolt	23 Aug 1978	507.65	315.44
9	Donald A. Vesco	1,496 cc Yamaha Silver Bird	28 Sep 1975	487.51	302.93
10	Donald A. Vesco	Yamaha	1 Oct 1974	453.36	281.71

* All from the USA

All the records listed here were achieved at the Bonneville Salt Flats, USA. To break a Fédération Internationale Motorcycliste record, the motorcycle has to cover a measured distance, making two runs within one hour, and taking the average of the two. American Motorcycling Association records require a turnaround within two hours.

▶ BUB Seven
Not your everyday motorcycle, Bub Seven was driven to record-breaking speeds by Chris Carr.

AIR SPEED

THE 10 LATEST AIR SPEED RECORDS HELD BY JETS*

	PILOT(S)#	LOCATION	AIRCRAFT	DATE	SPEED† KM/H	MPH
1	Eldon W. Joersz/ George T. Morgan Jr	Beale AFB, California, USA	Lockheed SR-71A	28 Jul 1976	3,529.560	2,193.167
2	Robert L. Stephens/ Daniel Andre	Edwards AFB, California, USA	Lockheed YF-12A	1 May 1965	3,331.507	2,070.102
3	Georgi Mossolov, USSR	Podmoskownoe, USSR	Mikoyan E-166	7 Jul 1962	2,681.000	1,665.896
4	Robert B. Robinson	Edwards AFB, USA	McDonnell F4H-1F Phantom II	22 Nov 1961	2,585.425	1,606.509
5	Joseph W. Rogers	Edwards AFB, USA	Convair F-106A Delta Dart	15 Dec 1959	2,455.736	1,525.924
6	Georgi Mossolov, USSR	Jukowski-Petrowskol, USSR	Mikoyan E-66	31 Oct 1959	2,388.000	1,483.834
7	Walter W. Irwin	Edwards AFB, USA	Lockheed YF-104A Starfighter	16 May 1958	2,259.538	1,404.012
8	Adrian E. Drew	Edwards AFB, USA	McDonnell F-101A Voodoo	12 Dec 1957	1,943.500	1,207.635
9	Peter Twiss, UK	Chichester, UK	Fairey Delta Two	19 Mar 1956	1,822.000	1,132.138
10	Horace Hanes	Palmdale, USA	F100C Super Sabre	20 Aug 1955	1,323.312	822.268

* As of 1 January 2011
# All pilots from the USA unless otherwise stated
† Over a straight course for ground-launched only, hence excluding X-15 records

The day before Joersz and Morgan set the current world record, Adolphus Bledsoe and John T. Fuller (both USA) travelled at 3,367.221 km/h (2,092.294 mph) in their Lockheed SR-71A, but this was over a closed circuit. This record still stands today. The speed of 1,323.312 km/h (822.268 mph) achieved on 20 August 1955 by Horace A. Hanes (USA) at Palmdale, USA, in a North American F-100C Super Sabre, was the first official supersonic record-holder.

TOP 10 FASTEST MANNED AIRCRAFT

	AIRCRAFT	TOP SPEED (MACH)
1	X-15	6.72
2 =	SR-71 Blackbird (YF-12)	3.2
=	MiG-25R Foxbat-B	3.2
=	X-2	3.2
5	XB-70 Valkyrie	3.1
6	MiG-31 Foxhound	2.83
7	MiG-25 Foxbat (Ye-155)	2.8
8 =	F-15 Eagle	2.5
=	F-111 Aardvark	2.5
10	X-1	2.435

▲ *Ready for launch*
The X-15 was part of the USAF/NASA X-series of experimental aircraft.

FASTEST X-15 FLIGHTS

Although some were achieved almost 50 years ago, the speeds attained by the rocket-powered X-15 and X-15A-2 aircraft in a programme of 199 flights in the period 1959–68 remain the greatest ever attained by piloted vehicles in the Earth's atmosphere. They were air-launched by being released from B-52 bombers, and thus do not qualify for the official air speed record, for which aircraft must take off and land under their own power. The X-15s attained progressively greater speeds, ultimately more than double that of the now long-standing conventional air speed record, and set an unofficial altitude record during Flight No. 91 on 22 August 1963, when Joseph A. Walker piloted an X-15 to 107,960 m (354,200 ft) – some 108 km (67 miles) high.

▲ *Armstrong's X-15*
Neil Armstrong flew over 200 different aircraft, including seven X-15 flights.

▲ *Flight of the Concorde*
An Anglo-French project, Concorde first flew in 1969 and entered regular service on 21 January 1976. It was retired in 2003.

TOP 10 FASTEST ROUTES OF CONCORDE*

	FROM	TO	DATE	SPEED KM/H	SPEED MPH
1	New York, USA	London, UK	7 Feb 1996	1,920.07	1,193.08
2	Caracas, Venezuela	Santa Maria, Acores, Portugal	20 Mar 1982	1,869.90	1,161.90
3	Caracas, Venezuela	Paris, France	24 Sep 1979	1,833.79	1,139.46
4	Barbados	London, UK	24 Nov 1977	1,826.38	1,134.86
5	Honolulu, Hawaii, USA	Guam	13 Oct 1992	1,813.43	1,126.81
6	New York, USA	Paris, France	21 Oct 1982	1,806.82	1,122.71
7	Rio de Janeiro, Brazil	Dakar, Senegal	29 Mar 1982	1,794.32	1,114.94
8	Acapulco, Mexico	Honolulu, Hawaii, USA	12 Oct 1992	1,775.76	1,103.41
9	Washington, DC, USA	Marrakech, Morocco	12 Feb 2000	1,771.52	1,100.77
10	Paris, France	New York, USA	1 Apr 1981	1,763.00	1,095.48

* Based on the fastest flight made between any two cities

Source: FIA

WATER SPEED

THE 10 **LATEST HOLDERS OF THE WATER SPEED RECORD – JET POWERED***

DRIVER / COUNTRY / BOAT / LOCATION / DATE	SPEED KM/H	SPEED MPH
1 Ken Warby, Australia Spirit of Australia Blowering Dam, Australia 8 Oct 1978	511.13	317.60
2 Ken Warby, Australia Spirit of Australia Blowering Dam, Australia 20 Nov 1977	463.78	288.18
3 Lee Taylor, USA Hustler Lake Guntersville, Alabama, USA 30 Jun 1967	459.02	285.22
4 Donald Campbell, UK Bluebird K7 Lake Dumbleyung, Australia 31 Dec 1964	444.71	276.33
5 Donald Campbell, UK Bluebird K7 Coniston Water, England, UK 14 May 1959	418.99	260.35
6 Donald Campbell, UK Bluebird K7 Coniston Water, England, UK 10 Nov 1958	400.12	248.62
7 Donald Campbell, UK Bluebird K7 Coniston Water, England, UK 7 Nov 1957	384.75	239.07
8 Donald Campbell, UK Bluebird K7 Coniston Water, England, UK 19 Sep 1956	363.12	225.63
9 Donald Campbell, UK Bluebird K7 Lake Mead, Nevada, USA 16 Nov 1955	347.94	216.20
10 Donald Campbell, UK Bluebird K7 Ullswater, England, UK 23 Jul 1955	325.60	202.32

* As of 1 January 2011

THE 10 **LATEST HOLDERS OF THE WATER SPEED RECORD – PROPELLER DRIVEN***

DRIVER# / BOAT / LOCATION / DATE / SPEED (KM/H / MPH)

1 Dave Villwock,
Miss Budweiser, Lake Oroville,
California, USA / 13 Mar 2004
354.849 / 220.493

2 Russ Wicks,
Miss Freei, Lake Washington,
Washington, USA / 15 Jun 2000
330.711 / 205.494

3 Roy Duby,
Miss US1,
Lake Guntersville,
Alabama, USA
17 Apr 1962
322.543 / 200.419

4 Bill Muncey,
Miss Thriftaway,
Lake Washington,
Washington, USA
16 Feb 1960
308.996 / 192.001

THE 10 **LATEST HOLDERS OF THE NON-STOP ROUND THE WORLD SAILING RECORD***

SKIPPER(S) / COUNTRY	YACHT	YEAR(S)	START/FINISH	AVERAGE SPEED (KNOTS)	DAYS
1 Franck Cammas, France	Groupama 3	2010	Brest, France	18.70	48
2 Bruno Peyron, France	Orange II	2005	Brest, France	17.89	50
3 Steve Fossett, USA	Cheyenne	2004	Brest, France	15.52	58
4 Bruno Peyron, France	Orange	2002	Brest, France	13.98	64
5 Olivier De Kersauson, France	Sport Elec	1997	Brest, France	12.66	71
6 Robin Knox-Johnston, UK & Peter Blake, New Zealand	Enza	1994–95	Brest, France	12.00	74
7 Bruno Peyron, France	Commodore Explorer	1993–94	Brest, France	11.35	79
8 Titouan Lamazou, France	Ecureuil D'Aquitaine II	1989–90	Sables D'Olonnes, France	8.23	109
9 Dodge Morgan, USA	American Promise	1985–86	St George's, Bermuda	7.07	150
10 John Ridgway, UK	English Rose V	1983–84	Ardmore, Scotland	6.48	193

* Eastbound; as of January 2011

Source: World Sailing Speed Record Council

5 Jack Regas,
Hawaii Kai III,
Lake Washington,
Washington, USA
30 Nov 1957
301.956 / 187.627

6 Art Asbury,
Canada,
Miss Supertest II,
Lake Ontario,
Canada
1 Nov 1957
296.988 / 184.540

7 Stanley Sayres
and Elmer
Leninschmidt,
Slo-Mo-Shun IV,
Lake Washington,
Washington, USA
7 Jul 1952
287.263 / 178.497

8 Stanley Sayres
and Ted Jones,
Slo-Mo-Shun IV,
Lake Washington,
Washington, USA
26 Jun 1950
258.015 / 160.323

9 Malcolm
Campbell, UK,
Bluebird K4,
Coniston Water,
England, UK
19 Aug 1939
228.108 / 141.740

10 Malcolm
Campbell, UK,
Bluebird K3,
Hallwiler See,
Switzerland
17 Aug 1938
210.679 / 130.910

* As of 1 January 2011
# USA unless otherwise stated

ROAD & RAIL

VW vehicles
The 5 sq km (1.9 sq mile) Wolfsburg plant in Germany – producer of the ever-popular VWs – uses 1,500 tonnes of sheet metal each day.

TOP 10 MOTOR-VEHICLE MANUFACTURERS

MANUFACTURER	MAIN COUNTRY OF PRODUCTION	VEHICLES (2009)
1 Toyota	Japan	7,234,439
2 General Motors	China	6,459,053
3 Volkswagen	Germany	6,067,208
4 Ford	USA	4,685,394
5 Hyundai	South Korea	4,645,776
6 PSA	France	3,042,311
7 Honda	Japan	3,012,637
8 Nissan	Japan	2,744,562
9 Fiat	Italy	2,460,222
10 Suzuki	India	2,387,537

Source: International Organization of Motor Vehicle Manufacturers

TOP 10 COUNTRIES WITH THE LONGEST ROAD NETWORKS

COUNTRY	TOTAL ROAD NETWORK KM	MILES
1 USA	6,506,204	4,042,768
2 China	3,583,715	2,226,817
3 India	3,320,410	2,063,207
4 Brazil	1,751,868	1,088,560
5 Japan	1,203,777	747,992
6 Canada	1,042,300	647,655
7 France	1,027,183	638,262
8 Russia	940,000	584,089
9 Australia	812,972	505,157
10 Spain	681,298	423,339
UK	394,428	245,086

Source: CIA, The World Factbook 2010

▶ **Driving high**
Shanghai's 11,671 km (7,252 miles) of highway include six elevated roads through the city centre.

TOP 10 **LONGEST RAIL NETWORKS**

COUNTRY	LENGTH KM	MILES
1 USA	226,427	140,695
2 Russia	87,157	54,157
3 China	77,834	48,364
4 India	64,015	39,777
5 Canada	46,688	29,011
6 Germany	41,896	26,033
7 Australia	37,855	23,522
8 Argentina	31,409	19,517
9 France	29,213	18,152
10 Brazil	28,857	17,931
UK	*16,454*	*10,224*

▶ *Cargo carriers*
Just 15% of the rail network in the United States is used for passenger journeys.

TOP 10 **BUSIEST UNDERGROUND RAILWAY NETWORKS**

CITY / PASSENGERS PER ANNUM (2010)*

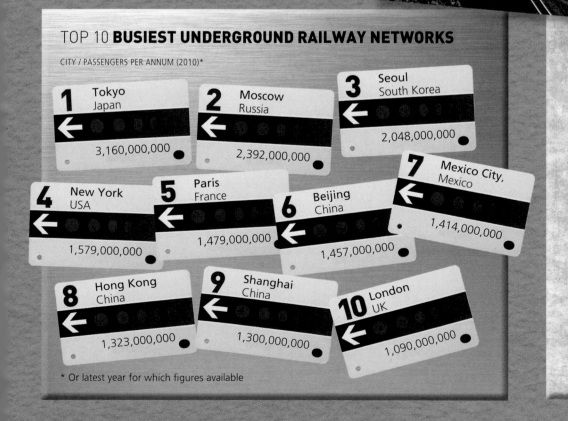

1 Tokyo
Japan
3,160,000,000

2 Moscow
Russia
2,392,000,000

3 Seoul
South Korea
2,048,000,000

4 New York
USA
1,579,000,000

5 Paris
France
1,479,000,000

6 Beijing
China
1,457,000,000

7 Mexico City,
Mexico
1,414,000,000

8 Hong Kong
China
1,323,000,000

9 Shanghai
China
1,300,000,000

10 London
UK
1,090,000,000

* Or latest year for which figures available

TOP 10 **ITEMS LOST ON LONDON TRANSPORT**

ITEM	NO. LOST
1 Books	129,158
2 Bags	116,749
3 Clothing	103,966
4 Valuables	73,998
5 Phones	65,912
6 Keys	39,011
7 Glasses	31,174
8 Umbrellas	30,378
9 Gloves	29,147
10 Jewellery	20,444

Source: Transport for London (TFL), 2005–10

THE 10 FIRST ROUND-THE-WORLD FLIGHTS

	PILOT(S) / AIRCRAFT	ROUTE (START/ END LOCATION)	TOTAL DISTANCE KM	MILES	DATES
1	Lt Lowell H. Smith/Lt Leslie P. Arnold (USA) Douglas World Cruiser, Chicago	Seattle, Washington, USA	42,398	26,345	6 Apr–28 Sep 1924
2	Lt Erik H. Nelson/Lt John Harding Jr (USA) Douglas World Cruiser, New Orleans	Seattle, Washington, USA	44,342	27,553	6 Apr–28 Sep 1924
3	Dr Hugo Eckener, Ernst Lehmann and crew (Germany), Airship, Graf Zeppelin	Lakehurst, New Jersey, USA	37,787	20,373	8–29 Apr 1929
4	Wiley Post and Harold Gatty (USA) Lockheed Vega, Winnie Mae	Roosevelt Field, Long Island, USA	24,903	15,474	23 Jun–1 Jul 1931
5	Wolfgang von Gronau, Ghert von Roth, Franz Hack, Fritz Albrecht (Germany), Dornier seaplane, Grönland-Wal D-2053	List, Germany	44,000	27,240	22 Jul–23 Nov 1932
6	Wiley Post (USA) Lockheed Vega, Winnie Mae (first solo)	Floyd Bennett Field, New York, USA	25,093	15,596	15–22 Jul 1933
7	Howard Hughes, Lt Thomas Thurlow, Henry P. McClean Conner, Richard Stoddart, Eddie Lund (USA), Lockheed 14, New York World's Fair 1939	Floyd Bennett Field, New York, USA	23,612	14,672	10–14 Jul 1938
8 =	Clifford Evans (USA) Piper PA-12, City of Washington	Teterboro, New, Jersey, USA	40,494	25,162	9 Aug–10 Dec 1947
=	George Truman (USA) Piper PA-12, City of the Angels	Teterboro, New, Jersey, USA	40,493	25,162	9 Aug–10 Dec 1947
10	Capt James Gallagher and crew of 13 (USA) Boeing B-50A, Lucky Lady II (first non-stop circumnavigation with in-flight refuelling)	Fort Worth, Texas, USA	37,742	23,452	26 Feb–2 Mar 1949

TOP 10 LONGEST WINGSPAN POWERED AIRCRAFT

	AIRCRAFT / MAX. TAKE-OFF WEIGHT	WINGSPAN M	FT	IN
1	H-4 Hercules 'Spruce Goose' 180,000 kg/400,000 lb	97.5	319	11
2	Antonov An-225 Mriya 640,000 kg/1,322,773 lb	88.4	290	2
3	Airbus A380-800F 590,000 kg/1,300,700 lb	79.8	261	8
4	Antonov An-124 Rusian 405,000 kg/892,872 lb	73.3	240	5
5	Convair B-36 Peacemaker 190,000 kg/410,000 lb	70.1	230	0
6	Bristol 167 Brabazon 130,000 kg/290,000 lb	70.0	229	11
7	Boeing 747-8 442,000 kg/975,000 lb	68.5	224	7
8	Lockheed C-5 Galaxy 381,000 kg/840,000 lb	67.3	222	9
9	Saunders-Roe SR45 Princess 156,500 kg/345,025 lb	66.9	219	6
10	Boeing 777-300ER 351,534 kg775,000 lb	64.8	212	7

▼ *Douglas World Cruiser*
With a range of 3,600 km (2,220 miles), the torpedo bomber could be fitted with floats or landing gear.

▲ *Airbus A380*
The A380 requires 530 km (330 miles) of wiring and 3,600 litres (950 gallons) of paint.

TOP 10 BUSIEST AIRPORTS

AIRPORT	PASSENGERS, 2008	CODE
1 ATLANTA, USA	88,032,086	ATL
2 LONDON HEATHROW, UK	66,037,578	LHR
3 BEIJING, CHINA	65,372,012	PEK
4 CHICAGO, USA	64,158,343	ORD
5 TOKYO, JAPAN	61,903,656	HND
6 PARIS, FRANCE	57,906,866	CDG
7 LOS ANGELES, USA	56,520,843	LAX
8 DALLAS/FORT WORTH, USA	56,030,457	DFW
9 FRANKFURT, GERMANY	50,932,840	FRA
10 DENVER, USA	50,167,485	DEN

Source: Airports Council International

TOP 10 LARGEST MOTOR YACHTS

	YACHT NAME	LAUNCH YEAR	M	LENGTH FT	IN
1	Eclipse	2010	169.8	557	0
2	Dubai	2006	162.0	531	5
3	Al Salamah	1999	139.2	456	10
4	Rising Sun	2004	138.4	454	1
5	Al Mirqab	2008	133.0	436	4
6	Octopus	2003	126.2	414	0
7	Savarona	1931	124.4	408	0
8	Crystal	2010	124.0	406	10
9	Alexander	1965	122.0	400	2
10	A	2008	119.0	390	4

Source: Power & Motoryacht 2010

TOP 10 LONGEST SHIP CANALS

	CANAL / COUNTRY	OPENED	LENGTH KM	MILES
1	Grand Canal, China	AD 283*	1,795	1,114
2	Erie Canal, USA	1825	584	363
3	Göta Canal, Sweden	1832	386	240
4	St Lawrence Seaway, Canada/USA	1959	290	180
5	Canal du Midi, France	1692	240	149
6	Main-Danube, Germany	1992	171	106
7	Suez, Egypt	1869	162	101
8	= Albert, Belgium	1939	129	80
	= Moscow-Volga, Russia	1937	129	80
10	Volga-Don, Russia	1952	101	63

* Extended from AD 605–10 and rebuilt between 1958–72

▶ Eclipse
Roman Abramovich's fifth yacht can house 62 guests with 50 crew, and features two helicopter pads and a mini submarine.

◀ Göta Canal
The Göta Canal in Sweden links Gothenburg on the west coast to Söderköping on the Baltic.

AIR DISASTERS

THE 10 FIRST POWERED AIRCRAFT FATALITIES

	VICTIM	NATIONALITY	LOCATION	DATE
1	Lt Thomas Etholen Selfridge	American	Fort Myer, USA	17 Sep 1908
2	Eugène Lefèbvre	French	Juvisy, France	7 Sep 1909
3	Ferdinand Ferber	French	Boulogne, France	22 Sep 1909
4	Ena Rossi	Italian	Rome, Italy	22 Sep 1909
5	Antonio Fernandez	Spanish	Nice, France	6 Dec 1909
6	Léon Delagrange	French	Croix d'Hins, France	4 Jan 1910
7	Hubert Le Blon	French	San Sebastián, Spain	2 Apr 1910
8	Hauvette Michelin	French	Lyons, France	13 May 1910
9	Aindan de Zoseley	Hungarian	Budapest, Hungary	2 Jun 1910
10	Thaddeus Robl	German	Stettin, Germany	18 Jun 1910

Although there had been many fatalities in the early years of ballooning and among pioneer parachutists, it was not until 1908 that anyone was killed in an aeroplane. On 17 September at Fort Myer, Virginia, Orville Wright was demonstrating his Type A *Flyer*. On board was a passenger, 26-year-old Lieutenant Thomas Etholen Selfridge of the Army Signal Corps. At a height of just 23 m (75 ft), one of the propellers struck a wire, sending the plane out of control. It crash-landed, injuring Wright and killing Lt Selfridge, who thus became powered flying's first victim.

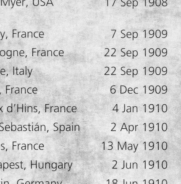

TOP 10 MOST FATAL PHASES OF COMMERCIAL FLIGHT

	PHASE	% OF FATAL ACCIDENTS*
1	Landing	21
2 =	Final approach	13
=	Taxi, load & unload	13
4	Takeoff	12
5	Initial approach	11
6	Initial climb	9
7	Cruise (second half)	6
8 =	Climb	4
=	Descent	4
=	Cruise (first half)	4

* 2000–09
Source: Boeing

The Worst Air Show Crashes

In front of an audience of 300,000 in Ramstein, Germany, on 28 August 1988, a mid-air collision occurred (pictured), which claimed the lives of 67 spectators and three pilots. Aircraft of the Italian Air Force display team, Frecce Tricolori, crashed on to the runway and tumbled into the spectator area. The deadliest incident occurred at Syknyliv airfield, Ukraine, on 27 July 2002, when a failed low-altitude rolling manoeuvre claimed the lives of 77 people. Both pilots ejected to safety and were sentenced to a combined 22 years in prison.

THE 10 **WORST AIR DISASTERS IN THE WORLD**

LOCATION / DATE / INCIDENT   NO. KILLED

1 New York, USA, 11 Sep 2001   c. 1,622
Following a hijacking by terrorists, an American Airlines Boeing 767
was deliberately flown into the North Tower of the World Trade
Center, killing all 81 passengers (including five hijackers), 11 crew
on board and an estimated 1,530 on the ground.

2 New York, USA, 11 Sep 2001   c. 677
As part of the coordinated attack, hijackers commandeered a
second Boeing 767 and crashed it into the South Tower of the
World Trade Center, killing all 56 passengers and nine crew on
board, and approximately 612 on the ground.

3 Tenerife, Canary Islands, 27 Mar 1977   583
Two Boeing 747s (PanAm and KLM, carrying 380 passengers and
16 crew, and 234 passengers and 14 crew respectively) collided
and caught fire on the runway of Los Rodeos airport after the pilots
received incorrect control-tower instructions.

4 Mt Osutaka, Japan, 12 Aug 1985   520
A JAL Boeing 747 on an internal flight from Tokyo to Osaka
crashed, killing all but four of the 509 passengers and all 15 crew.

5 Charkhi Dadri, India, 12 Nov 1996   349
A Saudi Arabian Airlines Boeing 747 collided with a Kazakh Airlines
Ilyushin IL 76 cargo aircraft on its descent and exploded, killing
all 312 (289 passengers and 23 crew) on the Boeing and all 37
(27 passengers and 10 crew) on the Ilyushin.

6 Paris, France, 3 Mar 1974   346
Immediately after take-off for London, a Turkish Airlines DC-10
suffered an explosive decompression when a door burst open,
and crashed at Ermenonville, north of Paris, killing all aboard.

7 Off the Irish coast, 23 Jun 1985   329
An Air India Boeing 747 on a flight from Vancouver to Delhi
exploded in mid-air, probably as a result of a terrorist bomb,
killing all 307 passengers and 22 crew.

8 Riyadh, Saudi Arabia, 19 Aug 1980   301
Following an emergency landing a Saudia (Saudi Arabian) Airlines
Lockheed TriStar caught fire. The crew was unable to open the
doors and all on board died from smoke inhalation.

9 Off the Iranian coast, 3 Jul 1988   290
An Iran Air A300 airbus was shot down in error by a missile fired
by the USS Vincennes, resulting in the deaths of all 274 passengers
and 16 crew.

10 Sirach Mountain, Iran, 19 Feb 2003   275
An Ilyushin 76 on a flight from Zahedan to Kerman crashed into
the mountain in poor weather. It was carrying 257 Revolutionary
Guards and a crew of 18, none of whom survived.

THE 10 **WORST AIRSHIP DISASTERS**

LOCATION / DATE / INCIDENT   NO. KILLED

1 Coast off New Jersey, USA, 4 Apr 1933   73
US Navy airship Akron crashed into the sea in
a storm, leaving only three survivors.

2 Over the Mediterranean, 21 Dec 1923   52
French airship Dixmude is assumed to have been
struck by lightning, broke up and crashed into the sea.

3 Near Beauvais, France, 5 Oct 1930   50
British airship R101 crashed into a hillside leaving
48 dead, with two dying later, and six survivors.

4 Coast off Hull, UK, 24 Aug 1921   44
Airship R38 broke in two on a training and test flight.

5 Lakehurst, New Jersey, USA, 6 May 1937   36
German Zeppelin Hindenburg caught fire when
mooring. Remarkably, 62 survived the blaze.

6 Hampton Roads, Virginia, USA, 21 Feb 1922   34
Roma, an Italian airship bought by the US Army, hit
power lines and crashed, killing all but 11 men on board.

7 Berlin, Germany, 17 Oct 1913   28
The first air disaster with more than 20 fatalities, German
airship LZ18 crashed after engine failure and an explosion
during a test flight at Berlin-Johannisthal.

8 Baltic Sea, 30 Mar 1917   23
German airship SL9 was struck by lightning on a flight
from Seerappen to Seddin and crashed into the sea.

9 Mouth of the River Elbe, Germany, 3 Sep 1915   19
German airship L10 was struck by lightning and
plunged into the sea.

10 Coast off Barnegat City, New Jersey,   18
USA, 6 Jul 1960
Largest-ever non-rigid airship US Navy Goodyear
ZPG-3W crashed into the sea. There were
three survivors.

▼ *Charkhi Dadri*
*Airborne Collision Avoidance
Systems are now compulsory
after the deadliest mid-air
collision in history.*

10
SPORT

100 METRES WORLD RECORD CENTENARY

On 6 July 1912, on the opening day of the men's 100 metres competition at the Stockholm Olympics, Philadelphia-born Don Lippincott became the first man to be recognized by the IAAF as the official holder of the world 100 metres record. Electronic timing was being used for the first time at the 1912 Olympic Games, and Lippincott won his heat in 10.6 seconds, a record not surpassed until 1920. The first man to run it in under 10 seconds was American Jim Hines, with a personal best of 9.95 on 14 October 1968, a record which stood for 15 years. The current holder, Usain Bolt, ran 9.58 seconds in Berlin on 16 August 2009. This beat his previous record by over a tenth of a second – the largest margin of improvement since electronic timing was introduced.

Olympics 2012

TOP 10 **MOST SUCCESSFUL HOST NATIONS AT THE SUMMER OLYMPICS***

	HOST	YEAR	GOLD	SILVER	BRONZE	TOTAL
1	USA	1904	78	84	82	244
2	USSR	1980	80	69	46	195
3	USA	1984	83	60	30	173
4	Great Britain	1908	56	51	39	146
5	USA	1932	41	32	30	103
6 =France		1900	26	41	34	101
=USA		1996	44	32	25	101
8	China	2008	51	21	28	100
9	Germany	1936	33	26	30	89
10	Sweden	1912	24	24	17	65

* Based on total medals won

▼ *China goes gold*
China dominated the 2008 diving events, winning seven gold medals.

Canada in 1976 is the only host nation not to have won a gold medal. They won five silver and six bronze medals. Mexico in 1968 won a record low number of medals by a host nation when they took just three gold, three silver and three bronze medals for a total of nine.

AUSTERE OLYMPICS

Because the 1948 Olympics were the first Games after World War II, and rationing was still in place in Britain, they became known as the Austerity Games.

	COUNTRY	GOLD	SILVER	BRONZE	TOTAL
1	USA	38	27	19	84
2	Sweden	17	11	18	46
3	France	11	6	15	32
4	Italy	9	12	10	31
5	Hungary	10	5	13	28
6	Great Britain	4	16	7	27

LONDON OLYMPICS 1908

Thanks to the 1908 London Olympics, the current distance of 26 miles 385 yards for the marathon was established. Scheduled for 26 miles from Windsor Park to the White City stadium, the finish line was moved back 385 yards so the race would finish in front of the royal box. And it was the marathon that produced high drama when Dorando Pietri (Italy) who, near total collapse at the end of the race, was helped over the line – only to be disqualified.

▼ *Olympic aquatics*
The 2012 Aquatics Centre at the Olympic Park in Stratford houses two 50-m pools.

LONDON OLYMPICS 2012

When it staged the 1908 and 1948 Olympics, London became the second city after Paris to host two Summer Games. In 2012 it will become the first city to host the world's greatest sporting event for a third time.

Voting for the 2012 Olympics Nine cities originally submitted applications to host the 2012 Summer Olympics: Havana (Cuba), Istanbul (Turkey), Leipzig (Germany), London (England), Madrid (Spain), Moscow (Russia), New York (USA), Paris (France) and Rio de Janeiro (Brazil). On 18 May 2004 the IOC Executive Board selected the five candidates: London, Madrid, Moscow, New York and Paris. The final decision on who should host the Games was made at the 117th IOC Session in Singapore on 6 July 2005. The voting went as follows:

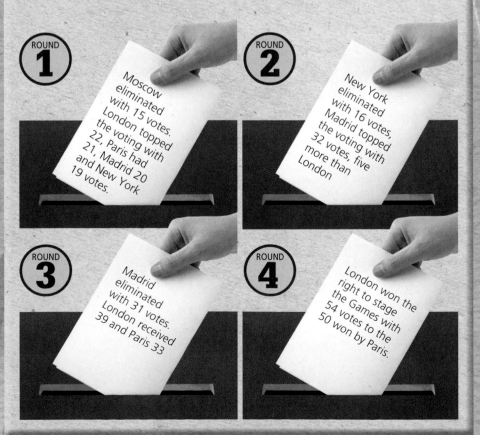

ROUND 1
Moscow eliminated with 15 votes. London topped the voting with 22, Paris had 21, Madrid 20 and New York 19 votes.

ROUND 2
New York eliminated with 16 votes, Madrid topped the voting with 32 votes, five more than London

ROUND 3
Madrid eliminated with 31 votes. London received 39 and Paris 33

ROUND 4
London won the right to stage the Games with 54 votes to the 50 won by Paris.

THE 10 LATEST SUMMER OLYMPIC HOST CITIES

2012 London, England
2008 Beijing, China **2004** Athens, Greece
2000 Sydney, Australia **1996** Atlanta, USA
1992 Barcelona, Spain **1988** Seoul, South Korea **1984** Los Angeles, USA
1980 Moscow, Russia
1976 Montreal, Canada

LONDON 2012 FACTFILE

Costs It is estimated that it will cost between £7–8 billion to host the 2012 Games. **The site area** The new 80,000-capacity Olympic Stadium in Stratford will host the athletics events and opening and closing ceremonies. **Competing nations** Over 10,000 athletes from 205 nations will be competing in 26 sports. **The torch** The Olympic torch arrives in Britain on 18 May 2012 and goes around the country before reaching the Olympic Stadium on 27 July.

ATHLETICS

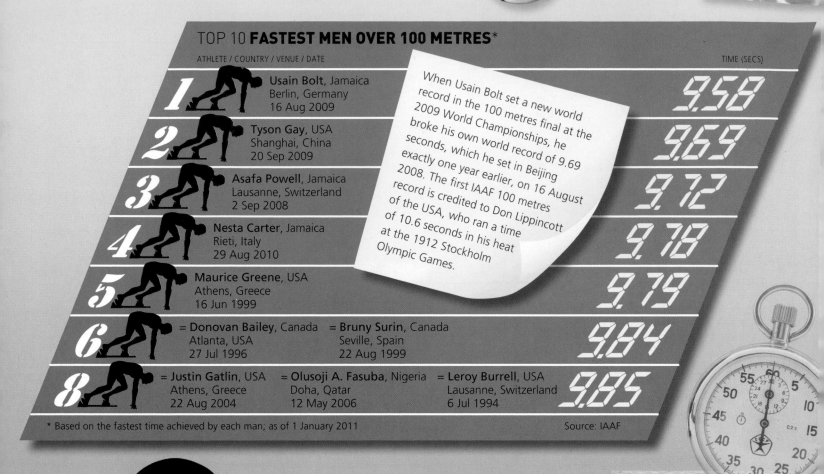

TOP 10 FASTEST MEN OVER 100 METRES*

ATHLETE / COUNTRY / VENUE / DATE

TIME (SECS)

1 **Usain Bolt**, Jamaica
Berlin, Germany
16 Aug 2009 — **9.58**

2 **Tyson Gay**, USA
Shanghai, China
20 Sep 2009 — **9.69**

3 **Asafa Powell**, Jamaica
Lausanne, Switzerland
2 Sep 2008 — **9.72**

4 **Nesta Carter**, Jamaica
Rieti, Italy
29 Aug 2010 — **9.78**

5 **Maurice Greene**, USA
Athens, Greece
16 Jun 1999 — **9.79**

6 = **Donovan Bailey**, Canada   = **Bruny Surin**, Canada
Atlanta, USA   Seville, Spain
27 Jul 1996   22 Aug 1999 — **9.84**

8 = **Justin Gatlin**, USA   = **Olusoji A. Fasuba**, Nigeria   = **Leroy Burrell**, USA
Athens, Greece   Doha, Qatar   Lausanne, Switzerland
22 Aug 2004   12 May 2006   6 Jul 1994 — **9.85**

> When Usain Bolt set a new world record in the 100 metres final at the 2009 World Championships, he broke his own world record of 9.69 seconds, which he set in Beijing exactly one year earlier, on 16 August 2008. The first IAAF 100 metres record is credited to Don Lippincott of the USA, who ran a time of 10.6 seconds in his heat at the 1912 Stockholm Olympic Games.

* Based on the fastest time achieved by each man; as of 1 January 2011

Source: IAAF

THE 10 LATEST HOLDERS OF THE MEN'S WORLD MILE RECORD*

	HOLDER / COUNTRY / WHERE SET	TIME (MIN:SEC)	DATE SET
1	Hicham El Guerrouj, Morocco — Rome, Italy	3:43.13	7 Jul 1999
2	Noureddine Morceli, Algeria — Rieti, Italy	3:44.39	5 Sep 1993
3	Steve Cram, UK — Oslo, Norway	3:46.32	27 Jul 1985
4	Sebastian Coe, UK — Brussels, Belgium	3:47.33	28 Aug 1981
5	Steve Ovett, UK — Koblenz, Germany	3:48.40	26 Aug 1981
6	Sebastian Coe, UK — Zürich, Switzerland	3:48.53	19 Aug 1981
7	Steve Ovett, UK — Oslo, Norway	3:48.8	1 Jul 1980
8	Sebastian Coe, UK — Oslo, Norway	3:48.95	17 Jul 1979
9	John Walker, New Zealand — Gothenburg, Sweden	3:49.4	12 Aug 1975
10	Filbert Bayi, Tanzania — Kingston, Jamaica	3:51.0	17 May 1975

* As of 1 January 2011

Source: IAAF

◀ *Hicham El Guerrouj*
Two-time Olympic champion Hicham El Guerrouj also broke 1500 and 2000 m records.

Long-standing Long-jump Records

When American Bob Beamon's staggering long jump of 8.90 metres at the 1968 Mexico Olympics bettered the old world record by a mammoth 55 cm (more than 21.5 in), it was a record that seemed likely to stand for a long time. And in fact it was nearly 23 years before Mike Powell of the USA broke the world record in August 1991. However, going into the 2012 London Olympics, Beamon's jump still stands as an Olympic record after 44 years, and is the longest-standing record in the history of the Games.

TOP 10 **FASTEST WOMEN'S MARATHONS***

	ATHLETE / COUNTRY / WHERE SET	WHEN SET	TIME (HR:MIN:SEC)
1	Paula Radcliffe, UK London, England	13 Apr 2003	2:15:25
2	Paula Radcliffe, UK Chicago, USA	13 Oct 2002	2:17:18
3	Paula Radcliffe, UK London, England	17 Apr 2005	2:17:42
4	Catherine Ndereba, Kenya Chicago, USA	07 Oct 2001	2:18:47
5	Paula Radcliffe, UK London, England	14 Apr 2002	2:18:56
6	Mizuki Noguchi, Japan Berlin, Germany	25 Sep 2005	2:19:12
7	Irina Mikitenko, Germany Berlin, Germany	28 Sep 2008	2:19:19
8	Catherine Ndereba, Kenya Chicago, USA	13 Oct 2002	2:19:26
9	Deena Kastor, USA London, England	23 Apr 2006	2:19:36
10	Yingjie Sun, China Beijing, China	19 Oct 2003	2:19:39

* As of 1 January 2011   Source: IAAF

TOP 10 **LONGEST LONG-JUMPS***

	ATHLETE / COUNTRY / WHERE SET	WHEN SET	DISTANCE (M)
1	Mike Powell, USA Tokyo, Japan	30 Aug 1991	8.95
2	Bob Beamon, USA Mexico City, Mexico	18 Oct 1968	8.90
3	Carl Lewis, USA Tokyo, Japan	30 Aug 1991	8.87
4	Robert Emmiyan, USSR Tsakhkadzor, USSR	22 May 1987	8.86
5	Carl Lewis, USA Indianapolis, USA	19 Jun 1983	8.79
6	= Carl Lewis, USA Indianapolis, USA	24 Jul 1982	8.76
	= Carl Lewis, USA Indianapolis, USA	18 Jul 1988	8.76
8	Carl Lewis, USA Indianapolis, USA	16 Aug 1987	8.75
9	= Larry Myricks, USA Indianapolis, USA	18 Jul 1988	8.74
	= Erick Walder, USA El Paso, USA	2 Apr 1994	8.74
	= Dwight Phillips, USA Eugene, Oregan, USA	17 Jun 2009	8.74

* As of 1 January 2011   Source: IAAF

At the 1991 World Championships, both Carl Lewis and Mike Powell seemed likely to beat Bob Beamon's long-standing world record. In round four, Lewis jumped 8.91 to better Beamon's distance but it was deemed to be wind-assisted. However, in the next round Powell jumped a legal 8.95 to shatter the 23-year-old world record.

When she broke her own world record in winning the 2003 London Marathon, Paula Radcliffe knocked a staggering 1 minute 53 seconds off her previous best mark, which she set in the Chicago Marathon six months earlier. Radcliffe won the London Marathon three times.

CRICKET

TOP 10 MOST RUNS IN TEST CRICKET

	PLAYER / COUNTRY	YEARS	MATCHES	RUNS*
1	Sachin Tendulkar, India	1989–2011	176	14,532
2	Ricky Ponting, Australia	1995–2011	152	12,363
3	Rahul Dravid, India/ICC	1996–2011	149	12,027
4	Brian Lara, West Indies/ICC	1990–2006	131	11,953
6	Jacques Kallis, South Africa/ICC	1995–2011	145	11,838
5	Allan Border, Australia	1978–1994	156	11,174
7	Steve Waugh, Australia	1985–2004	168	10,927
8	Sunil Gavaskar, India	1971–1987	125	10,122
9	Mahela Jayawardene, Sri Lanka	1997–2011	116	9,527
10	Shivnarine Chanderpaul, West Indies	1994–2011	129	9,063

* As of 1 April 2011.

TOP 10 MOST RUNS IN ONE-DAY INTERNATIONALS

	PLAYER / COUNTRY	YEARS	MATCHES	RUNS*
1	Sachin Tendulkar, India	1989–2011	452	18,093
2	Sanath Jayasuriya, Sri Lanka/Asia	1989–2009	444	13,428
3	Ricky Ponting, Australia/ICC	1995–2011	352	13,082
4	Inzamam-ul-Haq, Pakistan/Asia	1991–2007	378	11,739
5	Sourav Ganguly, India/Asia	1992–2007	311	11,363
6	Jacques Kallis, South Africa/Africa/ICC	1996–2011	307	11,002
7	Rahul Dravid, India/Asia/ICC	1996–2009	339	10,765
8	Brian Lara, West Indies/ICC	1990–2007	299	10,405
9	Mohammad Yousuf, Pakistan/Asia	1998–2011	288	9,720
10	Adam Gilchrist, Australia/ICC	1996–2008	287	9,619

* As of 1 April 2011

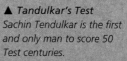

▲ **Tandulkar's Test**
Sachin Tendulkar is the first and only man to score 50 Test centuries.

Most World Cup Runs

The India v. England group game at Bangalore in the 2011 World Cup was the highest ever scoring match in the competition, with each side scoring 338 runs in a 676-run thriller. The highest individual team total is 413-5 by India against Bermuda at Port of Spain in 2007, and the highest individual innings is 188 not out by Gary Kirsten of South Africa against UAE at Rawalpindi in 1996.

TOP 10 **HIGHEST TEAM TOTALS IN TWENTY20 CRICKET**

	TEAM / OPPONENTS	VENUE	DATE	TOTAL*
1	Sri Lanka v. Kenya	Johannesburg	14 Sep 2007	260–6
2	Somerset v. Gloucestershire	Taunton	27 Jun 2006	250–3
3	Chennai v. Rajasthan	Chennai	3 Apr 2010	246–5
4	Nondescripts v. Sri Lanka Air Force Sports Club	Colombo	16 Oct 2005	245–4
5	Karachi Dolphins v. Lahore Eagles	Lahore	14 Oct 2010	243–2
6	Essex v. Sussex	Chelmsford	24 Jun 2008	242–3
7	South Africa v. England	Centurion	15 Nov 2009	241–6
8	Chennai v. Punjab	Mohali	19 Apr 2008	240–5
9	= Easterns v. Centrals	Bulawayo	16 May 2009	239–3
	= Sussex v. Glamorgan	Hove	23 Jun 2010	239–5

* As of 1 April 2011

► **Scoring partners**
Sri Lanka players
Mahela Jayawardene
and Kumar Sangakkara
after their record-
breaking partnership.

◄ **Good all-rounder**
Sanath Jayasuriya was
elected a member
of the Sri Lankan
parliament in 2010.

TOP 10 **HIGHEST PARTNERSHIPS IN TEST CRICKET**

	PARTNERS / COUNTRY / OPPONENTS / DATE	WKT	RUNS*
1	Kumar Sangakkara, Mahela Jayawardene Sri Lanka v. South Africa, 27 Jul 2006	3rd	624
2	Sanath Jayasuriya, Roshan Mahanama Sri Lanka v. India, 2 Aug 1997	2nd	576
3	Andrew Jones, Martin Crowe New Zealand v. Sri Lanka, 31 Jan 1991	3rd	467
4	= Bill Ponsford, Don Bradman Australia v. England, 18 Aug 1934	2nd	451
	= Mudassar Nazar, Javed Miandad Pakistan v. India, 14 Jan 1983	3rd	451
6	Conrad Hunte, Gary Sobers West Indies v. Pakistan, 26 Feb 1958	2nd	446
7	Marvan Atapattu, Kumar Sangakkara Sri Lanka v. Zimbabwe, 14 May 2004	2nd	438
8	Mahela Jayawardene, Thilan Samaraweera Sri Lanka v. Pakistan, 21 Feb 2009	4th	437
9	Jacques Rudolph, Boeta Dippenaar South Africa v. Bangladesh, 24 Apr 2003	3rd	429#
10	Neil McKenzie, Graeme Smith South Africa v. Bangladesh, 29 Feb 2008	1st	415

* As of 1 April 2011
# Stand unbroken

BASEBALL

▲ Star player
Hank Aaron was 41 when he appeared in his final All-Star game in 1975.

▲ Cubs in action
Despite being one of the oldest professional teams, the Cubs have not won the World Series since 1908.

TOP 10 MOST ALL-STAR GAME APPEARANCES

	PLAYER	YEARS	GAMES PLAYED*
1	= Stan Musial	1943–63	24
	= Willie Mays	1954–73	24
	= Hank Aaron	1955–75	24
4	= Ted Williams	1940–60	18
	= Brooks Robinson	1960–74	18
	= Cal Ripken	1983–2001	18
7	= Mickey Mantle	1953–68	16
	= Al Kaline	1955–74	16
	= Pete Rose	1965–85	16
10	= Yogi Berra	1949–62	15
	= Rod Carew	1967–84	15

* Up to and including 2010
Source: MLB

TOP 10 TEAMS WITH THE MOST GAMES PLAYED IN MAJOR LEAGUE BASEBALL*

	TEAM	YEARS	GAMES
1	Chicago Cubs	1876–2010	20,088
2	Atlanta Braves	1876–2010	20,053
3	St. Louis Cardinals	1882–2010	19,675
4	Cincinnati Reds	1882–2010	19,673
5	Pittsburgh Pirates	1882–2010	19,633
6	San Francisco Giants	1883–2010	19,557
7	Philadelphia Phillies	1883–2010	19,482
8	Los Angeles Dodgers	1884–2010	19,473
9	Detroit Tigers	1901–2010	17,175
10	Minnesota Twins	1901–2010	17,157

* In regular season games up to 2010
Source: MLB

The Cubs were known as the White Stockings when they formed in 1876.

The Chicago Cubs' first National League game was on 25 April 1876 when they beat the Louisville Grays 4–0.

TOP 10 **MOST CY YOUNG AWARDS**

	PLAYER	YEARS	AWARDS*
1	Roger Clemens	1986–2004	7
2	Randy Johnson	1995–2002	5
3 =	Steve Carlton	1972–82	4
=	Greg Maddux	1992–95	4
5 =	Sandy Koufax	1963–66	3
=	Tom Seaver	1969–75	3
=	Jim Palmer	1973–76	3
=	Pedro Martinez	1997–2000	3
9 =	Bob Gibson	1968–70	2
=	Tom Glavine	1991–98	2
=	Denny McLain	1968–69	2
=	Gaylord Perry	1972–78	2
=	Bret Saberhagen	1985–89	2
=	Johan Santana	2004–06	2
=	Tim Lincecum	2008–09	2
=	Roy Halladay	2003–10	2

The Cy Young Award is presented each year to the best pitcher in both the American League and National League. The award was first made in 1956 following the death the previous year of one of the game's all-time great pitchers, Cy Young. Originally only one award was made, but since 1967 there has been one award for the best pitcher in each league. The first recipient was Don Newcombe of the Brooklyn Dodgers.

▶ *Award-winner*
Steve Carlton played for six teams, but won all his Cy Young awards whilst at Philadelphia Phillies.

THE 10 **LATEST NO. 1 PICKS IN THE MLB DRAFT**

YEAR	PLAYER	POSITION	PICKED BY
2010	Bryce Harper	Outfielder	Washington Nationals
2009	Stephen Strasburg	Pitcher	Washington Nationals
2008	Tim Beckham	Shortstop	Tampa Bay Rays
2007	David Price	Pitcher	Tampa Bay Devil Rays
2006	Luke Hochevar	Pitcher	Kansas City Royals
2005	Justin Upton	Shortstop	Arizona Diamondbacks
2004	Matt Bush	Shortstop	San Diego Padres
2003	Delmon Young	Outfielder	Tampa Bay Devil Rays
2002	Bryan Bullington	Pitcher	Pittsburgh Pirates
2001	Joe Mauer	Catcher	Minnesota Twins

Source: MLB

▶ *Harper's home run*
As a 17-year-old in 2010, Bryce Harper hit 31 home runs in 66 games for his college team.

BASKETBALL

TEAM / YEARS / PLAYED / WON

1

Los Angeles Lakers
1949–2010
4,893 / 3,027

2

Boston Celtics
1947–2010
5,003 / 2,972

3

Philadelphia 76ers
1950–2010
4,828 / 2,569

4

New York Knickerbockers
1947–2010
4,999 / 2,483

5

Detroit Pistons
1949–2010
4,892 / 2,427

6

Atlanta Hawks
1950–2010
4,830 / 2,376

7

Sacramento Kings
1949–2010
4,893 / 2,300

8

Golden State Warriors
1947–2010
4,998 / 2,293

9

San Antonio Spurs
1968–2010
3,500 / 2,031

10

Phoenix Suns
1969–2010
3,412 / 1,914

* As of the end of the 2009–10 season

▲ *Leading Lakers*
The Lakers' win-loss percentage of .619 is the best of all NBA teams – past and present.

TOP 10 **MOST CAREER POINTS IN NBA PLAY-OFF GAMES**

PLAYER / YEARS	POINTS*
1 Michael Jordan 1985–98	5,987
2 Kareem Abdul-Jabbar 1970–89	5,762
3 Shaquille O'Neal 1994–2010	5,248
4 Kobe Bryant 1997–2010	5,052
5 Karl Malone 1986–2004	4,761
6 Jerry West 1961–74	4,457
7 Tim Duncan 1998–2010	3,914
8 Larry Bird 1980–92	3,897
9 John Havlicek 1963–77	3,776
10 Hakeem Olajuwon 1985–2002	3,755

* Up to and including the 2009–10 post season

Source: NBA

TOP 10 MOST POINTS IN A SINGLE NBA GAME*

PLAYER / TEAM / OPPONENTS / DATE	POINTS
1 Wilt Chamberlain, Philadelphia Warriors New York Knicks / 2 Mar 1962	100
2 Kobe Bryant, Los Angeles Lakers Toronto Raptors / 22 Jan 2006	81
3 Wilt Chamberlain, Philadelphia Warriors Los Angeles Lakers / 8 Dec 1961#	78
4 = Wilt Chamberlain, Philadelphia Warriors Chicago Packers / 13 Jan 1962	73
= Wilt Chamberlain, San Francisco Warriors New York Knicks / 16 Nov 1962	73
= David Thompson, Denver Nuggets Detroit Pistons / 9 Apr 1978	73
7 Wilt Chamberlain, San Francisco Warriors Los Angeles Lakers / 3 Nov 1962	72
8 = David Robinson, San Antonio Spurs Los Angeles Clippers / 24 Apr 1994	71
= Elgin Baylor, Los Angeles Lakers New York Knicks / 15 Nov 1960	71
10 Wilt Chamberlain, San Francisco Warriors Syracuse Nationals / 10 Mar 1963	70

* As of the end of the 2009–10 season
# Including three periods of overtime

TOP 10 MOST 3-POINT FIELD GOALS IN AN NBA SEASON*

PLAYER / TEAM / SEASON	3-PT FGS
1 Ray Allen Seattle Supersonics / 2005–06	269
2 Dennis Scott Orlando Magic / 1995–96	267
3 George McCloud Dallas Mavericks / 1995–96	257
4 Jason Richardson Charlotte Bobcats / 2007–08	243
5 Peja Stojakovic Sacramento Kings / 2003–04	240
6 = Peja Stojakovic New Orleans Hornets / 2007–08	231
= Mookie Blaylock Atlanta Hawks / 1995–96	231
8 = Reggie Miller Indiana Pacers / 1996–97	229
= Ray Allen Milwaukee Bucks / 2001–02	229
10 = Quentin Richardson Phoenix Suns / 2004–05	226
= Kyle Korver Philadelphia 76ers / 2004–05	226
= Rashard Lewis Orlando Magic / 2007–08	226

* Regular season up to and including 2009–10 season

◄ Shaquille O'Neal
In 2010, record-breaker Shaquille O'Neal moved to his sixth NBA team, Boston Celtics.

▲ Ray Allen
On 10 February 2011 Ray Allen's 2,562nd 3-point field goal of his career set a new NBA record.

COMBAT SPORTS

THE 10 LONGEST-REIGNING WORLD HEAVYWEIGHT CHAMPIONS*

	BOXER#	YEARS	REIGNS		DURATION	
				YRS	MTHS	DAYS
1	Joe Louis	1937–49	1	11	8	8
2	Muhammad Ali†	1964–79	3	8	11	15
3	Lennox Lewis, UK	1992–2004	3	8	2	18
4	Jack Dempsey	1919–26	1	7	2	20
5	Larry Holmes	1978–85	1	7	2	13
6	Wladimir Klitschko, Ukraine	2000–11	2	7	0	26
7	John L. Sullivan	1885–92	1	7	0	10
8	Jack Johnson	1908–15	1	6	3	11
9	Evander Holyfield	1990–2001	4	6	1	2
10	James J. Jeffries	1899–1903	1	5	11	5

* As of 1 January 2011
\# All boxers from the USA unless otherwise stated
† Formerly Cassius Clay

For many years boxing historians regarded the James Corbett v. John L. Sullivan bout on 7 September 1892 as the first world heavyweight contest under Queensberry Rules, but records now show that Sullivan's win over Dominick McCaffrey (USA) on 29 August 1885 was for the 'Championship of the World' and fought under Queensberry Rules.

The Longest World Boxing Championship Fights

Before the introduction of the Queensberry Rules in 1866, which stipulated that a round should last three minutes, a round lasted until such time as a fighter was knocked down. Consequently, contests often lasted many rounds; a 276-round contest between Jack Jones and Patsy Tunney at Cheshire, England in 1825 being the longest recorded. Under Queensberry Rules the longest world title fight was the 80-round featherweight bout that took place between Ike Weir and Frank Murphy at O'Brien's Opera House, Kouts, Indiana, in March 1889.

► Wladimir Klitschko
Both Wladimir Klitschko and his brother Vitali held world heavyweight titles in 2011.

THE 10 HIGHEST JUDO GRADES

GRADE	JAPANESE NAME
1 10th degree	Judan
2 9th degree	Kudan
3 8th degree	Hachidan
4 7th degree	Shichidan
5 6th degree	Rokudan
6 5th degree	Godan
7 4th degree	Yodan
8 3rd degree	Sandan
9 2nd degree	Nidan
10 1st degree	Shodan

The highest grade ever bestowed on a *Judoka* by the Kodokan is 10th degree, or 10th Dan as it is commonly known. Only 15 men have received this honour since the first, Yamashita Yoshiaka (also known as Yamashita Yoshitugu) on 26 October 1935.

▲ *Taekwondo*
Taekwondo was a Demonstration Sport in 1988 and 1992, and obtained full Olympic status in 2000.

◀ *Wrestlemania*
First held at Madison Square Garden in 1985, Wrestlemania is the sport's longest-running professional event.

TOP 10 OLYMPIC MEDAL-WINNING COUNTRIES AT TAEKWONDO*

	COUNTRY	GOLD	SILVER	BRONZE	TOTAL
1	South Korea	9	1	2	12
2	Chinese Taipei	2	1	4	7
3	USA	2	2	2	6
4 =	China	4	0	1	5
=	Mexico	2	1	2	5
6 =	Iran	2	0	2	4
=	Greece	1	3	0	4
=	Cuba	1	2	1	4
=	Turkey	0	2	2	4
=	France	0	1	3	4

* Based on total medals won up to and including the 2008 Beijing Olympics

TOP 10 ATTENDANCES AT WWE WRESTLEMANIA

	VENUE	YEAR	ATTENDANCE*
1	Pontiac Silverdome, Pontiac, Michigan	1987	93,173
2	Ford Field, Detroit, Michigan	2007	80,103
3	Citrus Bowl, Orlando, Florida	2008	74,635
4	Reliant Stadium, Houston, Texas	2009	72,744
5	University of Phoenix Stadium, Glendale, Arizona	2010	72,219
6	Georgia Dome, Atlanta, Georgia	2011	71,617
7	SkyDome, Toronto, Canada	2002	68,237
8	Reliant Astrodome, Houston, Texas	2001	67,925
9	SkyDome, Toronto, Canada	1990	67,678
10	Hoosier Dome, Indianapolis, Indiana	1992	62,167

* Up to and including Wrestlemania XXVII (2011)

ICE HOCKEY

TOP 10 GOALIES WITH THE MOST CAREER SHUTOUTS*

PLAYER / YEARS PLAYED / SHUTOUTS

1 Martin Brodeur
1991–2011
110

2 Terry Sawchuk
1949–70
103

3 George Hainsworth
1926–37
94

4 Glenn Hall
1952–71
84

5 Jacques Plante
1952–73
82

6 = Alec Connell
1924–37
81

= Tiny Thompson
1928–40
81

= Dominik Hasek
1990–2008
81

9 = Tony Esposito
1968–84
76

= Ed Belfour
1988–2007
76

* Regular season shutouts up to and including 2009–10

Source: NHL

▲ **Martin Brodeur**
Top goalie Brodeur has spent his entire NHL career with the New Jersey Devils.

◄ **Jaromír Jágr**
Jágr was the Czech Republic's flag bearer at the 2010 Winter Olympics.

TOP 10 MOST GAME-WINNING GOALS IN A CAREER*

	PLAYER	YEARS PLAYED	GAME-WINNING GOALS
1	Phil Esposito	1963–81	118
2	Jaromír Jágr	1990–2008	112
3	Brett Hull	1986–2006	110
4	Brendan Shanahan	1987–2009	109
5	= Teemu Selänne	1992–2011	97
	= Guy Lafleur	1971–91	97
7	Mats Sundin	1990–2009	96
8	Steve Yzerman	1983–2006	94
9	= Sergei Fedorov	1990–2009	93
	= Joe Nieuwendyk	1986–2007	93

* In regular season games up to and including 2009–10   Source: NHL

TOP 10 **MOST GOALS IN A SEASON***

PLAYER / TEAM / SEASON / GOALS

1 Wayne Gretzky
Edmonton Oilers
1981–82 — **92**

2 Wayne Gretzky
Edmonton Oilers
1983–84 — **87**

3 Brett Hull
St. Louis Blues
1990–91 — **86**

4 Mario Lemieux
Pittsburgh Penguins
1988–89 — **85**

5 = Phil Esposito
Boston Bruins
1970–71 — **76**

= Alexander Mogilny
Buffalo Sabres
1992–93

= Teemu Selänne
Winnipeg Jets
1992–93

8 Wayne Gretzky
Edmonton Oilers
1984–85 — **73**

9 Brett Hull
St. Louis Blues
1989–90 — **72**

10 = Wayne Gretzky
Edmonton Oilers
1982–83 — **71**

= Jari Kurri
Edmonton Oilers
1984–85

* In a regular season up to the end of 2009–10

Hart Memorial Trophy

The trophy is named after Dr David Hart, the father of former Montreal Canadiens manager-coach Cecil Hart, who presented the trophy to the NHL in the 1923–24 season. The first recipient was Frank Nighbor of the Ottawa Senators. Wayne Gretzky won the award a record nine times between 1980 and 1989.

▲ *Wayne Gretzky*
When he retired in 1999, Wayne Gretzky held more than 50 NHL regular season and play-off records.

TOP 10 **COACHES WITH THE LONGEST NHL CAREERS***

	COACH	FROM	TO	GAMES	SEASONS
1	Scotty Bowman	1968	2002	2,141	30
2	Dick Irvin	1929	1956	1,449	27
3	Al Arbour	1971	2008	1,607	23
4	= Mike Keenan	1985	2009	1,386	20
	= Jack Adams	1928	1947	964	20
	= Pat Quinn	1979	2010	1,400	20
7	Art Ross	1918	1945	758	18
8	= Bryan Murray	1982	2008	1,239	17
	= Ron Wilson	1994	2011	1,257	17
10	= Sid Abel	1953	1976	964	16
	= Billy Reay	1958	1977	1,102	16
	= Roger Neilson	1978	2002	1,000	16
	= Jacques Lemaire	1994	2010	1,213	16
	= Jacques Martin	1987	2011	1,182	16

* To the start of the 2010–11 season

SOCCER

▲ *Spain triumphs*
Spain's 2010 World Cup win over the Netherlands added to their Euro success in 2008.

TOP 10 COUNTRIES IN THE 2010 FIFA WORLD CUP*

	COUNTRY
1	Spain
2	Netherlands
3	Germany
4	Uruguay
5	Argentina
6	Brazil
7	Ghana
8	Paraguay
9	Japan
10	Chile

* Final ranking as published by FIFA

Source: FIFA

TOP 10 MOST WINS IN THE BARCLAYS PREMIER LEAGUE*

	CLUB	MATCHES PLAYED	MATCHES WON
1	Manchester United	715	460
2	Arsenal	716	387
3	Chelsea	715	372
4	Liverpool	715	356
5	Aston Villa	715	269
6	Tottenham Hotspur	716	268
7	Newcastle United	635	253
8	Blackburn Rovers	641	250
9	Everton	716	248
10	West Ham United	599	199

* From the formation of the League in 1992 to 1 January 2011

Source: Barclays Premier League

◄ *Ronaldo*
The World Cup's top scorer, Ronaldo retired in February 2011.

TOP 10 WORLD CUP GOALSCORERS

PLAYER / COUNTRY / YEARS / GOALS (FINAL STAGES 1930–2010)

Ronaldo
Brazil
1998–2006
15

= Gerd Müller
West Germany
1970–74
14

= Miroslav Klose
Germany
2002–10
14

Just Fontaine
France
1958
13

Pelé
Brazil
1958–70
12

= Sándor Kocsis
Hungary
1954
11

TOP 10 **RICHEST MANAGERS IN BRITISH FOOTBALL***

MANAGER / COUNTRY / TEAM / WORTH

1 **Fabio Capello**, Italy
England
£36,000,000

2 **Roy Keane**, Ireland
Ipswich Town
£28,000,000

3 **Alex Ferguson**, Scotland
Manchester United
£26,000,000

4 **Carlo Ancelotti**, Italy
Chelsea
£21,000,000

5 **Arsene Wenger**, France
Arsenal
£17,000,000

6 = **Sven-Goran Eriksson**,
Sweden
Leicester City
£15,000,000

= **Roberto Mancini**, Italy
Manchester City
£15,000,000

8 = **Ole Gunnar Solskjaer**,
Norway
Manchester United
Reserves
£10,000,000

= **Mark Hughes**, Wales
Fulham
£10,000,000

= **Harry Redknapp**, England
Tottenham Hotspur
£10,000,000

* At the start of the 2010–11 season

Source: FourFourTwo

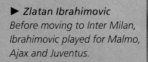

▶ *Zlatan Ibrahimovic*
Before moving to Inter Milan, Ibrahimovic played for Malmo, Ajax and Juventus.

TOP 10 **TRANSFERS WORLDWIDE***

PLAYER / COUNTRY	FROM	TO	YEAR	FEE (£)
1 **Cristiano Ronaldo**, Portugal	Manchester United	Real Madrid	2009	80,000,000
2 **Zlatan Ibrahimovic**, Sweden	Inter Milan	Barcelona	2009	60,700,000
3 **Kaká**, Brazil	AC Milan	Real Madrid	2009	56,000,000
4 **Fernando Torres**, Spain	Liverpool	Chelsea	2011	50,000,000
5 **Zinedine Zidane**, France	Juventus	Real Madrid	2001	47,700,000
6 **Luis Figo**, Portugal	Barcelona	Real Madrid	2000	37,400,000
7 **Hernán Crespo**, Argentina	Parma	Lazio	2000	35,700,000
8 **Andy Carroll**, England	Newcastle United	Liverpool	2011	35,000,000
9 **David Villa**, Spain	Valencia	Barcelona	2010	34,200,000
10 **Gianluigi Buffon**, Italy	Parma	Juventus	2001	33,000,000

* As of the end of the January 2011 transfer window

= **Jürgen Klinsmann**
Germany
1990–98
11

= **Helmut Rahn**
West Germany
1954–58
10

= **Teófilo Cubillas**
Peru
1970–78
10

= **Grzegorz Lato**
Poland
1974–82
10

= **Gary Lineker**
England
1986–90
10

= **Gabriel Batistuta**
Argentina
1994–2002
10

THE 10 OLDEST CURRENT NFL FRANCHISES

TEAM / NAME WHEN FRANCHISE GRANTED / FRANCHISE DATE

1 = Arizona Cardinals (Chicago Cardinals) 17 Sep 1920

= Chicago Bears (Decatur Staleys) 17 Sep 1920

3 Green Bay Packers 27 Aug 1921

4 New York Giants 1 Aug 1925

5 Detroit Lions (Portsmouth Spartans) 12 Jul 1930

6 Washington Redskins (Boston Braves) 9 Jul 1932

7 = Philadelphia Eagles 8 Jul 1933

= Pittsburgh Steelers (Pittsburgh Pirates) 8 Jul 1933

9 St. Louis Rams (Cleveland Rams) 12 Feb 1937

10 = Cleveland Browns* 4 Jun 1944

= San Francisco 49ers* 4 Jun 1944

* Charter member of the All-American Football Conference (AAFC)

Source: NFL

▲ *Cardinals v. Bears*
The Arizona Cardinals and the Chicago Bears have met 90 times in the NFL, with the Bears winning 57.

TOP 10 SUPER BOWL ATTENDANCES

TEAMS / YEAR / VENUE	ATTENDANCE
1 Pittsburgh Steelers v. Los Angeles Rams 1980 Rose Bowl, Pasadena	103,985
2 Washington Redskins v. Miami Dolphins 1983 Rose Bowl, Pasadena	103,667
3 Oakland Raiders v. Minnesota Vikings 1977 Rose Bowl, Pasadena	103,438
4 Green Bay Packers v. Pittsburgh Steelers 2011 Cowboys Stadium, Arlington	103,219
5 New York Giants v. Denver Broncos 1987 Rose Bowl, Pasadena	101,063
6 Dallas Cowboys v. Buffalo Bills 1993 Rose Bowl, Pasadena	98,374
7 Miami Dolphins v. Washington Redskins 1973 Memorial Coliseum, Los Angeles	90,182
8 San Francisco 49ers v. Miami Dolphins 1985 Stanford Stadium, California	84,059
9 San Francisco 49ers v. Cincinnati Bengals 1982 Pontiac Silverdrome, Michigan	81,270
10 Dallas Cowboys v. Miami Dolphins 1972 Tulane Stadium, New Orleans	81,023

TOP 10 MOST WINS IN THE NFL*

	TEAM	YEARS	WINS
1	Chicago Bears	1920–2010	704
2	Green Bay Packers	1921–2010	664
3	New York Giants	1925–2010	636
4	Washington Redskins	1932–2010	547
5	Pittsburgh Steelers	1933–2010	541
6	St. Louis Rams	1937–2010	511
7 =	Philadelphia Eagles	1933–2010	509
=	San Francisco 49ers	1946–2010	509
9	Detroit Lions	1930–2010	496
10	Arizona Cardinals	1920–2010	488

* Regular seasons, 1920–2010

The first of the Chicago Bears' 704 wins in the NFL was a 20–0 win over Moline Universal Tractors on Sunday 3 October 1920. The Bears were known as the Decatur Staleys at the time and the match was in the American Professional Football Association (APFA) – the forerunner of the NFL.

► **LaDainian Tomlinson**
LaDainian Tomlinson also holds the record for the most points in a regular season – 186.

◄ **Jake Delhomme**
Jake Delhomme's record-breaking pass in 2004 was to wide receiver Muhsin Muhammad, whose touchdown put the Panthers in the lead – for the only time in the match – in the fourth quarter. They went on to lose to the New England Patriots 29-32.

TOP 10 MOST TOUCHDOWNS IN AN NFL SEASON*

	PLAYER	TEAM	YEAR	TDS
1	LaDainian Tomlinson	San Diego Chargers	2006	31
2	Shaun Alexander	Seattle Seahawks	2005	28
3	Priest Holmes	Kansas City Chiefs	2003	27
4	Marshall Faulk	St. Louis Rams	2000	26
5	Emmitt Smith	Dallas Cowboys	1995	25
6 =	Priest Holmes	Kansas City Chiefs	2002	24
=	John Riggins	Washington Redskins	1983	24
8 =	O. J. Simpson	Buffalo Bills	1975	23
=	Jerry Rice	San Francisco 49ers	1987	23
=	Terrell Davis	Denver Broncos	1998	23
=	Randy Moss	New England Patriots	2007	23

* Regular season only, up to and including 2010

TOP 10 LONGEST PASSES IN THE SUPER BOWL*

	PLAYER	TEAM	YEAR	LENGTH YARDS
1	Jake Delhomme	Carolina Panthers	2004	85
2	Brett Favre	Green Bay Packers	1997	81
3 =	Jim Plunkett	Oakland Raiders	1981	80
=	Doug Williams	Washington Redskins	1988	80
=	John Elway	Dever Broncos	1999	80
6	David Woodley	Miami Dolphins	1983	76
7 =	Johnny Unitas	Baltimore Colts	1971	75
=	Terry Bradshaw	Pittsburgh Steelers	1979	75
9 =	Terry Bradshaw	Pittsburgh Steelers	1980	73
=	Kurt Warner	St. Louis Rams	2000	73

* Up to and including 2011

RUGBY

◀ **Lesley Vainikolo**
In 152 games for Bradford Bulls Vainikolo scored 149 tries and kicked one conversion.

TOP 10 MOST TRIES IN A SUPER LEAGUE REGULAR SEASON*

	PLAYER	CLUB	YEAR	TRIES
1	Lesley Vainikolo	Bradford Bulls	2004	36
2	Danny McGuire	Leeds Rhinos	2004	35
3	= Ryan Hall	Leeds Rhinos	2009	29
	= Pat Richards	Wigan Warriors	2010	29
5	Paul Newlove	St Helens	1996	28
6	= Kris Radlinski	Wigan Warriors	2001	27
	= Mark Calderwood	Leeds Rhinos	2005	27
8	= Matt Daylight	Gateshead Thunder	1999	25
	= Toa Kohe-Love	Warrington Wolves	1999	25
	= Darren Albert	St Helens	1999	25
	= Lesley Vainikolo	Bradford Bulls	2005	25
	= Justin Murphy	Catalans Dragons	2006	25

* Up to and including 2010

▼ **Toulouse**
The most successful French team, Toulouse have won the French Championship a record 17 times.

TOP 10 MOST APPEARANCES IN THE HEINEKEN CUP FINAL*

	CLUB / COUNTRY	YEAR(S)	WINS	RU	APPS
1	Toulouse, France	1996–2010	4	2	6
2	Leicester Tigers, England	1997–2009	2	3	5
3	Munster, Ireland	2000–08	2	2	4
4	= Brive, France	1997–98	1	1	2
	= London Wasps, England	2004–07	2	0	2
	= Biarritz, France	2006–10	0	2	2
	= Stade Français, France	2001–05	0	2	2
8	= Cardiff, Wales	1996	0	1	1
	= Bath, England	1998	1	0	1
	= Ulster, Ireland	1999	1	0	1
	= Colomiers, France	1999	0	1	1
	= Northampton Saints, England	2000	1	0	1
	= Perpignan, France	2003	0	1	1
	= Leinster, Ireland	2009	1	0	1

* Up to and including 2010

Although it is known as the Heineken Cup (in France, it is known as the 'H Cup' because of restrictions on alcohol sponsorship), the correct name for this trophy is the European Cup. It features teams from the English Premiership, Celtic League, French Top 14 and Italian Super 10.

TOP 10 POINTS SCORERS IN INTERNATIONAL RUGBY

PLAYER / COUNTRY / YEARS	TESTS	POINTS*
1 Jonny Wilkinson England/Lions 1998–2011	91 (6)	1,195 (67)
2 Dan Carter New Zealand 2003–10	79	1,188
3 Neil Jenkins Wales/Lions 1991–2003	91 (4)	1,090 (41)
4 Diego Dominguez Argentina/Italy 1989–2003	76	1,010
5 Ronan O'Gara Ireland/Lions 2000–11	110 (2)	1,006 (0)
6 Andrew Mehrtens New Zealand 1995–2004	70	967
7 Stephen Jones Wales/Lions 1998–2011	105 (6)	934 (53)
8 Michael Lynagh Australia 1984–95	72	911
9 Percy Montgomery South Africa 1997–2008	102	893
10 Matthew Burke Australia 1993–2004	81	878

* As of 1 April 2011

Figures in brackets indicate the number of appearances for the British and Irish Lions. Wilkinson lost his world record to Dan Carter in November 2010, but regained it when he converted a penalty against France at Twickenham on 26 February 2011.

TOP 10 TRY SCORERS IN THE IRB WORLD CUP*

	PLAYER	COUNTRY	YEARS	APPS	TRIES
1	Jonah Lomu	New Zealand	1995–99	11	15
2	Doug Howlett	New Zealand	2003–07	10	13
3 =	Rory Underwood	England	1987–95	15	11
=	Joe Rokocoko	New Zealand	2003–07	8	11
=	Chris Latham	Australia	1999–2007	7	11
6 =	David Campese	Australia	1987–95	15	10
=	Brian Lima	Samoa	1991–2007	18	10
8 =	Gavin Hastings	Scotland	1987–95	13	9
=	Jeff Wilson	New Zealand	1995–99	11	9
10 =	Christophe Dominici	France	1999–2007	15	8
=	Mils Muliaina	New Zealand	2003–07	10	8
=	Bryan Habana	South Africa	2007	7	8

* In all IRB World Cups 1987–2007

Source: IRB

▼ *Jonah Lomu*
In his 63 Tests for the All Blacks between 1994 and 2002, Jonah Lomu scored 37 tries, to put him in fifth place on the all-time New Zealand list.

TENNIS

▼ Rod Laver
Laver is the only person to complete two Grand Slams.

TOP 10 MOST WEEKS SPENT AT NO. 1 ON THE WTA RANKINGS

	PLAYER / COUNTRY	FROM	TO	WEEKS*
1	Steffi Graf, Germany	17 Aug 1987	30 Mar 1997	377
2	Martina Navratilova, Czechoslovakia/USA	10 Jul 1978	16 Aug 1987	332
3	Chris Evert, USA	3 Nov 1975	24 Nov 1985	260
4	Martina Hingis, Switzerland	31 Mar 1997	14 Oct 2001	209
5	Monica Seles, Yugoslavia/USA	11 Mar 1991	24 Nov 1996	178
6	Serena Williams, USA	8 Jul 2002	10 Oct 2010	123
7	Justine Henin, Belgium	20 Oct 2003	18 May 2008	117
8	Lindsay Davenport, USA	12 Oct 1998	29 Jan 2006	98
9	Amélie Mauresmo, France	13 Sep 2004	12 Nov 2006	39
10	Dinara Safina, Russia	20 Apr 2009	1 Nov 2009	26

* As of 1 January 2011

Source: WTA

TOP 10 MOST MEN'S SINGLES TITLES IN A CALENDAR YEAR*

	PLAYER / COUNTRY	YEAR	OUTDOOR	INDOOR	TOTAL
1	Rod Laver, Australia	1969	11	7	18
2	Guillermo Vilas, Argentina	1977	15	1	16
3	= Ilie Nastase, Romania	1973	11	4	15
	= Jimmy Connors, USA	1974	8	7	15
	= Ivan Lendl, Czechoslovakia	1982	6	9	15
6	= Björn Borg, Sweden	1979	8	5	13
	= John McEnroe, USA	1984	5	8	13
8	= Ilie Nastase, Romania	1972	7	5	12
	= Jimmy Connors, USA	1976	6	6	12
	= Thomas Muster, Austria	1995	11	1	12
	= Roger Federer, Switzerland	2006	9	3	12

* In the Open era, 1968–2010, as recognized by the ATP

Source: ATP

▼ Steffi Graf
Between 1986 and 1999 , Graf won a total of 107 singles tournaments.

Most Grand Slam Singles Titles in a Decade

Australia's Margaret Court (née Smith) holds the record for winning the most Grand Slam titles in one decade, winning 16 in the 1960s. The men's record is held by Switzerland's Roger Federer, who won 15 titles in the 2000s. The 1960s was a formidable decade for Australian players because, in addition to Court's record, Roy Emerson won 12 titles and Rod Laver 11.

► **Rafael Nadal**
Nadal is one of two Spanish players – along with Carlos Moya from Mallorca – to top the ATP rankings.

THE 10 **LAST PLAYERS TO WIN THREE OR MORE GRAND SLAM SINGLES TITLES IN A CALENDAR YEAR***

PLAYER / COUNTRY / TITLES WON	YEAR
1 Rafael Nadal, Spain French Open, Wimbledon, US Open	2010
2 Roger Federer, Switzerland Australian Open, Wimbledon, US Open	2007
3 Roger Federer, Switzerland Australian Open, Wimbledon, US Open	2006
4 Roger Federer, Switzerland Australian Open, Wimbledon, US Open	2004
5 Serena Williams, USA French Open, Wimbledon, US Open	2002
6 Martina Hingis, Switzerland Australian Open, Wimbledon, US Open	1997
7 Steffi Graf, Germany French Open, Wimbledon, US Open	1996
8 Steffi Graf, Germany French Open, Wimbledon, US Open	1995
9 Steffi Graf, Germany French Open, Wimbledon, US Open	1993
10 Monica Seles, Yugoslavia Australian Open, French Open, US Open	1992

* Up to and including 2010

TOP 10 **ATP WORLD TOUR MASTERS 1000 TITLES***

	PLAYER / COUNTRY	YEARS	TITLES
1	Rafael Nadal, Spain	2005–10	18
2	= Andre Agassi, USA	1990–2004	17
	= Roger Federer, Switzerland	2002–10	17
4	Pete Sampras, USA	1992–2000	11
5	Thomas Muster, Austria	1990–97	8
6	Michael Chang, USA	1990–97	7
7	= Boris Becker, Germany	1990–96	5
	= Jim Courier, USA	1991–93	5
	= Marcelo Ríos. Chile	1997–99	5
	= Gustavo Kuerten, Brazil	1999–2001	5
	= Marat Safin, Russia	2000–05	5
	= Novak Djokovic, Serbia	2007–09	5
	= Andy Roddick, USA	2003–10	5

* Singles titles 1990–2010

Source: ATP

The ATP World Tour Masters 1000 was inaugurated in 1990 and Stefan Edberg (Sweden) won the first event at Indian Wells. It has had several name changes throughout the years and changed to its current style in 2009. In the season-long series of nine events on the men's ATP tour, ranking points are more than for regular tour events but not as many as for Grand Slam events.

GOLF

THE 10 LAST MEN TO RECORD A ROUND OF 63 IN A MAJOR CHAMPIONSHIP*

	PLAYER / COUNTRY	MAJOR	VENUE	YEAR
1	Rory McIlroy, Northern Ireland	British Open	St Andrews	2010
2	Tiger Woods, USA	US PGA	Southern Hills	2007
3	Thomas Bjorn, Denmark	US PGA	Baltusrol	2005
4	Vijay Singh, Fiji	US Open	Olympic Fields	2003
5	Mark O'Meara, USA	US PGA	Atlanta	2001
6	José Maria Olazabal, Spain	US PGA	Valhalla	2000
7	Greg Norman, Australia	US Masters	Augusta	1996
8	Brad Faxon, USA	US PGA#	Riviera	1995
9	Michael Bradley, USA	US PGA#	Riviera	1995
10	Vijay Singh	US PGA	Inverness	1993

* Up to and including 2010
\# Faxon scored his 63 in the final round of the 1995 US PGA Championship; Bradley's 63 was in the first round.

▼ *Rory McIlroy*
McIlroy led the 2010 Open after his 63, but followed it with a second round 80.

▲ **Nick Faldo**
On his debut in the 1977 Ryder Cup, Nick Faldo won all three matches he played.

TOP 10 MOST RYDER CUP APPEARANCES*

	PLAYER	TEAM#	YEARS	APPEARANCES
1	Nick Faldo	E	1977–97	11
2 =	Christy O'Connor Sr	E	1955–73	10
=	Bernhard Langer	E	1981–2002	10
4	Dai Rees	E	1937–61	9
5 =	Peter Alliss	E	1953–69	8
=	Bernard Hunt	E	1953–69	8
=	Billy Casper	USA	1961–75	8
=	Neil Coles	E	1961–77	8
=	Bernard Gallacher	E	1969–83	8
=	Ian Woosnam	E	1983–87	8
=	Ray Floyd	USA	1969–93	8
=	Lanny Wadkins	USA	1977–93	8
=	Severiano Ballesteros	E	1979–95	8
=	Sam Torrance	E	1981–95	8
=	Colin Montgomerie	E	1991–2006	8
=	Phil Mickleson	USA	1995–2010	8

* As a player, up to and including 2010
\# USA = member of the US Ryder Cup team; E = member of the European Ryder Cup team (1979–2010), Great Britain & Ireland (1973–77) and/or Great Britain (1927–71)

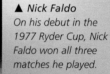

TOP 10 CAREER MONEY-WINNERS ON THE CHAMPIONS TOUR*

	GOLFER	YEARS	WINNINGS (US$)
1	Hale Irwin	1995–2010	25,570,804
2	Gil Morgan	1996–2010	19,855,653
3	Dana Quigley	1997–2010	14,715,857
4	Bruce Fleisher	1999–2010	14,592,350
5	Tom Kite	2000–10	14,525,662
6	Larry Nelson	1997–2010	13,928,229
7	Jim Thorpe	1999–2009	13,423,156
8	Allen Doyle	1998–2010	13,285,174
9	Tom Jenkins	1998–2010	13,097,063
10	Tom Watson	1999–2010	12,584,440

* As of 1 January 2011

Source: PGA Tour

The Champions Tour is a season-long series of tournaments organized by the PGA Tour in the USA and other parts of the world for golfers over the age of 50. It started life as the Senior PGA Tour in 1980 and changed its name to the Champions Tour in 2002.

TOP 10 MOST PGA CAREER WINS*

	PLAYER	YEARS	TOTAL
1	SAM SNEAD	1936–65	82
2	JACK NICKLAUS	1962–86	73
3	TIGER WOODS	1996–2009	71
4	BEN HOGAN	1938–59	64
5	ARNOLD PALMER	1955–73	62
6	BYRON NELSON	1935–51	52
7	BILLY CASPER	1956–75	51
8	WALTER HAGEN	1916–36	44
9	CARY MIDDLECOFF	1945–61	40
10	= GENE SARAZEN	1922–41	39
	= TOM WATSON	1974–98	39

* On the PGA Tour, up to and including 1 January 2011

All golfers in the Top 10 are from the USA. The most wins by a non-American is 34 by Vijay Singh (Fiji). The record on the European Tour is 50 by Severiano Ballesteros (Spain) between 1976 and 1995.

TOP 10 MOST WINS ON THE LPGA TOUR

	PLAYER*	YEARS	WINS#
1	Kathy Whitworth	1962–85	88
2	Mickey Wright	1956–73	82
3	Annika Sörenstam, Sweden	1995–2008	72
4	Patty Berg	1937–62	60
5	Louise Suggs	1946–62	58
6	Betsy Rawls	1951–72	55
7	Nancy Lopez	1978–97	48
8	JoAnne Carner	1969–85	43
9	Sandra Haynie	1962–82	42
10	Babe Zaharias	1940–55	41

* All golfers from the USA unless otherwise stated
# As of 1 January 2011

Source: LPGA

▶ Jack Nicklaus
As well as 73 Tour wins, Jack Nicklaus won 10 Champions Tour events, the last in 1996.

ON FOUR WHEELS

◄ *Jimmie Johnson*
In 2010, Johnson became the first man to win five consecutive NASCAR championships.

	DRIVER	FIRST WIN	LAST WIN	TOTAL WINS
1	Richard Petty	1960	1984	200
2	David Pearson	1961	1980	105
3 =	Bobby Allison	1966	1988	84
=	Darrell Waltrip	1975	1992	84
5	Cale Yarborough	1965	1985	83
6	Jeff Gordon	1994	2009	82
7	Dale Earnhardt	1979	2000	76
8	Rusty Wallace	1986	2004	55
9	Lee Petty	1949	1961	54
10	Jimmie Johnson	2002	2010	53

* Up to and including 2010

Source: NASCAR

TOP 10 **MOST POLE POSITIONS IN A FORMULA ONE CAREER**

DRIVER / COUNTRY / YEARS / POLES*

1 Michael Schumacher, Germany 1994–2006
68

2 Ayrton Senna Brazil 1985–94
65

3 = Jim Clark UK 1962–68
33

= Alain Prost France 1981–93
33

5 Nigel Mansell UK 1984–94
32

6 Juan Manuel Fangio, Argentina 1950–58
29

7 Mika Häkkinen, Finland 1997–2000
26

8 = Niki Lauda Austria 1974–78
24

= Nelson Piquet Brazil 1980–87
24

10 = Damon Hill UK 1993–96
20

= Fernando Alonso Spain 2003–10
20

* To the end of the 2010 season

The Sprint Cup Series is the leading series of races organized by NASCAR (National Association for Stock Car Auto Racing) in the United States. It was known as the Strictly Stock Series in 1949, the Grand National Series between 1950–70, the Winston Cup Series 1971–2003 and the NEXTEL Cup Series from 2004–07 before adopting its current style, NASCAR Sprint Cup Series, in 2008.

In 1992, Nigel Mansell started in pole position a record 14 times in one season. In the other two races he started, he was in second place on the grid in the Hungarian Grand Prix and in third place in the Canadian Grand Prix.

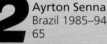

► *Michael Schumacher*
Since his return to Formula One in 2010, Schumacher has been unable to add to his record 68 poles.

THE 10 **LATEST WINNERS OF THE INDIANAPOLIS 500**

YEAR	DRIVER / COUNTRY	START POSITION	CAR	SPEED KM/H	MPH
2010	Dario Franchitti, UK	3	Dallara	226.990	141.045
2009	Hélio Castroneves, Brazil	1	Dallara	224.864	139.724
2008	Scott Dixon, New Zealand	1	Dallara	226.366	140.657
2007	Dario Franchitti, UK	3	Dallara	225.191	139.927
2006	Sam Hornish Jr, USA	1	Dallara	228.985	142.285
2005	Dan Wheldon, UK	16	Dallara	224.308	139.379
2004	Buddy Rice, USA	1	Panoz G Force	222.024	137.959
2003	Gil de Ferran, Brazil	10	Panoz G Force	228.633	142.066
2002	Hélio Castroneves, Brazil	13	Dallara	229.052	142.326
2001	Hélio Castroneves, Brazil	11	Dallara	224.142	139.275

▲ *Sebastian Vettel*
Vettel is the second German Formula One champion after Michael Schumacher.

TOP 10 **YOUNGEST FORMULA ONE CHAMPIONS***

	DRIVER / COUNTRY	SEASON	AGE# YRS	DAYS
1	Sebastian Vettel, Germany	2010	23	133
2	Lewis Hamilton, UK	2008	23	301
3	Fernando Alonso, Spain	2005	24	58
4	Emerson Fittipaldi, Brazil	1972	25	273
5	Michael Schumacher, Germany	1994	25	314
6	Niki Lauda, Austria	1975	26	197
7	Jacques Villeneuve, Canada	1997	26	200
8	Jim Clark, USA	1963	27	188
9	Kimi Räikkönen, Finland	2007	28	4
10	Jochen Rindt†, Austria	1970	28	140

* Up to and including 2010
# At first world title win
† Posthumous world champion (age at death)

ON TWO WHEELS

TOP 10 MOST CYCLING GRAND TOUR WINS*

	RIDER / COUNTRY	YEARS	TOUR	VUELTA	GIRO	TOTAL#
1	Eddy Merckx, Belgium	1968–74	5	1	5	11
2	Bernard Hinault, France	1978–85	5	2	3	10
3	Jacques Anquetil, France	1957–64	5	1	2	8
4 =	Lance Armstrong, USA	1999–2005	7	0	0	7
=	Fausto Coppi, Italy	1940–53	2	0	5	7
=	Miguel Indurain, Spain	1991–95	5	0	2	7
7 =	Gino Bartali, Italy	1936–48	2	0	3	5
=	Afredo Binda, Italy	1923–29	0	0	5	5
=	Alberto Contador, Spain	2007–10	3	1	1	5
=	Felice Gimondi, Italy	1965–76	1	1	3	5

* Aggregate wins in the three Grand Tours – Tour de France, Vuelta a España and Giro d'Italia
\# Up to and including 2010

TOP 10 MOST TOUR DE FRANCE APPEARANCES

	RIDER / COUNTRY	YEARS	RACES*
1	Joop Zoetemelk, Netherlands	1970–86	16
2 =	Lucien Van Impe, Belgium	1969–85	15
=	Guy Nulens, Belgium	1980–94	15
=	Viatcheslav Ekimov, Russia	1990–2006	15
=	George Hincapie, USA	1996–2010	15
=	Christophe Moreau, France	1996–2010	15
7 =	André Darrigade, France	1953–66	14
=	Raymond Poulidor, France	1962–74	14
=	Sean Kelly, Ireland	1978–92	14
=	Erik Zabel, Germany	1994–2008	14
=	Stuart O'Grady, Australia	1997–2010	14

* Up to and including 2010

Joop Zoetemelk won the Tour just once, in 1980. He finished second on a further six occasions, including his debut year, 1970.

TOP 10 MOST DAYS SPENT WEARING THE TOUR DE FRANCE LEADER'S JERSEY

RIDER / COUNTRY / DAYS*

1 Eddy Merckx, Belgium 111
2 Lance Armstrong, USA 83
3 Bernard Hinault, France 79
4 Miguel Indurain, Spain 60
5 Jacques Anquetil, France 52
6 Antonin Magne, France 39
7 Nicolas Frantz, Luxembourg 37
8 André Leducq, France 35
9 Louison Bobet, France 34
10 Ottavio Bottecchia, Italy 33

* Up to and including 2010

Source: Le Tour de France

▼ *Lance Armstrong*
Less than three years before his first Tour win, Lance Armstrong underwent surgery and chemotherapy for cancer.

Not surprisingly, Eddy Merckx holds the record for the most stage wins in the Tour de France – 34 between 1969 and 1975.

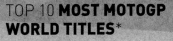
◀ *Antonio Cairoli*
Cairoli made his debut in 2002 and won his first world title in 2005.

TOP 10 **MOST MOTOCROSS WORLD TITLES**

	RIDER / COUNTRY	YEARS	MX1	MX2	MX3	500 CC	250 CC	125 CC	TOTAL*
1	Stefan Everts, Belgium	1991–2006	4	0	0	2	3	1	10
2	Joël Robert, Belgium	1964–72	0	0	0	0	6	0	6
3 =	Roger de Coster, Belgium	1971–76	0	0	0	5	0	0	5
=	Eric Geboers, Belgium	1982–90	0	0	0	2	1	2	5
=	Georges Jobé, Belgium	1980–92	0	0	0	3	2	0	5
=	Joël Smets, Belgium	1995–2003	0	0	1	4	0	0	5
7 =	Antonio Cairoli, Italy	2005–10	2	2	0	0	0	0	4
=	Harry Everts, Belgium	1975–81	0	0	0	0	1	3	4
=	Torsten Hallman, Sweden	1962–67	0	0	0	0	4	0	4
=	Heikki Mikkola, Finland	1974–78	0	0	0	3	1	0	4

* Up to and including 2010

Source: FIM (Fédération Internationale de Motocyclisme)

TOP 10 **MOST MOTOGP WORLD TITLES***

	RIDER / COUNTRY / YEARS	TITLES
1	Giacomo Agostini, Italy 1966–72, 1975	8
2	Valentino Rossi, Italy 2001–05, 2008–09	7
3	Michael Doohan, Australia, 1994–98	5
4 =	Geoff Duke, UK 1951, 1953–55	4
=	John Surtees, UK 1956, 1958–60	4
=	Mike Hailwood, UK 1962–65	4
=	Eddie Lawson, USA 1984, 1986, 1988–89	4
8 =	Kenny Roberts, USA 1978–80	3
=	Wayne Rainey, USA 1990–92	3
10 =	Umberto Masetti, Italy 1950, 1952	2
=	Phil Read, UK 1973–74	2
=	Barry Sheene, UK 1976–77	2
=	Freddie Spencer, USA 1983, 1985	2

* Moto GP 2002–10, 500cc 1949–2001

The Motorcross classes are:

MX1 for 2-stroke machines up to 250cc or 4-stroke machines up to 450cc

MX2 for 2-stroke machines up to 125cc or 4-stroke machines up to 250cc

MX3 for 2-stroke machines up to 500cc or 4-stroke machines up to 650cc

▶ *Valentino Rossi*
As of the the end of 2010, Rossi had taken 138 podiums out of 181 MotoGP starts.

HORSE SPORTS

THE 10 LATEST WINNERS OF THE UK TRIPLE CROWN*

YEAR	HORSE	JOCKEY#
1970	Nijinsky	Lester Piggott
1935	Bahram	Freddie Fox
1918	Gainsborough	Joe Childs
1917	Gay Crusader	Steve Donoghue
1915	Pommern	Steve Donoghue
1903	Rock Sand	Danny Maher
1900	Diamond Jubilee	Herbert Jones
1899	Flying Fox	Morny Cannon
1897	Galtee More	Charlie Wood
1893	Isinglass	Tommy Loates

* Up to and including 2010
# All jockeys from Great Britain

Workforce's winning distance of seven lengths was the biggest since Shergar's record 10-length victory in 1981. For Workforce's jockey, Ryan Moore, it was only his second Classic win – the first had taken place just 24 hours earlier, when he rode Snow Fairy to victory in the Oaks.

THE 10 FASTEST WINNING TIMES OF THE EPSOM DERBY*

	HORSE	YEAR	JOCKEY	TIME (MINS:SECS)
1	Workforce	2010	Ryan Moore	2:31.33
2	Lammtarra	1995	Walter Swinburn	2:32.31
3	Galileo	2001	Mick Kinane	2:33.27
4	Kris Kin	2003	Kieren Fallon	2:33.35
5	Royal Palace	1967	George Moore	2:33.36
6	North Light	2004	Kieren Fallon	2:33.72
7	Mahmoud	1936	Charlie Smirke	2:33.80
8	Kahyasi	1988	Ray Cochrane	2:33.84
9	High Rise	1998	Olivier Peslier	2:33.88
10	Reference Point	1987	Steve Cauthen	2:33.90

* Up to and including 2010

TOP 10 MONEY-WINNING JOCKEYS IN THE BREEDERS CUP

	JOCKEY*	YEARS	WINS	MONEY WON (US$)#
1	Pat Day	1984–2004	12	$23,033,360
2	Jerry Bailey	1986–2005	15	$22,006,440
3	Frankie Dettori, Italy	1990–2010	10	$17,831,172
4	Garrett Gomez	1994–2010	12	$17,758,600
5	Chris McCarron	1984–2001	9	$17,669,600
6	Mike Smith	1990–2010	13	$17,274,760
7	John Velazquez, Puerto Rico	1995–2010	9	$14,873,930
8	Gary Stevens	1984–2005	8	$13,723,910
9	Corey Nakatani	1990–2006	7	$9,965,480
10	Edgar Prado, Peru	1992–2010	4	$8,729,180

* All jockeys from the USA unless otherwise stated.
# Up to and including 2010
Source: Breeders' Cup

▲ Jerry Bailey
Texan Jerry Bailey's 15 Breeders Cup wins is an all-time record. He won the Classic five times throughout his career.

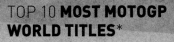

◄ *Antonio Cairoli*
Cairoli made his debut in
2002 and won his first
world title in 2005.

TOP 10 **MOST MOTOCROSS WORLD TITLES**

	RIDER / COUNTRY	YEARS	MX1	MX2	MX3	500 CC	250 CC	125 CC	TOTAL*
1	Stefan Everts, Belgium	1991–2006	4	0	0	2	3	1	10
2	Joël Robert, Belgium	1964–72	0	0	0	0	6	0	6
3 =	Roger de Coster, Belgium	1971–76	0	0	0	5	0	0	5
=	Eric Geboers, Belgium	1982–90	0	0	0	2	1	2	5
=	Georges Jobé, Belgium	1980–92	0	0	0	3	2	0	5
=	Joël Smets, Belgium	1995–2003	0	0	1	4	0	0	5
7 =	Antonio Cairoli, Italy	2005–10	2	2	0	0	0	0	4
=	Harry Everts, Belgium	1975–81	0	0	0	0	1	3	4
=	Torsten Hallman, Sweden	1962–67	0	0	0	0	4	0	4
=	Heikki Mikkola, Finland	1974–78	0	0	0	3	1	0	4

* Up to and including 2010

Source: FIM (Fédération Internationale de Motocyclisme)

TOP 10 **MOST MOTOGP WORLD TITLES***

	RIDER / COUNTRY / YEARS	TITLES
1	Giacomo Agostini, Italy 1966–72, 1975	8
2	Valentino Rossi, Italy 2001–05, 2008–09	7
3	Michael Doohan, Australia, 1994–98	5
4 =	Geoff Duke, UK 1951, 1953–55	4
=	John Surtees, UK 1956, 1958–60	4
=	Mike Hailwood, UK 1962–65	4
=	Eddie Lawson, USA 1984, 1986, 1988–89	4
8 =	Kenny Roberts, USA 1978–80	3
=	Wayne Rainey, USA 1990–92	3
10 =	Umberto Masetti, Italy 1950, 1952	2
=	Phil Read, UK 1973–74	2
=	Barry Sheene, UK 1976–77	2
=	Freddie Spencer, USA 1983, 1985	2

* Moto GP 2002–10, 500cc 1949–2001

The Motorcross classes are:

MX1 for 2-stroke machines up to 250cc or 4-stroke machines up to 450cc

MX2 for 2-stroke machines up to 125cc or 4-stroke machines up to 250cc

MX3 for 2-stroke machines up to 500cc or 4-stroke machines up to 650cc

► *Valentino Rossi*
As of the the end of
2010, Rossi had taken
138 podiums out of
181 MotoGP starts.

HORSE SPORTS

THE 10 LATEST WINNERS OF THE UK TRIPLE CROWN*

YEAR	HORSE	JOCKEY#
1970	Nijinsky	Lester Piggott
1935	Bahram	Freddie Fox
1918	Gainsborough	Joe Childs
1917	Gay Crusader	Steve Donoghue
1915	Pommern	Steve Donoghue
1903	Rock Sand	Danny Maher
1900	Diamond Jubilee	Herbert Jones
1899	Flying Fox	Morny Cannon
1897	Galtee More	Charlie Wood
1893	Isinglass	Tommy Loates

* Up to and including 2010
# All jockeys from Great Britain

Workforce's winning distance of seven lengths was the biggest since Shergar's record 10-length victory in 1981. For Workforce's jockey, Ryan Moore, it was only his second Classic win – the first had taken place just 24 hours earlier, when he rode Snow Fairy to victory in the Oaks.

TOP 10 MONEY-WINNING JOCKEYS IN THE BREEDERS CUP

	JOCKEY*	YEARS	WINS	MONEY WON (US$)#
1	Pat Day	1984–2004	12	$23,033,360
2	Jerry Bailey	1986–2005	15	$22,006,440
3	Frankie Dettori, Italy	1990–2010	10	$17,831,172
4	Garrett Gomez	1994–2010	12	$17,758,600
5	Chris McCarron	1984–2001	9	$17,669,600
6	Mike Smith	1990–2010	13	$17,274,760
7	John Velazquez, Puerto Rico	1995–2010	9	$14,873,930
8	Gary Stevens	1984–2005	8	$13,723,910
9	Corey Nakatani	1990–2006	7	$9,965,480
10	Edgar Prado, Peru	1992–2010	4	$8,729,180

* All jockeys from the USA unless otherwise stated.
# Up to and including 2010

Source: Breeders' Cup

THE 10 FASTEST WINNING TIMES OF THE EPSOM DERBY*

	HORSE	YEAR	JOCKEY	TIME (MINS:SECS)
1	Workforce	2010	Ryan Moore	2:31.33
2	Lammtarra	1995	Walter Swinburn	2:32.31
3	Galileo	2001	Mick Kinane	2:33.27
4	Kris Kin	2003	Kieren Fallon	2:33.35
5	Royal Palace	1967	George Moore	2:33.36
6	North Light	2004	Kieren Fallon	2:33.72
7	Mahmoud	1936	Charlie Smirke	2:33.80
8	Kahyasi	1988	Ray Cochrane	2:33.84
9	High Rise	1998	Olivier Peslier	2:33.88
10	Reference Point	1987	Steve Cauthen	2:33.90

* Up to and including 2010

▲ Jerry Bailey
Texan Jerry Bailey's 15 Breeders Cup wins is an all-time record. He won the Classic five times throughout his career.

The Hambletonian and Little Brown Jug are the two most prestigious races in the harness racing calendar. The Hambletonian, for three-year-old trotters, was first staged during the 1926 New York State Fair at Syracuse. The race is named after Hambletonian, the greatest sire in harness racing history. Since 1981 the permanent home of the race has been the Meadowlands Race Track in East Rutherford, New Jersey.

TOP 10 MOST WINS IN THE HAMBLETONIAN AND LITTLE BROWN JUG*

	DRIVER	YEARS	H#	LBJ#	TOTAL
1	John Campbell	1977–2006	6	4	10
2 =	Billy Haughton	1955–80	4	5	9
=	Mike Lachance	1988–2003	4	5	9
4	Stanley Dancer	1961–83	4	4	8
5	Ron Pierce	1993–2010	3	3	6
6 =	John Simpson Sr	1956–64	2	3	5
=	Frank Ervin	1949–66	2	3	5
8 =	Ben White	1933–43	4	0	4
=	Joe O'Brien	1955–73	2	2	4
10 =	Henry Thomas	1937–44	3	0	3
=	Del Cameron	1954–67	3	0	3
=	Howard Beissinger	1969–78	3	0	3
=	Bill O'Donnell	1985–86	1	2	3
=	Ron Waples	1983–92	1	2	3
=	Jack Moiseyev	1991–96	1	2	3

* Up to and including 2010
# H = Hambletonian; LBJ = Little Brown Jug

▲ **Hambletonian**
The Hambletonian is one of three races that make up the Triple Crown for harness racing trotters.

TOP 10 OLYMPIC EQUESTRIAN NATIONS*

	COUNTRY	DRESSAGE	EVENTING	JUMPING	TOTAL
1	Germany	11	4	6	21
2	Sweden	7	7	3	17
3	France#	3	3	6	12
4 =	USA	0	6	5	11
=	West Germany†	7	1	3	11
6	Netherlands	3	5	2	10
7	Italy#	0	3	4	7
8 =	Australia	0	6	0	6
=	Great Britain	0	5	1	6
=	USSR	4	1	1	6

* Based on gold medals won in the three main disciplines: Dressage, Three-Day Eventing and Show Jumping, up to and including 2008
# France and Italy totals include one shared gold in the now-discontinued High Jump event held in 1900
† Not including the five gold medals won by the United Germany team, 1956–64

▲ **Galloping to gold**
The most successful German in Equestrian Events is Dr Reiner Klimke, who won six Dressage gold medals between 1964 and 1988. He also won two bronze medals.

WATER SPORTS

TOP 10 MOST WORLD AND OLYMPIC DIVING GOLD MEDALS*

	DIVER / COUNTRY	M/F	YEARS	OLYMPIC GAMES	WORLD CHAMPS	TOTAL
1	Guo Jingjing, China	F	2001–09	4	10	14
2	Greg Louganis, USA	M	1978–88	4	5	9
3	Dmitri Sautin, Russia	M	1994–2003	2	5	7
4	=Fu Mingxia, China	F	1991–2000	4	2	6
	=Wu Minxia, China	F	2001–09	2	4	6
6	=Klaus Dibiasi, Italy	M	1968–76	3	2	5
	=Gao Min, China	F	1986–92	2	3	5
	=Qin Kai, China	M	2007–09	1	4	5
	=Wang Feng, China	M	2001–09	1	4	5
10	=Pat McCormick, USA	F	1952–56	4	0	4
	=Phil Boggs, USA	M	1973–78	1	3	4

* In individual and synchronized events at the Olympic Games 1904–2008 and the World Aquatics Championships 1973–2009

TOP 10 OLYMPIC AND WORLD CHAMPIONSHIP WATER POLO MEDAL-WINNING COUNTRIES

	COUNTRY	GOLD	SILVER	BRONZE	TOTAL*
1	Hungary	13	10	4	27
2	USA	4	7	7	18
3	Italy	8	4	4	16
4	Yugoslavia	5	5	4	14
5	USSR	4	3	4	11
6	=Russia	0	1	7	8
	=Spain	3	4	1	8
8	Netherlands	2	3	2	7
9	Belgium	0	4	2	6
10	Australia	2	1	2	5

* Up to and including the 2008 Olympic Games and 2009 World Aquatics Championships

TOP 10 MOST WORLD AQUATIC CHAMPIONSHIP TITLES*

	SWIMMER / COUNTRY	YEARS	IND.	RELAY	TOTAL
1	Michael Phelps, USA	2001–09	13	9	22
2	Ian Thorpe, Australia	1998–2003	6	5	11
3	=Grant Hackett, Australia	1998–2005	7	3	10
	=Aaron Peirsol, USA	2001–09	7	3	10
5	=Kornelia Ender, East Germany	1973–75	4	4	8
	=Libby Lenton, Australia	2005–07	4	4	8
7	=Jim Montgomery, USA	1973–78	2	5	7
	=Kristin Otto, East Germany	1982–86	3	4	7
	=Jenny Thompson, USA	1991–2003	3	4	7
	=Michael Klim, Australia	1998–2007	2	5	7
	=Leisel Jones, Australia	2001–07	4	3	7
	=Ryan Lochte, USA	2005–09	3	4	7

* In individual long course events and relays up to and including 2009

◄ *Guo Jingjing* Chinese diving champion Guo Jingjing was just 18 when she won her first Olympic medal – a silver at Sydney in 2000.

TOP 10 MOST FORMULA ONE POWERBOAT WORLD TITLES

	DRIVER / COUNTRY	YEARS*	TITLES
1	Guido Cappellini, Italy	1993–2009	10
2	Scott Gillman, USA	1997–2006	4
3	Renato Molinari, Italy	1981–84	3
4	=Jonathan Jones, UK	1991–98	2
	=Sami Seliö, Finland	2007–10	2
6	=Bob Spalding, UK	1985	1
	=Fabrizio Bocca, USA	1992	1
	=Gene Thibodaux, USA	1986	1
	=Jay Price, Qatar	2008	1
	=John Hill, UK	1990	1
	=Roger Jenkins, UK	1982	1

* There was no championship 1987–89

Source: UIM

THE 10 FASTEST WINNING TIMES IN THE SYDNEY TO HOBART RACE*

	YACHT / COUNTRY	YEAR	ELAPSED TIME#
1	Wild Oats XI, Australia	2005	1:18:40:10
2	Nokia, Denmark	1999	1:19:48:02
3	Wild Oats XI, Australia	2008	1:20:34:14
4	Wild Oats XI, Australia	2007	1:21:24:32
5	Alfa Romeo, Australia/New Zealand	2002	2:04:58:52
6	Wild Oats XI, Australia	2010	2:07:37:20
7	Wild Oats XI, Australia	2006	2:08:52:33
8	Alfa Romeo II, Australia/New Zealand	2009	2:09:02:10
9	Nicorette, Sweden	2000	2:14:02:09
10	Morning Glory, Germany	1996	2:14:07:10

* Up to and including 2010
# days:hours:minutes:seconds

The first Sydney to Hobart race took place in 1945 and was initially going to be an informal cruise, until British naval officer John Illingworth suggested it should be a race. It starts in Sydney Harbour at 1.00 pm on Boxing Day each year, and takes in 628 nautical miles. One of the toughest yacht races in the world, it is regarded as a sporting icon in Australia, alongside the Melbourne Cup and Ashes Test matches.

► Guido Cappellini
Between 1993 and 1996 Italian Cappellini won the Formula One Powerboat world title a record four consecutive years. He also won three consecutive titles in 2001–03.

WINTER SPORTS

TOP 10 MOST ALPINE SKIING WORLD CUP RACE WINS (MEN)

	SKIER / COUNTRY	FIRST/LAST WIN	WINS*
1	Ingemar Stenmark, Sweden	1974–89	86
2	Hermann Maier, Austria	1997–2008	54
3	Alberto Tomba, Italy	1987–98	50
4	Marc Girardelli, Luxembourg	1983–96	43
5	Pirmin Zurbriggen, Switzerland	1982–90	40
6	Benjamin Raich, Austria	1999–2009	35
7	Bode Miller, USA	2001–10	32
8	Stephan Eberharter, Austria	1998–2004	29
9	Phil Mahre, USA	1976–1983	27
10	Franz Klammer, Austria	1973–1984	26

* Up to and including 2011

Source: FIS

The very first winner of a men's World Cup event was Heinrich Messner of Switzerland, who won the slalom at Berchtesgaden, West Germany, on 5 January 1967.

◀ **Hermann Maier**
Austria's Hermann Maier won four overall World Cup titles, two Olympic gold medals and three World Championship gold medals.

▼ **Vreni Schneider**
Switzerland's Vreni Schneider was voted her country's 'Sportswoman of the 20th Century'.

TOP 10 MOST ALPINE SKIING WORLD CUP RACE WINS (WOMEN)

	SKIER / COUNTRY	FIRST/LAST WIN	WINS*
1	Annemarie Moser-Pröll, Austria	1970–80	62
2	Vreni Schneider, Switzerland	1984–95	55
3	Renate Götschl, Austria	1993–2007	46
4	Anja Pärson, Sweden	1998–2011	42
5	Lindsey Vonn (née Kildow), USA	2004–11	41
6	Katja Seizinger, Germany	1991–98	36
7	Hanni Wenzel, Liechtenstein	1973–84	33
8	Erika Hess, Switzerland	1981–86	31
9	Janica Kostelic, Croatia	1999–2006	30
10	Marlies Schild, Austria	2004–11	29

* Up to and including 2011

Source: FIS

The first winner of a women's World Cup race was Nancy Greene of Canada, who won the slalom in West Germany, on 7 January 1967.

TOP 10 **MOST INDIVIDUAL SKI-JUMPING MEDALS AT THE NORDIC WORLD SKI CHAMPIONSHIPS**

	JUMPER / COUNTRY	YEARS	G	S	B	TOTAL*
1	Birger Ruud, Norway	1931–48	5	2	0	7
2	Adam Malysz, Poland	2001–11	4	1	1	6
3	Jens Weissflog, Germany	1985–95	2	1	2	5
4	= Janne Ahonen, Finland	1997–2005	2	0	2	4
	= Martin Schmitt, Germany	1999–2009	2	2	0	4
	= Sven Eriksson, Sweden	1931–36	0	1	3	4
	= Jari Puikkonen, Finland	1980–89	1	2	1	4
	= Masahiko Harada, Japan	1993–99	2	1	1	4
	= Reidar Andersen, Norway	1930–37	0	3	1	4
	= Andreas Goldberger, Austria	1993–97	0	2	2	4
	= Helmut Recknagel, West Germany	1958–62	2	0	2	4
	= Matti Nykänen, Finland	1982–89	1	1	2	4
	= Simon Ammann, Switzerland	2007–11	1	1	2	4

* Up to and including the 2011 championship

Source: FIS

▼ *Adam Malysz*
Despite his World Championship successes, Poland's Adam Malysk has not yet won an Olympic gold medal. He took a bronze and silver at Salt Lake City in 2002, and two silver medals at Vancouver in 2010.

THE 10 **FASTEST WINNING TIMES IN THE MEN'S 500 METRES SPEED-SKATING OLYMPIC FINAL**

SKATER / COUNTRY / YEAR / VENUE / TIME (SECS)

1 Casey FitzRandolph,
USA
2002
Salt Lake City, USA
34.62

2 Joey Cheek,
USA
2006
Turin, Italy
34.88

3 Tae-Bum Mo,
South Korea
2010
Vancouver, Canada
34.91

4 Hiroyasu Shimizu,
Japan
1998
Nagano, Japan
35.68

5 Aleksandr Golubev,
Russia
1994
Lillehammer, Norway
36.33

6 Uwe-Jens Mey,
East Germany
1988
Calgary, Canada
36.45

7 Uwe-Jens Mey,
Germany
1992
Albertville, France
37.14

8 Eric Heiden,
USA
1980
Lake Placid, USA
38.03

9 Sergey Fokichev,
USSR
1984
Sarajevo, Yugoslavia
38.19

10 Yevgeniy Kulikov,
USSR
1976
Innsbruck, Austria
39.17

EXTREME SPORTS

The Ironman competition consists of a 2.4-mile open water swim, 112-mile cycle race and a full marathon of 26 miles 385 yards. The fastest time is 8 hours 4 minutes 8 seconds by Luc Van Lierde of Belgium in 1996. The women's record is 8 hours 54 minutes 2 seconds by Britain's Chrissie Wellington in 2009. Paula Newby-Fraser (Zimbabwe) holds the record for the most wins – 8. The men's record is 6, held jointly by Dave Scott and Mark Allen (both USA).

▲ **Hawaiian extremes**
The Ironman World Championship has been held in Hawaii every year since 1978.

All winners are from the USA unless otherwise stated. The Olympia championships are international bodybuilding events organized by the International Federation of Body Building and Fitness (IFBB).

TOP 10 MOST WINNERS OF THE BODYBUILDING OLYMPIA CHAMPIONSHIPS*

	BODYBUILDER / YEARS	WINS
1	= Lee Haney 1984–91	8
	= Lenda Murray# 1990–2003	8
	= Ronnie Coleman 1998–2005	8
4	Arnold Schwarzenegger Austria 1970–80	7
5	= Cory Everson# 1984–89	6
	= Dorian Yates, UK 1992–97	6
	= Iris Kyle# 2004–10	6
8	= Kim Chizevsky# 1996–99	4
	= Jay Cutler 2006–10	4
10	= Sergio Oliva, Cuba 1967–69	3
	= Frank Zane 1977–79	3

* Men's and women's championships
\# Female champions

Source: IFBB

THE 10 LATEST WINNERS OF THE IRONMAN WORLD CHAMPIONSHIP

YEAR	MALE / COUNTRY	FEMALE / COUNTRY
2010	Chris McCormack, Australia	Mirinda Carfrae, Australia
2009	Craig Alexander, Australia	Chrissie Wellington, UK
2008	Craig Alexander, Australia	Chrissie Wellington, UK
2007	Chris McCormack, Australia	Chrissie Wellington, UK
2006	Normann Stadler, Germany	Michellie Jones, Australia
2005	Faris Al-Sultan, Germany	Natascha Badmann, Switzerland
2004	Normann Stadler, Germany	Natascha Badmann, Switzerland
2003	Peter Reid, Canada	Lori Bowden, Canada
2002	Tim DeBoom, USA	Natascha Badmann, Switzerland
2001	Tim DeBoom, USA	Natascha Badmann, Switzerland

▼ **Ronnie Coleman**
Coleman's eight Mr Olympia wins were in consecutive years.

1

TOP 10 **LEADING GOLD MEDALLISTS AT THE SUMMER X GAMES***

ATHLETE# / COUNTRY / SPORT / YEARS	GOLDS
1 **Dave Mirra**, USA BMX 1996–2005	13
2 **Travis Pastrana**, USA Moto X/rally car racing 1999–2010	10
3 **Tony Hawk**, USA Skateboarding 1995–2003	9
4 **Andy Macdonald**, USA Skateboarding 1996–2002	8
5 = **Fabiola da Silva**, Brazil In-line skating 1996–2007	7
= **Pierre-Luc Gagnon**, Canada Skateboarding 2002-10	7
7 = **Bucky Lasek**, USA Skateboarding 1999–2006	6
= **Jamie Bestwick**, England BMX 2000–10	6
9 = **Bob Burnquist**, Brazil Skateboarding 2001–08	5
= **Biker Sherlock**, USA Street luge 1996–98	5

* Up to and including X Games XVI in 2010.
# All male except Fabiola da Silva

Andy Macdonald holds the record for winning the most X Games medals – 15 in total. The first ESPN Extreme Games (now X Games) for 'alternative' sports were held in June/July 1995. The Games are held every year and since 1997 there has also been an annual Winter X Games.

▶ *Travis Pastrana*
Pastrana won the first three Moto X Freestyle titles in 1999, 2000 and 2001.

TOP 10 **FASTEST WINNING TIMES OF THE IDITAROD TRAIL SLED-DOG RACE***

	MUSHER#	YEAR	TIME
1	John Baker	2011	8d 18h 46m 39s
2	Martin Buser, Switzerland	2002	8d 22h 46m 02s
3	Lance Mackey	2010	8d 23h 59m 09s
4	Doug Swingley	2000	9d 00h 58m 06s
5	Doug Swingley	1995	9d 02h 42m 19s
6	Lance Mackey	2007	9d 05h 08m 41s
7	Jeff King	1996	9d 05h 43m 13s
8	Jeff King	1998	9d 05h 52m 26s
9	Martin Buser, Switzerland	1997	9d 08h 30m 45s
10	Jeff King	2006	9d 11h 11m 36s

* Up to and including 2011
# All mushers from the USA unless otherwise stated

Source: The Iditarod

▼ *Alaskan extremes*
The Iditarod is held annually, beginning on the first Saturday in March, and is a 1,868-km (1,161-mile) race across Alaska from Willow, near Anchorage, to Nome. First held in 1973 as a test of the best sled-dog mushers and teams, it has now evolved into a highly competitive race.

SPORTS MISCELLANY

TOP 10 HIGHEST-EARNING SPORTSWOMEN

SPORTSWOMAN*	SPORT	EARNINGS (US$)#
1 Maria Sharapova, Russia	Tennis	24,500,000
2 Serena Williams, USA	Tennis	20,200,000
3 Venus Williams, USA	Tennis	15,400,000
4 Danica Patrick, USA	Auto racing	12,000,000
5 Kim Yu-Na, South Korea	Figure skating	9,700,000
6 Annika Sorenstam, Sweden	Golf	8,000,000
7 Ana Ivanovic, Serbia	Tennis	7,200,000
8 Jelena Jankovic, Serbia	Tennis	5,300,000
9 Paula Creamer, USA	Golf	5,200,000
10 Lorena Ochoa, Mexico	Golf	5,000,000

* All from the USA unless otherwise stated
\# Based on earnings from prize money, endorsements and appearance fees in the 12 months to August 2010

Source: *Forbes* magazine

◀ *Maria Sharapova*
Sharapova has won three Grand Slam events: Wimbledon and the US and Australian Opens.

TOP 10 HIGHEST-EARNING SPORTSMEN

SPORTSMAN*	SPORT	EARNINGS (US$)#
1 Tiger Woods	Golf	105,000,000
2 Floyd Mayweather	Boxing	65,000,000
3 Kobe Bryant	Basketball	48,000,000
4 Phil Mickelson	Golf	46,000,000
5 David Beckham, UK	Soccer	43,700,000
6 Roger Federer, Switzerland	Tennis	43,000,000
7 LeBron James	Basketball	42,800,000
8 Manny Pacquiao, Philippines	Boxing	42,000,000
9 Eli Manning	Football	39,900,000
10 Terrell Suggs	Football	38,300,000

* All from the USA unless otherwise stated
\# Based on money earned from salaries, bonuses, prize money, endorsements and licensing income in the 12 months to July 2010
Source: *Forbes* magazine

◀ *Floyd Mayweather*
Mayweather received around $25 million for fighting Oscar de la Hoya in 2007.

THE 10 LATEST WINNERS OF THE BBC SPORTS PERSONALITY OF THE YEAR AWARD

YEAR / WINNER / SPORT

2010 Tony McCoy
Horse racing

2009 Ryan Giggs
Association Football

2008 Chris Hoy
Cycling

2007 Joe Calzaghe
Boxing

2006 Zara Phillips
Equestrian

2005 Andrew Flintoff
Cricket

2004 Kelly Holmes
Athletics

2003 Jonny Wilkinson
Rugby Union

2002 Paula Radcliffe
Athletics

2001 David Beckham
Association Football

Source: BBC

The BBC Sports Personality of the Year Award is presented in front of a live audience every December, with the winner being chosen following votes cast by viewing members. The recipient must either be born in Britain, or reside or partake in their particular sport in the UK. The award was first made in 1954.

TOP 10 MOST WATCHED SINGLE SPORTS EVENTS ON BRITISH TELEVISION

	EVENT	YEAR	AUDIENCE
1	World Cup Final, England v. West Germany	1966	32,300,000
2	FA Cup Final replay, Chelsea v. Leeds United	1970	28,490,000
3	World Heavyweight title fight, Muhammad Ali v. Joe Frazier	1971	27,300,000
4	World Cup, England v. Portugal	1966	26,500,000
5	World Cup, England v. West Germany	1970	26,300,000
6	European Cup Final, Manchester United v. Benfica	1968	26,000,000
7	European Cup Final, Leeds United v. Bayern Munich	1975	24,200,000
8	Winter Olympics Ice Dance Final, Torvill & Dean	1994	23,960,000
9	European Cup Final, Liverpool v. FC Brugge	1978	23,900,000
10	World Cup, England v. Argentina	1998	23,780,000

MOST VALUABLE SPORTING BRANDS

Forbes magazine works out value of sporting-team brands as a percentage of a team's overall value that is derived from its name, to calculate the most valuable sporting brands. In 2010, Manchester United were deposed by the New York Yankees thanks to their 27th World Series title, which pushed up the brand's merchandising revenue to US$328 million. Currently ranking third is Spanish soccer team Real Madrid, whose seven-year $1.4 billion television deal is the largest in professional sports. The Dallas Cowboys and European football teams Barcelona, Bayern Munich and Arsenal all hold Top 10 positions.

◄ *New York Yankees*
The Yankees are the most successful team in Major League Baseball.

FURTHER INFORMATION

THE UNIVERSE & THE EARTH

Caves
caverbob.com
Lists of long and deep caves

Disasters
emdat.be
Emergency Events Database covering major disasters since 1900

Encyclopedia Astronautica
astronautix.com
Spaceflight news and reference

Islands
worldislandinfo.com
Information on the world's islands

Mountains
peaklist.org
Lists of the world's tallest mountains

NASA
nasa.gov
The main website for the US space agency

Oceans
oceansatlas.org
The UN's resource on oceanographic issues

Planets
nineplanets.org
A multimedia tour of the Solar System

Rivers
rev.net/~aloe/river
The River Systems of the World website

Space exploration
spacefacts.de
Manned spaceflight data

LIFE ON EARTH

Animals
animaldiversity.ummz.umich.edu
A wealth of animal data

Birds
avibase.bsc-eoc.org
A database on the world's birds

Conservation
iucn.org
The leading nature conservation site

Endangered
cites.org
Lists of endangered species of flora and fauna

Extinct
nhm.ac.uk/nature-online/life/dinosaurs-other-extinct-creatures
Dinosaurs and other extinct animals

Fish
fishbase.org
Global information on fish

Food and Agriculture Organization
fao.org
Statistics from the UN's FAO website

Forests
fao.org/forestry
The FAO's forestry website

Insects
entnemdept.ufl.edu/walker/ufbir
The University of Florida Book of Insect Records

Sharks
flmnh.ufl.edu/fish/sharks
The Florida Museum of Natural History's shark attack files

THE HUMAN WORLD

Crime (UK)
homeoffice.gov.uk
Home Office crime and prison population figures

Leaders
terra.es/personal2/monolith
Facts about world leaders since 1945

Military
globalfirepower.com
World military statistics and rankings

Nobel Prizes
nobelprize.org
The official website of the Nobel Foundation

Population (UK)
statistics.gov.uk/hub/population
UK population figures

Religion
worldchristiandatabase.org
World religions data (subscription required)

Royalty
royal.gov.uk
The official site of the British monarchy

Rulers
rulers.org
A database of the world's rulers and political leaders

Supercentenarians
grg.org/calment.html
A world listing of those who have reached 110 or older

World Health Organization
who.int/en
World health information and advice

TOWN & COUNTRY

Bridges and tunnels
en.structurae.de
Facts and figures on the world's buildings, tunnels and other structures

Bridges (highest)
highestbridges.com
Detailed facts and stats on the world's highest bridges

Buildings
emporis.com/en
The Emporis database of high-rise and other buildings

Country and city populations
citypopulation.de
A searchable guide to the world's countries and major cities

Country data
cia.gov/library/publications/the-world-factbook
The CIA's acclaimed *World Factbook*

Country populations
un.org/esa/population/unpop
The UN's worldwide data on population issues

Development
worldbank.org
Development and other statistics from around the world

Population
census.gov/ipc
International population statistics

Skyscrapers
skyscraperpage.com
Data and images of the world's skyscrapers

Tunnels
lotsberg.net
A database of the longest rail, road and canal tunnels

CULTURE & LEARNING

Art
artnet.com
World art info, with price database available to subscribers

The Art Newspaper
theartnewspaper.com
News and views on the art world

The British Library
Catalogues and exhibitions in the national library

Education (UK)
education.gov.uk/researchandstatistics
Official statistics relating to education in the UK

Languages
ethnologue.com
Online reference work on the world's 6,909 living languages

The Man Booker Prize
themanbookerprize.com
Britain's most prestigious literary prize

Museums and galleries
culture24.org.uk
Exhibitions and cultural events in the UK

Newspapers
wan-press.org
The World Association of Newspapers' website

Oxford English Dictionary
oed.com
Accessible online to most UK public library subscribers

UNESCO
unesco.org
Comparative international statistics on education and culture

MUSIC

All Music Guide
allmusic.com
A comprehensive guide to all genres of music

Billboard
billboard.com
US music news and charts data

BRIT Awards
brits.co.uk
The official website for the popular music awards

The British Phonographic Industry Ltd
bpi.co.uk
Searchable database of gold discs and other certified awards

Grammy Awards
naras.org
The official site for the famous US music awards

Gramophone
gramophone.co.uk
The online site of the classical music magazine

MTV
mtv.co.uk
MTV UK music online

New Musical Express
nme.com
The online version of the music magazine

PRS for Music
prsformusic.com
The organization that collects performance royalties for musicians

Rock and Roll Hall of Fame
www.rockhall.com
The museum of the history of rock

ENTERTAINMENT

Academy Awards
oscars.org
The official 'Oscars' website

BAFTAs
bafta.org
The home of the BAFTA Awards

BBC
bbc.co.uk
Gateway to BBC TV and radio, with a powerful search engine

Film Distributors' Association
launchingfilms.com
Trade site for UK film releases and statistics

Golden Globe Awards
hfpa.org
Hollywood Foreign Press Association's Golden Globes site

Internet Movie Database
The best of the publicly accessible film websites; IMDbPro is available to subscribers

London Theatre Guide
londontheatre.co.uk
A comprehensive guide to West End theatre productions

Screen Daily
screendaily.com
Daily news from the film world at the website of UK weekly *Screen International*

Variety
variety.com
Extensive entertainment information (extra features available to subscribers)

Yahoo! Movies
uk.movies.yahoo.com
Charts plus features, trailers and links to the latest UK film releases

THE COMMERCIAL WORLD

The Economist
economist.com
Global economic and political news

Energy
bp.com
Online access to the *BP Statistical Review of World Energy*

Environment
epi.yale.edu
The latest Environmental Performance Index rankings

Internet
internetworldstats.com
Internet World Stats

Organization for Economic Co-operation and Development
oecd.org
World economic and social statistics

Rich lists
forbes.com
Forbes magazine's celebrated lists of the world's wealthiest people

Telecommunications
itu.int
Worldwide telecommunications statistics

UK tourist attractions
alva.org.uk
Information and visitor statistics on the UK's top tourist attractions

The World Bank
worldbank.org
World development, trade and labour statistics, now freely accessible

World Tourism Organization
world-tourism.org
The world's principal travel and tourism organization

ON THE MOVE

Aircraft crashes
baaa-acro.com
The Aircraft Crashes Record Office database

Airlines
airfleets.net
Statistics on the world's airlines and aircraft

Airports
airports.org
Airports Council International statistics on the world's airports

Air safety
aviation-safety.net
Data on air safety and accidents

Air speed records
fai.org/records
The website of the official air speed record governing body

Car manufacture
oica.net
The International Organization of Motor Vehicle Manufacturers' website

Metros
metrobits.org
An exploration of the world's metro systems

Rail
uic.org
World rail statistics

Railways
railwaygazette.com
The world's railway business in depth from *Railway Gazette International*

Shipwrecks
shipwreckregistry.com
A huge database of the world's wrecked and lost ships

SPORT

Athletics
iaaf.org
The world governing body of athletics

Cricket
espncricinfo.com
Comprehensive live cricket information

Cycling
uci.ch
The Union Cycliste Internationale, the competitive cycling governing body

FIFA
fifa.com
The official website of FIFA, the world governing body of soccer

Formula One
formula1.com
The official F1 website

Olympics
olympic.org
The official Olympics website

Premier League
premierleague.com
The official website of the Premier League

Rugby
itsrugby.co.uk
Comprehensive rugby site

Skiing
fis-ski.com
Fédèration Internationale de Ski, the world governing body of skiing and snowboarding

Tennis
lta.org.uk
The official site of the British Lawn Tennis Association

INDEX

PICTURE CREDITS

Activision
65t Activision Blizzard.

American Motorcyclist Association
189b.

AKG
138-139b Paramount Pictures/album/akg-images;144b Warner Bros./album/akg-images; 152t Photo: Pixar Animation Studios/Walt Disney Pictures/Album/akg-images.

The Art Archive
117t The Art Archive / Musée d'Orsay Paris / Alfredo Dagli Orti .

Bridgeman Art Library
118t Private Collection/Bridgeman Art Library.

Corbis
10b © Mike Agliolo; 11 © Mark M. Lawrence; 18l © Maggie Steber/National Geographic Society; 19l © Russ Heinl/All Canada Photos; 20 © Paul Harris/JAI; 22tl © George Steinmetz; 22c © George Hammerstein; 23t © Stringer/Russia/Reuters; 23b © Matthieu Paley; 25l © Ed Darack/Science Faction; 24b © Jim Zuckerman; 26t © Frans Lemmens; 26b © Ocean; 28 © Andrew McConnell/Robert Harding World Imagery; 28b © Cezaro de Luca/epa; 29b © Ziyah Gafic/VII Network; 30b © Adi Weda/epa; 32-33 © Gerd Ludwig; 34l © Louie Psihoyos/Science Faction; 36c © Brian J. Skerry/National Geographic Society; 37c & 37t© DLILLC; 38-39b © Toshiki Sawaguchi/epa; 39br © Jeff Vanuga; 39tr ©Remy Steinegger/Reuters; 41c © Fred Buyle/Realis Agence; 40-41b © Gallo Images; 40tl © Paul A. Souders; 42-43t © Tom Brakefield; 43b © Frans Lanting; 44t © Thomas Marent/Visuals Unlimited; 45t © Tobias Bernhard; 46tl © Denis Scott; 47tr © Joe McDonald; 48b ©LWA-Dann Tardif; 52t © Frans Lanting; 53c © Beawiharta/Reuters; 54-55 © Matthias Kulka; 57r © Bettmann; 58t © Alessandro Della Bella/Keystone; 59br © Robert Gilhooly/epa; 60b © Gideon Mendel/ActionAid; 62b © Jalil Rezayee/epa; 63t © Imaginechina; 64-65 background © Gideon Mendel/In Pictures; 66bl © Yann Arthus-Bertrand; 67tl © Alai Bazil/epa; 67br © Alan Crowhurst/epa; 68tl © Bettmann; 68b © Mark Wilson/Pool; 69b © Luke MacGregor/Reuters; 70cl © Bettmann; 70cr © Hulton-Deutsch Collection; 70b © Bettmann; 71br © Underwood & Underwood; 72t © Reuters; 73tl © HO/Reuters; 73tr © Luis Galdamez/Reuters; 74-75t © Shepard Sherbell/SABA; 76-77 background © Hulton-Deutsch Collection; 77br © Bettmann; 77c © Bettmann; 76t © Hulton-Deutsch Collection; 80t © Paul Bowen/Science Faction; 80b © Korea News Service/X01654/Reuters; 81b © Ed Darack/Science

Faction; 83t © Paolo Whitaker/X00921/Reuters; 82-83 background © John Van Hasselt; 84-85 © Zhang Chao/Xinhua Press; 86b © Jose Fuste Raga; 87t © Danny Lehman; 88b © Philippe Lissac/Godong; 89b © Martin Harvey; 90b © Khaled Al-Hariri/X00374/Reuters; 91b © Christophe Calais; 92t © Jose Fuste Raga; 92-93b © Joson; 93c © Stuart Freedman/In Pictures; 95t; 96t © Michael Fiala/Reuters; 99t © Richard Klune; 98c © Joseph Sohm; Visions of America; 98t © YNA/epa; 100b © Martial Trezzini/epa; 101b © Martin Jones; 104t © Louise Gubb; 105t © Guo Cheng/XinHua/Xinhua Press; 107t © Kimberly White/Reuters; 109t © Blaine Harrington III; 109c © Blue Lantern Studio; 112tr © HO/Reuters; 112b © Hulton-Deutsch Collection; 113b © Marco Secchi; 115t © Katie Orlinsky; 116b © Robert Holmes; 117b; 119t © Michele Asselin; 118br © Luke MacGregor/Reuters; 120-121 © Rick Maiman/Sygma; 122br © Sunset Boulevard; 123bl © Sozufe Adeleri /Retna Ltd ./Retna Ltd.; 123t © G.J. McCarthy /Dallas Morning News; 124t © Alfredo Aldai/epa; 124b © Michael Ochs Archives; 126t © Giulia Muir/epa; 127t, 130tl & 133b © Neal Preston; 129r © Tim Mosenfelder; 130b © Kirsty Umback; 132-133 background © Owen Franken; 134 © Rune Hellestad; 135t © Barry Lewis/In Pictures; 135br & 136t © Reuters; 137tl © Jörg Carstensen/dpa; 142t © Walter McBride ./Retna Ltd.; 143b © Robbie Jack; 162tl © Schenectady Museum; Hall of Electrical History Foundation; 163bl © Tracey Nearmy/epa; 163tr © Robert Wallis; 165b © Britta Pedersen/dpa; 166t © Kim Kyung-Hoon/Reuters; 172b © Karen Kasmauski; 172-173 background © Jeremy Horner; 174t © Kim Komenich/San Francisco Chronicle; 175tr © Micheline Pelletier; 175bl © Underwood & Underwood; 177tr © Emilio Suetone/Hemis; 180t © Akhtar Soomro/epa; 181bt © Jean-Pierre Lescourret; 182b © Omar Sobhani/Reuters; 184-185 © William Manning; 184t © Blaine Harrington III; 188b © Bettmann; 189t © Wu Hong/epa; 190t © Philip Wallick; 191t & 190-191 background © Dean Conger; 194b © Randy Faris; 195t © Deon Reynolds/Monsoon/Photolibrary; 197 © Christophe Boisvieux; 197 inset © Marcus Brandt/epa; 198tr © Lake County Museum; 200c © Bettmann; 200b © Fueger/dpa; 201 © Kapoor Baldev/Sygma; 202-203 © Kay Nietfeld/epa; 204b © Chen Kai/Xinhua Press; 207t © London 2012/Handout/Reuters; 209t © Olivier Maire/epa; 211r © Reuters; 214t © Bettmann; 214b © Jeanine Leech/Icon SMI; 216t © Andrew Gombert/epa; 216b © Icon Sports Media; 217 © Icon SMI; 218b © Marius Becker/epa; 219t © Zou Zheng/Xinhua Press; 220t © Dave Sandford/NHL Images/Reuters; 222b © Paulo Whitaker/Reuters; 222t © Matthew Ashton/AMA; 223t © Christian

Liewig; 225t © M.J. Masotti Jr./Reuters; 227b © Reuters; 228b © Adam Stoltman; 229t © Justin Lane/epa; 230b © Gerry Penny/epa; 231b © The Augusta Chronicle/ZUMA Press; 232t © George Tiedemann/GT Images; 232-233 © Schlegelmilch;234b © Tim de Waele; 235t © Robin Van LonkHuijsen/epa; 235b © Kai Fösterling/ epa; 237t © Tony Kurdzuk/Star Ledger; 239b © Chen Shaojin/Xinhua Press; 240t © Christophe Karaba/epa; 240b © Jean-Yves Ruszniewski/TempSport; 242t © Bruce Omori/epa; 242b © Reuters; 243t © Bo Bridges; 244t © Ben Radford; 245b © Justin Lane/epa.

ESO
10tl; 12-13 background Y. Beletsky; 13r G. Hüdepohl.

Fotolia
9b © Tristan3D; 17l © Martha Andrews; 18-19 © Eric Isselée; 22l © Yong Hian Lim; 24t © Marta; 26t & 49tl © Eric Isselée 26-27 © Mytho; 27t © zwo; 28t © Antony McAulay; 29t © electriceye; 28-29 background © Tomáš Hašlar; 31t © Kirill Zdorov; 33 inset © SkyLine; 33br © raven; 36b © patpitchaya; 37b © hperry; 38t © Taalvi; 41b © Jakub Krechowicz; 42c © lunamarina; 44b © picturetime; 46b © patrimonio designs; 46c © iPics; 48tl © biglama; 49tr © valdis torms; 50cr © Oleksiy Ilyashenko; 50tl © MilkMilk777; 50t © hazel proudlove; 50cl © gtranquillity; 50b © Konstantin Sutyagin; 51cl © TMAX; 51bl © Tomboy2290; 53br © Herbie; 52-53b © Hagit Berkovich; 56 © cameraman; 56r © TheSupe87; 57c © anankkml; 57b © Olaru Radian; 58b © Irochka; 59bl © Maxim_Kazmin; 58-59 background © zphoto; 60t © Ben Chams; 61b © electriceye; 62tl © TheKid; 62c © Sprinter81; 63b © Taffi; 62-63 background © eyewave; 64l © klikk; 64br ©Ruth Black; 65bl ©godfer; 65c © ben; 66t © JAMCO Design; 66-67 background © Konovalov Pavel ; 67tr © DoctorJools; 67tr © Andy Lidstone; 68-69 background © KonstantinosKokkinis; 70tl © Carsten Reisinger; 70tr © Lance Bellers; 70-71 background © Tyler Olson; 72 © SpbPhoto; 72b © Herbert Berends; 73r © picsfive; 73br © Domen Colja; 73c © Tommroch; 74t & 74bl © Gina Sanders; 75tl © Sebastian Kaulitzki; 74-75 background © Tracy King; 77l © ann triling; 78-79 background © life_artist; 79t © sabri deniz kizil; 79b © Danicek; 79tl © Dariusz Kopestynski; 80-81 background © zphoto; 82b © Pixlmaker; 82r © Elena Kovaleva; 85 © Maximo Sanz; 86t © RabidBadger; 86-87 background © Daniel Fleck; 87b © Galyna Andrushko; 88t © Marco Birn; 88t © Anchels; 89t © nezezon; 90t © Kristina Afanasyeva; 91t © Manish; 91tr © Alex; 94bc © Sylvie Thenard; 94bc © Ilja Mašík; 95b © Andrea Seemann;